# The Origins of Exceptional Abilities

For Nick and Lucy

# The Origins of Exceptional Abilities

Michael J. A. Howe

Basil Blackwell

Copyright © Michael J. A. Howe 1990

First published 1990
First published in USA 1990

Basil Blackwell Ltd
108 Cowley Road, Oxford, OX4, 1JF, UK

Basil Blackwell, Inc.
3 Cambridge Center
Cambridge, Massachusetts 02142, USA

All rights reserved. Except for the quotation of short passages for the purposes of criticism and review, no part of this publication may be reproduced, stored in a retrieval system, or transmitted, in any form or by any means, electronic, mechanical, photocopying, recording or otherwise, without the prior permission of the publisher.

Except in the United States of America, this book is sold subject to the condition that it shall not, by way of trade or otherwise, be lent, re-sold, hired out, or otherwise circulated without the publisher's prior consent in any form of binding or cover other than that in which it is published and without a similar condition including this condition being imposed on the subsequent purchaser.

*British Library Cataloguing in Publication Data*
A CIP catalogue record for this book is available from the British Library.

*Library of Congress Cataloging in Publication Data*
Howe, Michael J. A., 1940–
The origins of exceptional abilities / Michael J. A. Howe.
p. cm.
Includes bibliographical references.
ISBN 0-631-16827-3
1. Gifted children. 2. Nature and nurture. I. Title.
BF723.G5H68 1990
155.455 – dc20

90-31388
CIP

Typeset in 10 on 12 pt Sabon
by Graphicraft Typesetters Ltd., Hong Kong
Printed in Great Britain by
Billing and Sons Ltd, Worcester

# Contents

| | |
|---|---|
| Preface and Acknowledgements | vii |
| 1 Introduction | 1 |
| 2 Barriers to Understanding | 21 |
| 3 Accelerating the Acquisition of Abilities | 62 |
| 4 Family Backgrounds | 97 |
| 5 Child Prodigies | 126 |
| 6 Motivation and Temperament | 176 |
| 7 The Contribution of Intelligence towards Explaining High Abilities | 197 |
| 8 Final Words | 224 |
| References | 241 |
| Author Index | 255 |
| Subject Index | 259 |

# Preface and Acknowledgements

Some psychological questions are readily answered. They submit to well-designed experimental research in which influential variables are carefully controlled and their outcomes accurately measured. Elegant investigations have produced some neat solutions. But the really interesting questions, and the most important ones, are not so tractable. These questions are too large to be easily resolved. They sprawl and are too untidy, too messy. In the search for answers, no single approach or methodology is sufficient.

'What are the causes of exceptional human abilities?' is one of the large and sprawling questions. It has not proved at all easy to resolve. But its importance is enormous: we simply cannot ignore it. Answering that question is the main aim of this book.

Ignorance often limits our horizons because it prevents us from seeing what might be possible. In connection with the kinds of achievements that we regard as being outstanding or extraordinary, we are easily convinced that the most striking feats must depend on circumstances which, except for certain rare individuals, are entirely unattainable. Some of the most widespread beliefs about exceptional people revolve around the view that certain individuals are not only remarkable but inherently so, while the remainder of us are doomed to ordinariness. But such a view can be challenged: there is firm evidence that even the most extraordinary human abilities do not justify our assuming that any person who displays them must have been born exceptional. Efforts to explain why certain individuals become outstandingly able often start off on the wrong foot, because we fail to question preconceived notions that may be quite wrong. For instance, we may find ourselves asking why one dazzling musician has been fortunate enough to be so innately gifted, whereas we might be wiser to start by querying the initial assumption that the notion of innate gifts must have a role in a scientific explanation.

Perhaps because it is often so difficult to explain why one particular individual, rather than someone else, has gained remarkably impressive abilities, there is a temptation to believe that the causes of the most exceptional human accomplishments are largely mysterious, and will always remain so. It is true that human genius cannot be readily explained. The causes are not at all simple or straightforward, and the production of impressive abilities cannot be reduced to any easy formula that can be widely applied. But, as I show in this book, much *is* known about the circumstances that give rise to the most impressive abilities: although the causes are complicated and incompletely understood they are very far from being totally obscure. In practical terms, this means that even though we cannot construct an educational production-line that will reliably manufacture genius, it is well within our power to take steps that will greatly increase the likelihood of any child becoming a young person who is by current standards unusually competent in one or more valued areas of expertise. With a small amount of help and guidance, the majority of ordinary parents are capable of doing a great deal to help make that possible.

Exceptional abilities provide one of the most valuable of all mankind's resources. So it is surprising how very few nations have developed or even articulated systematic policies designed to extend the numbers of young people who grow up capable of the kinds of individual achievements which we now regard as being outstanding. One reason for this failure lies in the above-mentioned belief that the causes are either mysterious or closely bound to innate and inherited characteristics, and that consequently it is unrealistic to expect that deliberate interventions aimed at increasing the numbers of extremely competent individuals will actually succeed. In fact, however, although our knowledge is incomplete, sufficient is known to make it possible to design and implement educational policies that would produce large increases in the numbers of individuals who master the most difficult human skills and abilities. There is no real justification for failing to move in this direction.

A second reason for the lack of progress towards devising policies that would add to the numbers of highly capable young people stems from the view that the formal school-based educational system provides the main, if not the only, vehicle for pedagogic improvements. And since, by and large, schools seem to be doing the best they can, the room for improvement may appear to be strictly limited. But that reasoning is flawed. To a considerable extent it is the child's home and the child's own family that provide the kinds of opportunities which make it possible for some children to become exceptionally capable.

And to an equal extent it is realistic to regard the family background as providing the region of greatest scope for the kinds of changes that would extend those advantages to more children.

As an environment for learning, the child's home is in many ways ideal. Only at home is it likely that a child will have opportunities to interact regularly and frequently, on a one-to-one basis, with adults who have a thorough knowledge of that child as an individual. Even the best teachers and the best schools are seriously handicapped by the impossibility of their matching such opportunities. That is not to deny that many teachers are highly successful at helping children to reach important educational goals. But, as an under-used potential source of opportunities that could produce major gains in young children's educational progress, it is probably correct to say that, for many children, the home background now offers more scope for improvements than schools do. For obvious reasons that is especially true in relation to progress in the crucial earliest few years of life. Of course, there are some families in which the parents are already unusually successful at giving their children frequent opportunities and regular encouragement for early learning. There are also a few families in which the parents' own educational limitations may seriously restrict the extent to which they are capable, even with assistance, of helping their children in this way. But the vast majority of today's parents, if they were made fully aware of the possible benefits to be obtained as a result of their making efforts to aid their children's progress, and if they were to be provided with a reasonable amount of guidance about ways to assist learning in young children, would be capable of achieving a great deal more than they currently do towards helping their children to learn.

I should emphasize that in stressing the need for policies designed to implement ways to increase the number of individuals capable of impressive achievements, I am *not* asking for policies that simply aim to encourage or identify 'gifted' children. As I show in this book, current thinking that surrounds notions of 'gifts' and 'giftedness' is often confused and unhelpful in a number of ways. Other things apart, those terms usually imply acceptance of the idea that outstanding capabilities are beyond the reach of any but a few inherently special individuals. That view needs to be abandoned in order to make way for effective policies.

Many people have contributed to this book in one manner or another, and I am grateful to all of them. The numerous students who have read or talked about my sometimes opinionated assertions on the issues covered here have made a large number of helpful contributions. A number of my colleagues in the Psychology Department at Exeter University have been similarly generous. Amongst those who have helped me in one way or another I would especially like to thank Bob Brown, Ian Gordon, Rachel Kirby, Stephen Lea, Rod Maliphant, Steve Reicher, Leslie Reid, Alan Slater, Paul Webley, and Brian Young. (Without Rachel and Stephen I would never have survived the computer crises that have threatened my sanity with some regularity.) Philip Carpenter and Kim DiDonato read early drafts and gave valuable advice. A visit by Ralf Krampe of the Max-Planck Institut in Berlin gave me insights into some important recent investigations of the effectiveness of practice being conducted by himself and Anders Ericsson. In Britain generally, I have learned much about outstandingly able individuals from discussions with Ian Hunter, John Radford, John Sloboda, Joan Freeman, and Colin Berry. Sadly, that short group of names comes all too close to being an exhaustive list of British psychologists who have a serious commitment to conducting research into the causes of outstanding abilities.

Many of my intellectual debts are to American researchers. I am especially grateful to Steve Ceci, who over the years has not only been a good friend but has constantly stimulated me with fresh and often surprising evidence about the nature of abilities in the human species. He also read part of the manuscript, and made a number of valuable comments. Howard Gardner's kindness in accommodating me with Project Zero during a short visit to Harvard University made it possible for me to have valuable conversations with a number of individuals in the vicinity of Cambridge, including Jeanne Bamberger, Lynn Goldsmith, Bob Sternberg, and Bill Fowler. To the last-named I am especially indebted, since his careful re-examination of some of the findings obtained by pioneering researchers in the years between the two world wars has provided an invaluable but largely unrecognized service to anyone who is at all seriously interested in discovering why individuals differ in their capabilities. I also owe a debt to Howard Gruber, whose book *Darwin on Man* convinced me that we can and must study the lives of people as individuals if we are ever fully to understand how the most exceptional achievements come to be made.

Finally, I wish to thank Sylvia Howe. Her love and support have meant the world to me throughout the twenty-eight years since we first met.

Michael J. A. Howe

# 1

# Introduction

From time to time someone proposes that we humans only use a small part of the mental capacity that is available in our brains. The suggestion is intriguing: the prospect of vast untapped reservoirs of ability existing in every person is a tantalizing one. Everyone knows that people who are exceptionally able make immense contributions to human life, so it is hard to ignore a claim which implies that the capacity of any ordinary person to think and learn can be hugely expanded. Should we take it seriously? Is it likely that the revolutions that have taken place in manufacturing, in communicating, and in the processing of information, will be followed by yet another revolution, one that results from a controlled explosion of the capabilities of individual people in their millions?

Perhaps this is a realistic possibility, perhaps not. Psychologists have found it hard to find firm grounds for confirming or rejecting it. That may seem surprising, since consequences that are profoundly important for individual children and the world they inhabit hinge on the issue.

Why has it been so difficult to reach a firm conclusion? Essentially, the failure to agree on either this particular matter or a variety of related ones that are equally important arises from the fact that too many fundamental questions about the origins of exceptional abilities have remained unanswered. The communication of psychological knowledge about the development of human abilities has been uneven. It has left big gaps in our understanding of the causes of outstanding achievements. Not enough is known about the causes that lead to differences between people and help make each individual unique.

The issue I have raised is just one of a number of urgent questions about extraordinary abilities. There are many others. What are the causes of exceptional capabilities? Why are some people smarter than others, or better at sports, or music? To what extent is it possible to accelerate a child's early development? Is there truth in the assertion that 'Any child can be a genius'? Can the highest levels of individual achievement be reached in the absence of special innate gifts or 'natural' talents? Or, conversely, is it true that some children possess certain innate talents which will inevitably emerge, whatever the circumstances of a child's early life? All of these questions are important ones, and in each case the value of having a firm and verified answer is immense. Yet there has been remarkably little agreement, even among those educators, psychologists, and other professionals who might be expected to be well-informed. Their responses have been varied and contradictory.

But *why* has there been so little agreement? One conceivable reason is that we simply cannot say why some people are more capable than others because no-one knows what are the causes of variability between individuals. Another possibility is that the knowledge does exist, but that it has not been effectively brought to bear on the questions I have raised. Broadly speaking, whilst it is true that our understanding of these matters is far from being complete, the second of the alternatives is nearer to the truth.

The purpose of this book is to enquire into the origins of exceptional human abilities. My aim is to provide explanations for the differences that arise between people in their skills, their knowledge, and their achievements. The book is especially concerned with the circumstances in which exceptional capabilities are first acquired by children and young people. It examines the reasons why outstanding accomplishments are achieved by some individuals, but not by others. It also investigates the background factors that enable certain young children to make exceptional progress in their earliest years, thereby gaining the advantages that prepare a person to make substantial achievements in adulthood. Of particular concern are the background circumstances that give rise to so-called 'child prodigies'. These exceptional young people often, although not always, develop into unusually accomplished or creative adults. The book also surveys research which has assessed the effectiveness of deliberate efforts by parents and others to encourage accelerated early development in their children.

In view of the sheer importance of having a detailed and precise knowledge of the circumstances that give rise to exceptional abilities it may seem surprising that large areas of ignorance and uncertainty have been allowed to remain. Part of the blame for the fact that progress has been so uneven may lie with our own unquestioned assumptions and preconceptions. The everyday psychology of commonsense and folklore can establish itself in our minds in ways which bar the way towards a fuller understanding. Some of our habitual thinking about exceptional achievements may be rooted in fundamental misconceptions about the nature and causes of human accomplishments. The chances are that understanding will best be advanced by approaches which combine scientific rigour with an insistence on taking nothing for granted.

There are pressing reasons for wanting to add to what we already know. Doing so is especially valuable because that knowledge can be utilized in order to increase the numbers of individuals who become capable of achievements that we nowadays regard as being exceptional. Of all natural resources, none is more crucial than the abilities of individual human beings. We urgently need a better understanding of how the most remarkable achievements are actually brought about. Human accomplishments, particularly the most impressive ones, do not only benefit the individuals who make them: the marvellous feats of a small number of people can enrich the lives of many. So there are huge gains to be made from increasing the number of those young men and women who succeed in acquiring the capabilities that are needed for making outstanding achievements. It is virtually certain that increases in knowledge and understanding, when applied imaginatively, will make it possible to nurture exceptional abilities more effectively, and help to extend to numerous young people the opportunity to reach very high levels of competence. Although there remain many unanswered questions about the origins of exceptional abilities, and about the extent to which progress can be accelerated, it is clear that the vast majority of young people, if they are given sufficient opportunities and enough help and encouragement, are capable of reaching considerably higher levels of competence at any of a variety of important skills than most children currently achieve.

The practical desire to know more about the underlying causes of excellence, and to explain how those causes actually operate in real life, can also be seen as one facet of a broader scientific undertaking – the effort to understand the psychological development of individual people. Everyone's life is a kind of journey. Its route determines what we do with our lives. How, we want to know, do people become the individuals they turn out to be, and how did each of us develop into the person we now are? How did one young infant become the adult you, and another infant turn into the person that is me?

## Contrasting Viewpoints

Experimental research into human learning and cognitive development has been intensively pursued for several decades, but psychologists are far from being unanimous in their views about the origins of exceptional abilities. Opinions are not only diverse but often conflicting. The contrasts in views are seen especially clearly in the differing reactions to recent assertions concerning the benefits to be gained by providing intensive education in the earliest years of childhood.

Much publicity has been given to the claim that most young children can reap huge benefits from parental efforts to provide what is sometimes termed a 'hot house' regime of early experiences. Broadly speaking, that term can be applied to any intensive child-rearing programme that has been deliberately designed to promote early acquisition of useful knowledge and basic intellectual skills. We are told by some authors that it is possible to accelerate very considerably the development of *any* young child's skills, and that the key to such acceleration lies in the efforts of parents or teachers to give intensive tuition, support, and encouragement in the child's first years.

It has even been asserted that, given appropriate early training, virtually any child is capable of becoming a genius. For instance, viewers of a British television series, *Hot House People*, were encouraged to believe that all children should be 'programmed for genius', that every child born has a greater potential intelligence than Leonardo da Vinci ever used, that education should begin in the womb, that it is possible to give any baby 'encyclopaedic knowledge', and much else in the same vein (Walmsley and Margolis, 1987). As we shall see later, claims of this kind have been voiced in the past as well as recently. But they are becoming increasingly frequent, and more and more confident.

Are these claims true or false? There is no doubt that there is much that is wrong or misguided, or potentially harmful, in some of the assertions of those who advocate 'hothousing' approaches. Other considerations aside, parents and teachers would be wise to avoid imposing any kind of programme which emphasizes formal instruction at an early age at the expense of informal play and talk and other interactions between parents and children, or which restricts a child's opportunities to make friends, gain social skills, and develop a sense of humour.

All the same, the basic claim that children are capable of making considerably more progress in their earliest years than most children today actually do make is a sound one, and it certainly deserves to be considered seriously. It may also turn out to be true that children whose parents provide an unusually rich mixture of teaching, encouragement, and other opportunities in the early years is likely to gain advantages that will permanently elevate the quality of the individual's life. On the other hand statements of that kind may be found to be unjustified. It is vital to have evidence that makes it possible to assess the truth of falsity of the various claims that have been made.

## 1 The Hereditarian Position

A not-uncommon response to the assertion that strenuous parental efforts to help and encourage young children can yield enormous benefits is to say that such a claim is self-evidently nonsense. One reason for believing this is the fact that the assertion seems to contradict a number of widely accepted views concerning the contributions of innate or inherited characteristics to exceptional abilities. For example, many people believe that a person cannot be a great musician, or an eminent mathematician, or an exceptional artist, unless he or she is fortunate enough to be born with an appropriate aptitude or natural gift. It is thought that biological factors lead to certain individuals, but not others, being innately talented.

Similarly, some individuals are said to be better endowed than other people with more or less permanent characteristics of general intelligence. And, it is sometimes argued, 'talent will out' wherever it exists, in which case a gifted young person will have no particular need for intensive efforts by parents or others to encourage the development of the gift during a child's earliest years. Conversely, it would appear, in an individual without innate talent or high intelligence, the effort to create exceptional ability is doomed to fail, because such a child is inherently and immutably inferior. And if that is so, subjecting children who lack special talents to an intensive, 'hot house' regime of early tuition is likely to be a cruelly destructive and self-defeating exercise. As well as failing to achieve their goals, unsuccessful efforts to manufacture special abilities in ordinary children could do harm by depriving young people of many of the joys of childhood and subjecting them to unnecessary pressures for which they are not at all prepared.

The belief that it is pointless and harmful to submit ordinary young children to experiences designed to accelerate early mental development has had the support of a number of influential scientists. In the first half of this century psychological research by Lewis Terman and Arnold Gesell in the United States and by Cyril Burt in Britain appeared to supply intellectual buttressing for this view. These researchers all saw intellectual development as an 'unfolding' process that took place within strict constraints that were imposed by an individual's innate natural endowment. Gesell and his co-workers undertook a number of experimental studies which were designed to examine the effectiveness of attempts to accelerate development. The experiments typically involved comparing the progress of a child who was given special early training with that of an untrained twin, who acted as a control. According to Gesell, the findings showed that efforts to bring about acceleration were, by and large, unsuccessful.

Terman and Burt took rigidly hereditarian positions. Lewis Terman claimed that his viewpoint was confirmed by the results of a large-scale longitudinal investigation that was conducted in California by himself and a team of assistants. His view that a child's native endowment was all-important was supported, Terman argued, by the fact that individuals identified as being mentally superior whilst they were young children usually continued to maintain above-average intellectual skills throughout their lives.

Cyril Burt, who bears some responsibility for the introduction of the 'eleven-plus' examination in Britain, believed that human intelligence was largely fixed in early childhood, and unchangeable. He was convinced that the similarity of the intelligence-test scores obtained by twins who had been brought up in different families provided evidence to support his belief that differences between individuals in their abilities are largely accounted for by inherited factors. For this reason Burt insisted that only limited gains could be produced by interventions designed to enrich a child's early experiences.

But for a number of reasons, these men's views no longer have the dominating position they once held. In Terman's case, it is now clear that some of the findings which appeared to provide support for his beliefs about the importance of native endowments, are in fact equally compatible with alternative explanations of the causes of high abilities. Other researchers have drawn attention to findings which emphasize the importance of a person's experiences and opportunities, rather than natural endowments. It turns out that the children in Terman's huge Californian study who were identified as being superior, on the basis of intelligence test scores, were no more successful in their subsequent lives than they would have been if they had been selected on a completely random basis from children with similar social and economic family backgrounds, taking no account at all of their intelligence-test scores or other indications of their presumed giftedness or superiority (Sorokin, 1957; Ceci, 1990). Gesell's position is weakened by the fact that in a substantial number of instances his own experimental results (accurately reported by him, but largely ignored in his discussions of the findings) seem to contradict his views. As will be seen in chapter 3, it is clear that in many instances the accelerated learning that Gesell and his co-workers initiated did have substantial long-term effects after all (Fowler, 1983). And Burt's influence, once enormous, has been seriously undermined by the discovery that some of the findings he reported are of doubtful validity.

All the same, the views expressed by Terman, Gesell, and Burt have been very influential indeed. To some extent they continue to be. Although many psychologists nowadays would be critical of these writers' positions, it remains true that when people are discussing extraordinary abilities, the explanatory concepts that are most frequently introduced in order to account for them include ones that these three researchers would have favoured, namely innate talents and aptitudes, inborn gifts, and natural abilities. But it is now clear that those constructs cannot provide an entirely satisfactory explanation for the emergence of exceptional human abilities.

It is not that inherited influences are unimportant. It would be totally wrong to assume that by rejecting some of the hereditarian and deterministic ideas of Terman, Gesell, and Burt we become forced to accept the opposing belief that everything depends on a child's environment. (In this instance, as in others, the finding that one explanatory account is not entirely correct does not justify the too-common response of leaping to the conclusion that a competing alternative account must be right.) Individual differences are by no means entirely due to environmental differences: the differing achievements of individual people almost certainly depend to some extent on factors that are inborn, and there is a substantial body of research findings that firmly points to the existence of hereditary influences on human abilities. Also, there is evidence that predictions about young children's patterns of abilities can be made on the basis of knowledge about individual differences which are present as early as the first month or so of infants' lives (Korner, 1971; Escalona, 1973) or soon afterwards (Slater, Cooper, Rose & Morison, 1989). These two kinds of information provide good reasons for insisting that even if the idea that there exist innate gifts or talents, or 'natural' abilities, is largely fictitious, by no means all of the important ingredients of a child's experiences come from the external environment alone. Inborn qualities also make a contribution.

## 2 An Emphasis on Experience

In contrast to those psychologists and educators who are unimpressed by claims that any child who is given sufficient opportunities and enough encouragement is capable of outstanding accomplishments, there are others whose response to such claims is not nearly so dismissive. Without denying that hereditary factors can be influential (and without denying that some aspects of 'hothousing' approaches which assume that environmental factors are all-important are more likely to be harmful than helpful) they take the position that talents and abilities, far from being inborn, are to a considerable extent manufactured from the experiences of an individual child.

Views of this kind have always had a few advocates. Albert Einstein was convinced that no special innate gift underlay his own abilities: he attributed them to his enormous curiosity (Gruber, 1982). Samuel Johnson is quoted by Boswell as remarking that whilst there may exist some inborn variability in people's minds, such differences are nothing in comparison to what is formed by education (Bloom, 1976). More recently, Stephen Gould has remarked that the idea that innate causes largely account for the differences in what people achieve is not just mistaken but gravely harmful as well. In his words,

> few tragedies can be more extensive than the stunting of life, few injustices deeper than the denial of an opportunity to strive or even to hope, by a limit imposed from without, but falsely identified as lying within. (Gould, 1984, pp. 28–9)

In previous centuries a minority of parents and teachers have held similar views to Gould's, but usually in the face of a climate of opinion which held that a person's achievements largely depended on natural gifts and aptitudes. A hundred years before Gould made his statement, John Stuart Mill had written in his *Autobiography* that,

> the prevailing tendency to regard all the marked distinctions of human nature as innate, and in the main indelible ... [in the face of 'irresistible proofs' to the contrary] is one of the chief hindrances to the rational treatment of great social questions, and one of the greatest stumbling blocks to human improvement. (Mill, 1971, p. 162)

Another nineteenth-century iconoclast was an Austrian cleric, who deliberately set out to make his son, born in 1800, into an exceptionally able person. The father wrote a lengthy account of the way in which he educated his child, an experiment which seems to have been highly successful: the son, Karl Witte, was to become a highly distinguished scholar. It is clear from the description that by today's standards the parental teaching methods followed by the elder Witte were sensible and down-to-earth. They were calculated to encourage the child and appeal to his curiosity whilst avoiding pressure, fatigue, or boredom, but were not otherwise unconventional. Essentially, the approach that was taken was to provide many opportunities for learning and systematically implement down-to-earth procedures which followed from the father's observation:

> What an immeasurable amount a child will learn in six, eight, or ten years, that is, in 3,650 days, in 36,500 hours, reckoning the day at ten hours, if every conversation with

him or in his presence teaches him something! (Witte, 1975, p. 86)

The parents of a number of individuals who first distinguished themselves as child prodigies and subsequently went on to become outstanding thinkers have shared the belief that their children were by no means inherently exceptional, and that their hugely distinguished adult careers were made possible by the unusual educational opportunities that were provided in early childhood. For example, James Mill, John Stuart Mill's parent, insisted (as did the elder Karl Witte) that his son had no special natural abilities. So too did the father of Norbert Wiener, who was a remarkable prodigy as a child and later became an outstanding mathematician and the founder of the science of cybernetics.

These fathers would have agreed with the views of the Russian psychologist L. S. Vygotsky, who demonstrated that the mature capacities and accomplishments of the human brain are very profoundly shaped by man-made culture. Vygotsky (1962) showed that human cultures, internalized by children largely through the mediation of social interactions, not only provide access to skills and knowledge but also determine the fundamental sign systems that underlie knowledge and thought, as well as the particular languages in which meanings are expressed, and the sense and significance of even such basic concepts as space and time.

Without denying that the human brain is subject to biological constraints, Vygotsky drew attention to the endless variety of its possibilities. He emphasized the remarkable diversity of ways in which human minds can become furnished, and thereby equipped for achievements of one kind or another. One contribution of Vygotsky's writing has been to remove any reason for doubting that differences between individuals in the lives they experience can be sufficiently profound to account for the variability (immense as it is) between people in what their mental systems become capable of achieving.

## *Genes and Experiences: a Contradiction?*

Is it possible to claim that individuals' abilities are largely manufactured from their experiences rather than innate talents, and at the same time admit that inherited or innate qualities affect a child's development? These assertions appear to be mutually contradictory.

That is not necessarily the case. The issues are rather complex, and will be considered more fully at later stages, especially in chapter two and chapter seven. But some brief comments at this point may help to clarify matters initially. It is important to realize that whilst it is clear that inherited factors do have an impact on the development of individuals, rather little is known about *how* that impact is exerted. It appears likely that when genetic differences in children lead to differences in their cognitive abilities, that often happens because genes have affected cognition indirectly rather than directly. For example, it seems less likely that genetic differences lead to variablility in the rate of neural transmission, for instance, or the speed or power of the physiological mechanisms that underlie cognitive processing, than that they help to determine attributes such as activity level in infants, temperament, or perceptual sensitivity. Differences in any of the latter can, in certain circumstances, contribute to differences between children in their abilities, but because the effects are indirect rather than direct ones, the outcomes are not fixed or inevitable and can often be modified by appropriate environmental interventions. The view that genetic causes of variability always take the form of irreversible and unmodifiable 'blueprints' is mistaken.

### AN UNPLANNED EXPERIMENT

Far too often, people have accepted uncritically beliefs about the importance of this or that factor simply because they seem plausible, or appear to be true, or are widely considered by others to be true. And there is a certain unwillingness to admit that we may still not have the answers to various key questions. The truth of the matter is that many of those questions about high abilities to which 'everyone knows' the answer – or seems to – have in fact never been satisfactorily explained. Quite often, when we think that we know the solution to a question, a closer investigation reveals that we do not. In order to understand the reasons why some young children, but not others, turn into extraordinarily capable adults, it is necessary to re-examine some views that are widely accepted as being the definitive truth, to collect large amounts of detailed empirical evidence, and to bring to the examination and analysis of that evidence a clarity of thought that has not always been evident beneath the confident statements that people have made about the origins of human talents.

Ultimately, questions about the possible causes of superior abilities have to be decided on the basis of evidence about what actually happens in human lives. And in order to acquire the necessary evidence, it is often necessary to undertake empirical research. Typically, the research takes the form of controlled experiments or systematic observations. Occasionally, however, the circumstances of daily life helpfully intervene by providing unplanned 'natural' experiments, making us less dependent on being able to to undertake deliberate empirical investigations. For instance, historical sources happen to have provided some fascinating ready-made data which can help us to establish the truth or falsity of the assertion that no-one can become an exceptionally able musician unless he or she is lucky enough to have inherited certain rare gifts.

In the year 1703, the young composer Antonio Vivaldi arrived at a Venetian orphanage known as la Pietà. He had been hired to teach the violin to the orphan girls who lived there. Vivaldi encountered a state of affairs which many modern teachers would find hard to believe. The orphanage authorities placed enormous emphasis on the value of music. They made sure that the orphans regularly listened to music, were encouraged to gain musical skills, and had opportunities to receive the necessary training. As a result of these felicitous circumstances, about a third of the older girls became extraordinarily accomplished musicians. Visitors to Venice who were lucky enough to attend one of the frequent concert performances that took place at the la Pietà orphanage, which included the technically intimidating new works that Vivaldi and other composers were producing at that time, were dazzled by the orphans' virtuosity. The concerts at la Pietà were judged to be of a quality that matched the most impressive musical performances to be encountered anywhere in the world (Koldener, 1970; Kunkel, 1985).

All this happened despite the fact that, being mostly illegitimate and from backgrounds of destitution and squalor, the orphan girls of la Pietà were probably far from being genetically well-endowed, so far as any inherited precursors of musical excellence are concerned. One cannot be absolutely certain about the matter, but there are no grounds for believing that the orphan girls who became such excellent musicians would have inherited superior natural talents, aptitudes, or innate musical gifts.

So the musical achievements of the orphans of la Pietà in the early eighteenth century contribute evidence to the present-day debate about the causes of exceptionality. Their brilliance seems to contradict the view – still widely held today, almost 250 years after Vivaldi's death – that all human talents, and perhaps musical ones especially, are born rather than made. The data yielded by this eighteenth-century unplanned experiment encourage us to question the belief that outstanding skills cannot be forged from the experiences of an individual's life.

But the view that all depends on inherited natural talents continues to have its defenders. Confronted by an account of the blossoming of musical skills at la Pietà, or by a description of the more recent successes of children musically trained by the Suzuki method (Peak, 1986; Taniuchi, 1986), some observers have pointed out, quite correctly, that neither approach has produced a musician of the quality of Yehudi Menuhin or Artur Rubinstein. Whilst conceding that training and encouragement may, after all, produce quite remarkable abilities, they insist that the most brilliant achievements of all may nevertheless demand qualities that are innately extraordinary.

The point is a fair one, although a critic might argue that such a response to a fairly convincing demonstration that striking feats can emerge in the absence of any unusual innate predisposition is not unlike that of a believer who 'knows' that each of ten illnesses is a consequence of demonic possession, and reacts to the news that nine of the ten have been proved to be caused by viruses by insisting that demonic possession must be the cause of the tenth. It does seem unlikely that the biological foundations that underlie the most outstanding achievements are fundamentally different from those possessed by people who gain achievements that are undeniably exceptional, if not quite so very rare. After all, no-one would suggest that someone who wins a gold medal at the Olympic games must have been born possessing qualities that are totally distinct from those of the competitor who gains the silver medal. Chance, fortune, and many other external factors can help to decide which of a number of very able people will happen to be the ones who receive the very highest accolades.

## *Regions of Ignorance*

The questions that have been raised about the origins and causes of exceptional abilities are too numerous and complex to be resolved by any one experiment or investigation. Many issues are involved. As soon as one starts trying to answer the questions in any detail it becomes clear that no single method or approach can be relied upon to supply all the information that is required. In order to make progress towards increased understanding of the various forces that can contribute to some individuals becoming capable of striking accomplishments, it will be necessary to make use of evidence taken from a variety of different sources.

In some instances the most definitive answers are provided by the findings of experimental research. On other occasions information obtained from alternative kinds of investigations is more useful. For example, if we need to know about the progress of someone's life over a lengthy period of time it is unlikely that data gained from brief experiments will provide all the information we require. The chances are that the kinds of relatively detailed information about a person that can be obtained in interviews, or biographical accounts, will prove more valuable (Freeman, 1979; Bloom, 1985). And quite often, the evidence that would make it possible to provide a really firm answer to a particular query that has been raised simply does not exist. In such cases it may be necessary to fall back on any available information that is at all relevant, even though such data may have only an indirect bearing upon the question, and, so far as answering it is concerned, may be suggestive rather than definitive.

There are other complications as well. For example, difficult problems are encountered when one tries to form generalizatons about the origins of those human achievements that are interesting precisely because they are so untypical, and which may only be gained by individuals who are extraordinary (if not unique) in important respects. Another problem is that some of the empirical methodologies favoured by psychologists are ruled out by the sheer length of time that may be necessary for acquiring the most impressive human abilities: this can take many years.

There is, therefore, no realistic alternative to taking an eclectic approach in deciding on the research methods to be followed and the sources of information to be drawn upon. The eclecticism of the present book is a matter of necessity, not choice. The reader will need to be tolerant of the fact that substantial differences will be encountered between chapters (and to a lesser extent within the same chapter) in the kinds of evidence that are surveyed and discussed. Sometimes the emphasis will be on data from recent experimental studies; on other occasions information from biographical or autobiographical sources, or interviews, will predominate. Since no one source of knowledge comes near to providing all the factual data that would enable the task to be completed, the broad strategy will be to look at findings from any source of information that offers the promise of providing useful evidence.

## Contents of the Book

In the following chapters I explore the origins of exceptional achievements from a number of perspectives. To understand exceptional accomplishments it is often helpful to look fairly closely at the lives of the individuals who achieve them. In some parts of the book, particularly chapters 4 to 6, there is considerable emphasis on studies of individual people. Certain chapters, notably chapter 3, place more stress on experimental investigations. Other chapters give more attention to conceptual issues.

Chapter 2 begins by identifying some widespread preconceptions about superior abilities. In some instances these turn out to be misconceptions, some of which have had the unfortunate effect of making the task of understanding superior abilities, and the people who display them, more difficult than it needs to be. One barrier to understanding stems from the fact that we ordinary people are understandably awed and dazzled by those individuals who are capable of rare feats that are far beyond our own modest capabilities. A result of this is that we can become so preoccupied with the sheer extraordinariness of outstanding abilities that we convince ourselves that the people who display them must be virtually a race apart, quite exceptional from the day they are born. Consequently, there is a strong temptation to believe that the rules and principles underlying the acquisition of mundane abilities by ordinary people simply do not apply to these rare individuals and their immensely superior accomplishments. But as it happens, the ways in which extraordinary people gain exceptional abilities are by no means totally different from the ways in which ordinary people acquire unexceptional skills. Most importantly, we can learn much about the origins and causes of outstanding abilities by attending to the elements they share with ordinary abilities. Becoming too preoccupied with the sheer exceptionality of the most outstanding feats may be self-defeating.

Another set of barriers and obstacles to genuine understanding are primarily linguistic. Some of the language terms and speech patterns that people introduce in everyday talk about exceptional accomplishments can get in the way of our understanding. For instance, certain of the words we use for describing exceptional people can make it appear self-evident that particular explanations must be correct. Thus, simply because phrases such as 'natural talent' or 'innate aptitude' exist, a reader may find it hard to resist making the inference that these words must refer to something concrete and real, some quality or essence that helps account for someone's ability. One source of confusion here is the common tendency to reify. To do so is to assume, quite wrongly, that wherever there exists a word in our language there must also be some underlying concrete 'thing' to which it refers. Another common fallacy is to assume that terms which *describe* phenomena (for instance, 'talented') can at the same time *explain* those same phenomena.

Other language-induced misunderstandings are caused by the fact that the verbal labels which are introduced in order to describe people are not always the objective descriptions they appear to be. For example, to call someone a 'genius' is in practice more an accolade than a description. Rather than being a straightforward indication of a person's abilities, it is actually more an indication of how that person's accomplishments have been received. This may depend upon luck and fashion, in addition to exceptional ability as such.

Another, very different, group of confusions and misunderstandings that hinder people's efforts to understand the origins of superior abilities springs from faulty thinking about the nature of inherited influences on human abilities. As I mentioned earlier, it is often assumed that hereditary factors must operate in a direct, all-or-nothing fashion, and that outcomes of genetic effects are irreversible, unchangeable and closed to environmental influences. In actuality that is not true at all, a fact which has profound implications for any practical enterprise that sets itself the goal of extending the accomplishments of ordinary people.

To a large extent, a person's own experiences determine what that individual learns, achieves, and becomes. But those researchers who have depended on the experimental and observational methods typically followed in psychological research into human development have found it hard to find ways of taking an individual's experiences into account. It can be relatively easy to obtain measures of a person's environment, but environment and experience are by no means the same thing. Consequently, this crucial influence has tended to be neglected. Detailed descriptive studies which examine the lives of particular individuals in some detail can help to remedy this deficiency.

Many of the questions that we ask ourselves about the acquisition of superior abilities are, at least ostensibly, straightforwardly empirical ones. They include 'to what extent does intensive childhood education succeed in meeting such-and-such a goal?' and 'how much does intellectual development depend on the extent to which parents encourage a child and provide appropriate opportunities for learning?' Chapter 3 examines the empirical evidence in relation to a number of queries about the practical effectiveness of interventions that have been designed either to accelerate the development of abilities in children or to help adults to gain extraordinary skills. To any reader who has hitherto believed that certain basic skills, such as language, are not readily or substantially affected by parental interventions designed to accelerate early progress, the research findings may come something of a shock.

The majority of the findings surveyed in chapter 3 come from experimental studies, involving individuals varying in age from infancy to adulthood. Many different kinds of learning and development have received attention. Some studies have examined the influence of intensive training on reading. Others concentrate on physical mobility and motor coordination. Yet other investigations have assessed the outcomes of various kinds of intervention on perceptual abilities, memory skills, numerical abilities, or language development.

Chapter 4, which raises questions about the family backgrounds of individuals whose abilities are remarkable, examines some consequences of the fact that exceptional abilities *are* exceptional. To understand the origins of unusual skills fully it is helpful at times to shift the direction of our gaze away from the achievements as such and towards the other attributes of the individual people who perform them. So far as the goal of understanding exceptionally able individuals is concerned, approaches to research that depend on normative methods, and make generalizations from the averaged observations of performance by a large sample of subjects, have a rather limited value. So, once again, it is also valuable to be able to draw upon detailed descriptions of individuals.

A reason for needing to examine the lives of particular people in some depth is the simple fact that in order to explain anything, it is first necessary to have a precise description of it. In psychology it is all too easy to fail to give sufficient emphasis to the careful description of what is being investigated. There is a tendency to rush in with explanatory models and experimental research well before a detailed descriptive knowledge has been gained of the phenomena that are, it is hoped, to be explained. As Wittgenstein pointed out, 'the existence of experimental methods makes us think we have the means of solving the problems that trouble us: though problems and methods pass one another by' (quoted in Gardner, 1985).

The need for an initial stage of investigation in which emphasis is placed on the need for detailed descriptive knowledge is especially important when what is to be explained is not only highly complex and multi-faceted but also largely unique. By following the progress of a particular person's life, it becomes possible to obtain a long-term perspective on significant events. Such a perspective, which is inevitably absent in short-term experimental studies that yield findings based on the averaged scores of a number of subjects, gives a necessary background against which particular changes can be interpreted and their real implications for the individual appreciated.

One particular advantage of gaining detailed information about the progressing lives of particular individuals is that insight is provided into the ways in which people actually experience their lives. People differ in the pathways via which they travel from one point in life to another, and the different ways in which individuals act serve to shape experiences that are entirely unique to them (Rutter, 1989). Parts of chapters 4, 5, and 6 include relatively detailed examinations of aspects of individual's lives. Chapter 4 concentrates on the ways in which the family background contributes to the acquisition of special skills and abilities. Unsurprisingly, the likelihood of becoming an unusually capable adult is closely linked to family characteristics and values. Much depends upon the opportunities that members of the family help to make available. It is somewhat unusual – perhaps surprisingly so – for a young person to achieve striking intellectual success unless the family circumstances experienced during childhood offered some encouragement, incentive, or stimulation for intensive learning. The particular ways in which people's capabilities reflect the influence of the family and home background are highly diverse, but in one way or another the effects of the family upon the individual's abilities are usually profound.

Chapter 5 is about child prodigies. The chapter begins by tracing the development of several individuals. The vast majority of child prodigies are the children of parents who place high value on education and make considerable efforts to stimulate and encourage their offspring, particularly in early childhood. A substantial proportion of child prodigies continue to be exceptionally able and productive throughout their lives. In certain spheres of endeavour, such as music, it is unusual for a person to reach the highest levels of success unless marked precocity has been evident in childhood. Biographical and autobiographical accounts of people who have been child prodigies show that a number of the personal problems and difficulties experienced by them have stemmed from the unusual circumstances of their childhoods. In particular, the transition from childhood to adulthood can present especially formidable difficulties for children of parents who combine close involvement with their education with unusually high expectations. These parents often find it hard to give their children the freedom to learn to manage independently and to discover how to choose their own goals and make personal decisions.

Chapter 6 investigates the ways in which broadly motivational factors contribute to exceptional abilities. It is tempting to assume that not only the manifestations of intellectual achievements but their causes as well are primarily intellectual in form. But to a surprising extent, whilst it is of course true that outstanding individuals are 'clever', 'intelligent' and so on, the drives and the personal qualities that set in motion those efforts that eventually produce such achievements are not intellectual ones. Qualities of temperament, personality, and character are just as crucial. There has rarely, if ever, been a great achievement by an individual in the absence of an unusually strong sense of direction on the part of the person concerned. Almost always, people who gain outstanding accomplishments are exceptional not only in their intellectual abilities, but also in their single-mindedness, the strength of their commitment and determination, their dedication, and their ability to persevere in the face of difficulties and to concentrate on reaching their goals whilst resisting distractions. These broadly motivational factors that drive human activities are just as crucial to a person's success as specifically intellectual qualities are.

Biographical evidence makes it clear that whilst motivational influences always play a vital role in making exceptional human achievements possible, there are huge variations in their precise form and in the ways in which a person's progress is affected by them. They differ, not only between one individual and another, but also in a single person, between different stages of life. For example, whilst it is certain that Newton, Darwin, and Einstein were all 'highly motivated' to reach the goals they set themselves, the particular factors that goaded them towards a lifetime of study, and the particular reasons that spurred them on, were totally different. Also, in the case of any one individual, we are likely to find that one set of incentives were largely responsible for, say, guiding a young child towards working at the activities that enabled her or him to become an unusually competent young musician, whilst very different incentives were necessary for the child to make the transition to being an outstanding adult performer.

Our understanding of exceptional abilities is inevitably bound up with the way we think about human abilities in general. It is generally assumed that someone's intellectual accomplishments are constrained by that person's general ability, or 'intelligence'. A related assumption is that the concept of general intelligence has a necessary role in any attempt to account for differences in abilities between people. Chapter 7 challenges both these beliefs. It raises questions such as, 'in what (if any) fundamental ways are exceptionally able individuals different from people who have no special abilities?' I argue that whilst measures of intelligence are extremely valuable for descriptive and predictive purposes, the concept of intelligence has no genuinely explanatory function. Contrary to what is widely believed, there is no firm evidence that general intelligence exists as a quality that is either unitary or capable of exerting any kind of causative or controlling influence on specific abilities. The assumption that the concept of intelligence can help to explain abilities as well as describe them may actually impede our efforts to discover why people actually differ. I also suggest that the belief that the concept of intelligence can help to explain why people differ in ability has had the effect of obscuring the important fact that the different abilities of any individual are not only unconstrained by that person's measured general intelligence, but are also to a marked extent autonomous and independent of one another.

Chapter 8 concludes the book. It examines the reasons for many parents having failed to carry out simple procedures that could substantially aid their young children's progress. The chapter then looks at some of the approaches taken by parents who have been successful at helping their children to learn. It ends by drawing attention to the importance of sheer chance in many people's lives.

## Conclusion

Three final points. The first is to do with the fact the most of the abilities that receive attention in the following chapters are, in the broadest sense, intellectual. We should never forget that in order to enjoy a fulfilling and productive life, a person must gain many other qualities as well. These include emotional and expressive capabilities, and many social skills and sensitivities that make it possible for someone to get on with other people and establish friendships and deep personal relationships. Other essential qualities include a sense of purpose and direction, various abilities that are required for making plans, getting practical things done, making sensible decisions, and acting independently, as well as a sense of humour, and much else besides. Any individual who has been deprived of the kinds of experiences that help these qualities to develop – perhaps as a result of experiencing an insensitive or too intense 'hot house' regime in childhood – will undoubtedly suffer, as a number of the descriptions of child prodigies in chapter 5 make sadly clear.

The second point is a special instance of the one above. Especially when children are very young, it is always possible that an intervention designed to encourage the child to gain one ability may have the effect of impeding the acquisition of another ability that is equally crucial. A problem of this kind was encountered in a series of experiments conducted by B. L. White (1971) and his colleagues. They were interested in accelerating infants' progress towards gaining the ability to reach out towards objects and pick them up – a skill which is basic to many abilities that involve using objects as implements. Having established that in order for a child to reach out for objects successfully it is necessary to sustain visual attention to visual items, White prepared some distinctive patterned visual stimuli, and found that these were effective in encouraging the infants to make long visual fixations. Unfortunately, however, the children who were given this form of visual enrichment took more time, rather than less, compared with children in a control group, to reach an acceptable standard of performance at a visually directed reaching task.

What caused this paradoxical outcome? Subsequent research showed White where he had gone wrong. It emerged that the period during which the infants were provided with the enriching visual materials corresponded with a stage in their lives when they normally spend a good deal of time simply looking at their hands. This activity almost certainly helps infants gain skills needed in order to be able to reach out for objects, and since White's patterned visual stimuli distracted the infants' attention away from their hands the stimuli impeded rather than helped the acquisition of the ability to reach out.

The above example shows how important it is recognize that gaining a compound skill is not just a matter of collecting the necessary components and combining them to produce the desired outcome. It is also necessary to take into account the order in which the sub-skills are needed. Particularly in the case of infant learning, this may only be possible when substantial descriptive knowledge of normal development is already available.

Third, and finally, it is quite possible that a child who acquires substantial intellectual resources at an unusually young age will have a greater than average need for emotional, social, and other non-intellectual capabilities, in order to cope with the special challenges that an extraordinary child is likely to encounter. Fortunately, at least some of the learning activities that help to accelerate the acquisition of cognitive skills also contribute to one or more of the broader capabilities listed above. For example, talking to a child may simultaneously help develop a parent–child relationship, give the child the vocabulary to articulate her emotions, promote self-expression, stimulate thinking as well as language, provide a foundation for learning to read, and, in some instances, instil a love of language and a deep interest in the way things are said (McCabe, 1987). Even so, there are very real dangers in an early education that is directed too exclusively towards developing a child's intellect.

# 2

# Barriers to Understanding

In attempts at scientific explanation it is not unusual for progress to be held back by the failed explanatory efforts of previous generations. These can persist as shadows in the mind, forming barriers to new efforts to understand things better. Old concepts such as 'phlogiston' and 'the ether' have sometimes acted in this way. So too, in psychology, have the four 'humours' and the 'faculties' of the mind.

Our efforts to explain psychological phenomena may also be impeded by the fact that issues which are broadly psychological are so ubiquitous amongst the things we talk about and think about in everyday life. Because they are, we each carry around with us a bundle of 'commonsense' everyday beliefs, attitudes, and assumptions about psychological matters. Most of the time these serve us very well, but they can act as obstacles to our attempts to gain a deeper knowledge. If a person has always taken it for granted that something is true, that individual is likely to feel that it 'must' be, or is 'obviously' correct. It is not at all easy for someone to make the mental changes that are needed in order to accommodate an alternative view. One of the aims of this chapter is to illustrate some of the ways in which common non-scientific everyday beliefs about exceptional abilities may stand in the way of a more rigorous explanation and make the task of discovering the real causes appear to be more difficult than it actually is.

## Being Extraordinary

One particular mental obstacle to understanding extraordinary achievements takes the form of a tendency to be preoccupied with their sheer extraordinariness. This can sometimes stampede us into reaching a conclusion about the likely explanation of an outstanding ability before we have even begun to investigate it. Because feats of genius can be dazzling, and far beyond what most people can even imagine achieving, we can find ourselves awed, gaping at them open-mouthed. It may be hard to resist concluding that the individuals who perform such feats must be virtually a separate race, set above other people, totally different from everyone else. In his fascinating book on child prodigies, David Feldman (1986) quotes the reaction of an orchestral violinist on hearing a brilliant eleven-year-old violin prodigy. 'I was so overcome by what she did in rehearsal ... If I practised for three thousand years I couldn't play like that. None of us could.' (Feldman, 1986, p. 289). And as John Sloboda (1985) points out in his book *The Musical Mind*, most people have a similar reaction on learning, for instance, of Mozart's feat of writing out the complete score of Allegri's *Miserere* after listening to two choral performances.

There is a strong temptation to leap to the conclusion that underlying displays like these, ones that can strike ordinary people as strange or mysterious, infinitely superior and apparently inexplicable, there must exist some inborn qualities that are correspondingly rare and exceptional. How otherwise *can* they be explained? Surely, it is argued, if we are to account for someone being capable of feats that are of an order of excellence which is far beyond our own capabilities, we shall have to assume that the person who performed them must have been born with special gifts that are similarly remarkable.

When attention is directed exclusively towards what is extraordinary about exceptional people, such a conclusion may seem inevitable. But as Sloboda and others have pointed out, if instead of concentrating on the differences between extraordinary individuals and others we start to examine their similarities as well, it soon becomes apparent that alternative explanations might be possible, after all. And there is much to be said for a research strategy which incorporates the view that it is fruitful to look for commonalities between exceptional abilities and unexceptional ones. At the very least, such a strategy prevents investigators from rushing to conclude that exceptional skills must be fundamentally and inherently special even before there has been an opportunity to examine in any detail the actual nature of the abilities we find so dazzling.

## *Some exceptional Musicians*

Even with the most remarkable individuals, feats which at first appear to be quite impossible to explain can seem less inconceivable once we start to examine the life of the individual who achieved them. Take

Mozart, for example. He was unarguably a composer of genius, and it is widely believed that he was a brilliant performer and composer by the time he was four, and endowed from the time of his birth with miraculous musical gifts. But, even with Mozart, a more detailed knowledge of his life opens up the possibility that the origins of his abilities were not entirely mysterious. He was indeed a capable performer at the piano from a very early age. He did start composing when he was extremely young. Yet contrary to myth his achievements were by no means effortless or unprompted. Thousands of hours of practice were necessary.

His father, Leopold Mozart, a talented instrumentalist and a renowned and extremely ambitious teacher of music, went to enormous lengths to ensure that the son became a successful musician. Recent biographers have shown that the single-minded Leopold, whose earlier efforts to teach Mozart's older sister, Nannerl, had been highly successful, 'dedicated much of his life to making his son into an important musician in the best way he knew' (Hildesheimer, 1983, p. 67), and promoting Wolfgang's career. The young Wolfgang Mozart had very few opportunities to play outdoors or to make friends with children of his own age. He was subjected to a very unusual childhood regime. In all probability, from his very earliest years a large proportion of the child's time was devoted to musical activities and practice, and more practice, carefully directed by the father. And from the time he was six the young prodigy and his sister were dragged around Europe on money-making tours. To advertise them Leopold designed posters on which, 'In order to increase the sensational aspect of their act, Leopold reduced the children's ages by one year on the announcements. Indeed, these read like circus posters' (Hildesheimer, 1983, p. 31).

Of course, no-one would deny for one moment that Mozart was an exceptionally creative individual. Knowing how hard his father pushed him does nothing to alter this fact, but it does affect our efforts to explain how his genius might have been formed. We are no longer compelled to see Mozart's music as some kind of heaven-sent miracle, impossible to explain except by vague references to ill-understood innate gifts. No day-to-day record exists of the routine of Mozart's earliest days, and we can only guess at how his first years were actually filled. Yet what we do know makes it certain that the experiences of a very unusual early childhood in which music was always present had a crucial influence.

But what of the memory feat by Mozart that I mentioned earlier? Can that, too, be explained? Perhaps it can. To an untrained observer the task appears to be one of recalling an immensely long sequence of separate notes or bars. It is important to realize that for a highly skilled individual like Mozart, whose musical education may have filled as much as 20,000 or 30,000 hours, the task would not have appeared to be anything like that. For Mozart, what was being remembered would have been meaningful and significant in numerous ways, and the constituent parts would have been highly familiar. Outstandingly skilled musicians can count on being able to recognize meanings and patternings and musical structures in music, making it unnecessary to memorize vast numbers of lower-level items (Chase and Simon, 1973; Sloboda, 1985). As will become apparent later in this chapter, there are a number of published reports in which it is shown that ordinary people who have spent only 1,000 hours in training, and in some instances as little as 100 hours, may be able to perform feats of memorization, ones that appear to a naïve observer to be 'impossible' and quite magical. Similarly, chess masters are able to remember around 50,000 separate chess positions. This apparently astonishing ability depends on the fact that the individual's mental representation of a position is far from being a simple copy of the physical board: it is more accurately regarded as being an abstract structural description of significant relationships between groups of chess pieces.

But to return to Mozart, however uncommon his first experiences were and however intensive his training, it is hard to understand how he could have produced masterpieces of musical composition in early childhood, as he is supposed to have done. Here the reality is somewhat different from what has been reported. Contrary to the myth that Mozart composed great masterworks at the age of four or five, one investigation has revealed that none of the compositions by him that are now regarded as being major works were actually written earlier than the twelfth year of his musical career (Hayes, 1981). So it was only after many years of rigorous training to be a composer that he began to produce his greatest music. Like everyone else, Mozart needed a very long period of preparation in order to reach his peak.

A similar conclusion emerged when Hayes submitted the musical output of 76 major composers to the same kind of analysis. The standard that was adopted for regarding a composition as being one that we now judge to be of major importance was that it should be sufficiently highly regarded nowadays for several recordings of it to be currently available. (This excludes items that can be found in the catalogues because they have been recorded for their novelty value, and ones that are included simply as fillers.) Using this criterion, it turned out that only three of the 76 composers had produced major works by the tenth year of their composing career. (The three are Satie, who produced 'Trois Gymnopédies' in his eighth year as a composer, and Shostakovich and Paganini, each of whom composed a notable masterwork after a mere nine preparatory years.) The message is clear: all musical composers, with no exceptions at all, have to go through a very long period of learning their craft. There are no short cuts to musical greatness, not even for the most brilliant musicians. Although popular accounts of remarkable individuals like Mozart may suggest otherwise, the belief that certain talented individuals are able to produce masterpieces without having to invest the years of careful preparation that ordinary people require in order to reach high levels of expertise is simply mistaken.

The fact of the matter is that not only composers but all creators of outstanding human achievements, from artists and writers to scientists and mathematicians, reach the highest levels of competence only after many years of painstaking learning. The most striking feats depend on skills that take thousands of hours of practice. Often, vast quantities of knowledge need to be gained as well. Chess masters, for instance, all have to acquire an ability to perceive the significance of numerous different chess positions. Their ability to recognize any of around 50,000 distinct patterns, each comprising several chess pieces (Simon and Chase, 1973) is only possible because a vast array of knowledge will have been acquired in the course of years of training, during which something in the region of 20,000 hours will have been devoted to the game. Consequently, even the most exceptional players of all take at least ten years of concentrated training to reach the highest levels of chess mastery.

## Myths about Exceptional People

The above observations provide a sharp challenge to the belief that people who achieve exceptional feats must be inherently different from everyone else. Yet that belief persists. There are number of apparent facts that seem to lend credence to it. A number of them deserve to be examined.

### 1 Effortless Creation

The first of these so-called facts is the belief that for a few special individuals the creative activities that lead to the production of works of genius may require no conscious effort at all. It would appear that some fortunate individuals do not experience the intense struggle that most people have to go through in order to create great achievements. A number of reports, including some autobiographical ones, speak of effortless insights that occur quite spontaneously, in the arts and sciences alike. An especially well-known instance of the apparently 'unconscious' production of a masterpiece is described in Coleridge's account of the writing of 'Kubla Khan'. Another is Kekule's report of his discovery of the benzene ring. Both accounts seem to suggest that most, if not all, of the creative work must have been done while its author was sleeping. Kekule's discovery is said to have appeared to him in a vivid dream about snakes. Coleridge claimed that the poem appeared in his mind in a finished form on his awakening from a deep sleep. In the words of his own report, written in 1816, of events which took place in 1797.

> The Author continued for about three hours in a profound sleep, at least of the external senses, during which time he had the most vivid confidence, that he could not have composed less than from two to three hundred lines; if that indeed can be called composition in which all the images rose up before him as *things*, with a parallel production of the concurrent expressions, without any sensation or consciousness of effort. On awakening he appeared to himself to have a distinct recollection of the whole, and taking his pen, ink, and paper, instantly and eagerly wrote down the lines that are here preserved. (Quoted by Perkins, 1981, p. 10)

But on closer examination the picture that emerges is not nearly so simple as this. In the case of 'Kubla Khan', it becomes apparent that Coleridge's part in the production of the poem was almost certainly neither passive nor spontaneous (Lowes, 1927; Perkins, 1981). Like a number of the Romantics, Coleridge combined an appetite for laborious work with an inclination to strike a pose of being capable of effortless masterpieces, even if that involved major departures from the literal truth (Howe, 1982). Coleridge's account of the writing of 'Kubla Khan' is partly untrue. Evidence that he engaged in editorial work on an early version proves that, his own story notwithstanding, the poem did not suddenly appear to him in its finished form. He drew upon a number of different sources, which supplied not only certain of the images but also some of the actual phrases that appear in the published poem.

And Kekule was almost certainly not actually dreaming when he made his discovery, but understandably lost in thought about the scientific problem which had been preoccupying him over a long period of time (Perkins, 1981; Weisberg, 1986). In reality, the making of a masterpiece always involves a great deal of deliberate conscious effort. That is not to deny that we are unaware of much of the mental work that our brains engage in. David Perkins asks,

> If creating is supposed to be unconscious, does this mean that the course of thought behind the achievement was not deliberately carried out, or not in fact conscious at the time, or never conscious even afterwards, or closed in principle to awareness? What people usually seem to have in mind is that the creative process is wholly closed to awareness ... A more reasonable sense in which the creative process is unconscious might be this: not surprisingly, makers are not routinely conscious of how they proceed. They attend to their work, not to the thought processes that are getting the work done. (Perkins, 1981, p. 39)

Progress towards new discoveries is neither regular nor predictable, and ideas can take shape in sudden leaps of thought, with no prior warning, sometimes on awakening, or following a period of daydreaming or semi-sleep (Rothenberg, 1979). Mental activities that take place during periods of sleep or day-dreaming may often be crucial. But no outstanding human achievement has ever been produced without a great deal of conscious work on its creator's part.

## 2 Sudden Emergence

Another reason for many people believing that the causes of certain individuals' extraordinary abilities lie in special inborn talents or aptitudes is that children's special abilities are sometimes reported to have appeared very suddenly. The sudden emergence of a full-blown skill in a very young child, in circumstances that have provided no opportunities for learning and practice, would certainly be hard to explain. It is understandable that instances in which new abilities have unexpectedly emerged, apparently in the absence of any relevant previous experiences, have prompted witnesses to conclude that some form of innate gift must be the cause.

But although there have been many instances in which extraordinary abilities *appear* to have been acquired in the absence of practice, it is doubtful whether this ever happens. It is noteworthy that the descriptions are usually anecdotal, and often they are reported by people who are claiming to remember events in the distant past. Also, for a number of reasons, observers of unexpected abilities can sometimes be misled (Ericsson and Faivre, 1988). Firstly, the fact that a child is suddenly discovered performing some new task may be misinterpreted by doting parents as implying that the actual acquisition of the skill was equally sudden. In addition, parents and others may have reasons for wanting to believe that a child's special abilities are mysterious, magical, or miraculous (see chapter 4). And thirdly, especially in the case of feats that are very unusual, it is easy to overestimate the amount of practice that is necessary for achieving standards of performance, which, compared with what most people can do, are genuinely exceptional. Ericsson and Faivre suggest that a child, perhaps confined to bed through illness, who practises for an hour or so per day at, say, mental arithmetic, or a memory skill, may easily surprise adults who are suddenly made aware that the child has gained an unusual ability.

Perhaps because the idea of mysterious skills suddenly and inexplicably emerging is one that many people find intriguing, contradictory information is sometimes forgotten or not recorded. For example, several published accounts of a mentally-handicapped and blind young man named Leslie Lemke report the events described in the following version:

> When Leslie was about 20 years old, May [his adoptive mother] and her husband were awakened at three a.m. on a winter morning to the sound of someone playing Tchaikovsky's Piano Concerto No. 1 on their piano. The music was played by Leslie, who had never played the piano before or even shown any interest in the instrument. (Rimland and Fein, 1988, p. 476.)

But that is not quite the true story. In fact, as Bernard Rimland and Deborah Fein add in a footnote inserted after their account had gone to press, a recent interviewer, Darold Treffert (1989), learned that,

> Leslie had been exposed to the piano starting at age seven or eight. He was able to play folk songs before the 'miracle' night. May ... already quite elderly at the time, and confused by the extraordinary event of his playing classical music for the first time, without practice, overlooked his prior piano work. (Rimland and Fein, 1988, p. 476)

In all probability it is safe to assume that all reports of the sudden emergence of unpractised skills are fallacious. The reports often involve either faulty remembering or a less than complete knowledge of the circumstances in which the skill was actually acquired.

## 3 Racial Differences

A very different area of knowledge has been a third source of information that has misled some readers into thinking that the causes of variability in individuals in their accomplishments must lie in inherent and unbridgeable differences between people. Certain very marked differences between European and African infants, observed in a number of cross-cultural research studies examining their early progress, have been interpreted as demonstrating that variability in people's patterns of competence must be innately determined, by factors that reflect individuals' varying racial origins.

There are certain well-documented differences, apparently related to race, in the rate at which movement-based abilities develop in young children. For example, it is known that many African infants gain skills such as sitting and walking appreciably earlier than infants in Europe and America do. It has been widely concluded that inborn (and therefore probably hereditary) causes must be at the root of these differences in early capabilities, and, by implication, central among the causes of human variability in adult achievements.

The suggestion that inborn factors are the cause of the observed differences between babies is a plausible one. The question of whether or not that view is actually correct was addressed in a programme of research carried out in Kenya by Charles Super (1976). He studied the development of infants in a farming community of the Kipsigi tribe. Super's findings confirmed that Kipsigi infants do indeed gain motor skills such as walking, standing, and sitting without support about one month earlier than babies in other continents.

But he also observed that certain other skills, such as lifting the head, and crawling, are acquired later rather than earlier by Kipsigi babies, compared with other infants. These findings establish that the forwardness of the African infants is specific to certain particular abilities: there is no generalized motor-skill precocity. And most importantly, Super also showed that those skills that Kipsigi infants gain earlier than others are ones that are deliberately taught by Kipsigi mothers. In fact, their language contains specialized words that are called upon for the purpose of giving instruction in sitting and walking. The Kipsigi culture has established standardized methods for teaching these abilities.

Super also confirmed that the progress of all infants at skills that involve limb movements and coordination depends on the training they receive from their mothers. When he compared patterns of early crawling in different African tribes, Super found that there was a substantial correlation ($r = -.77$) between the proportion of the mothers who said they taught crawling to their babies and the average age at which crawling actually began. After incorporating a measure of the opportunities that were provided for practising crawling, Super observed that there was an even higher correlation ($r = -.9$) between the availability of instruction and the age at which a baby began to crawl. (The availability of opportunities was assessed by counting the occasions on which babies were simultaneously awake and lying down.)

In the light of the evidence gathered by Super it is almost certain that the reasons for the accelerated motor development observed in Kipsigi infants lie in cultural and environmental factors, and not inborn mechanisms. The same applies to other instances of precocious development of physical skills by African babies. In each of the instances Super investigated, the pattern of emergence of motor skills was found to reflect the pattern of infant care. The culture determines how the infants are trained. Typically, they are encouraged to acquire particular skills, sometimes at the expense of others.

Of course, we cannot be absolutely sure that the faster development by Kipsigi infants and other babies of those skills that are specifically trained proves that the special training is the sole cause of increased progress. It is just conceivable that there is another explanation. For example, Kipsigi mothers might happen to notice that their infants are 'naturally' good at certain skills and subsequently decide to encourage further progress in those particular areas of achievement. To rule out the possibility of this alternative explanation being the correct one it would be necessary to ascertain that babies who are genetically similar to the trained babies but who are *not* given special training do not display similar precocity. Fortunately, Super had data at hand for checking on this. He was able to examine infants in families which shared the same genetic background as the babies with precocious motor skills, but had a different way of life, one that involved child-rearing practices that were more similar to European ones. He found that these infants, who did not receive the special training in motor skills received by infants living in the traditional villages, did not display any precocity at all at the skills at which the traditionally-raised infants excelled. This further evidence confirms that the African infants' superior early progress at sitting, standing and walking is caused by training and experience, not by inborn qualities.

## *Do exceptional Abilities demand inherent Exceptionality?*

Super's investigations of African infants show that even those substantial differences between people that strike the uninformed observer as being convincing proof that inherent causes are involved may, after all, be due to variability in environment and experience. So the belief that the sheer extraordinariness of exceptional skills provides grounds for assuming that there must exist fundamental inherent differences between people in capacity to achieve, is refuted by evidence from several independent sources. First, contrary to myth, even geniuses have to undergo years of hard training, just like everyone else. Secondly, the idea that for a few special individuals creative achievements can be effortless happens to be untrue. Thirdly, the belief that certain large differences between babies' patterns of competence prove that differences between individuals' abilities are inherent, turns out to be entirely false.

Despite the fact that the most remarkable human accomplishments seem to be totally different from anything that most people can even conceive of achieving, there are no genuine grounds for concluding that the underlying qualities must necessarily be inherently exceptional. However much we may marvel at the apparent strangeness of those whose achievements are most outstanding, we should bear in mind that progress towards a better understanding of how these remarkable abilities are gained is most likely if we direct at least some attention to the ways in which exceptional individuals depend on skills that are similar to, rather than contrasting with, those of ordinary people.

## Extraordinary Skills in Ordinary People

The idea that any person whose accomplishments are exceptional must be inherently quite different from ordinary human beings is one that many people find hard to abandon. They would be quick to point out that whilst it may be true that Mozart and the other composers had to work for years at their craft, it is also true that another person who was given the same opportunities that Mozart received would not necessarily become a great musician.

The point is well taken. Still, there are yet more grounds, in addition to the ones I have already mentioned in the present chapter and the previous one, for challenging the assumption that the simple fact that someone has an exceptional ability can ever form proof that the person must have started life inherently extraordinary. Some particularly interesting evidence shows that remarkable skills can sometimes be encountered in circumstances where it is possible to be certain that the individual who performs them has no inherently superior qualities at all. Consider the three following observations, each of which describes the performance of a very remarkable feat. Each demands very rare skills and goes far beyond anything that we would expect an ordinary person to be able to do.

First, in one psychological investigation it was discovered that one young man was able to remember lists of up to 80 random digits.

After one presentation of a list he could recall the whole sequence without making any errors at all. Now, it has long been assumed that people's natural ability to retain items in memory is unchangeable, and there is firm evidence that the maximum list length that most people can recall is around eight or nine items. So there appears to be no way of avoiding the conclusion that this particular young man, who successfully recalled lists about ten times as long as those which the average person could remember, must have possessed a fundamentally exceptional capacity to remember. It is hard to think of any other explanation for someone being able to recall ten times as much information as other people could.

Secondly, in another study, which involved a kind of video game in which coloured objects moved around a screen, volunteers tried to identify various kinds of briefly presented visual stimuli. The design of the study included certain visual masking events which had the effect of making the stimuli very hard to perceive. But the investigators found that one particular individual could always identify all the items with perfect accuracy, even under difficult conditions. His expertise contrasted very sharply with that of the other participants: most of them could only identify the items correctly if they were presented for two or three times as long as this person required. So once more, it would appear that the individual, like the young man in the previous example, must have possessed certain mental abilities that were inherently superior to those of ordinary people.

Thirdly, in yet another investigation, a five-year-old child was observed to swim and dive with tremendous skill, and to operate with impressive mastery a canoe that was known to be extremely hard for most adults to control. The feats performed by this particular child were so immensely superior to anything that children of the same age are normally able to achieve that, once again, the conclusion that special inherent capabilities must have been present appears to be inescapable.

Each of these three instances presents a situation which seems to point quite unambiguously to the existence of some special inborn gifts or inherent capabilities that ordinary individuals lack. If it could be shown that, despite all appearances, none of the three brilliant performers whom I have just described had any kind of innate endowment that was at all unusual, the case for arguing that the sheer extraordinariness of the achievements of a genius is sufficient proof that the underlying abilities must be inherently superior to those of other people would be seriously undermined.

As it happens, we do know that in each of the above three cases the person concerned was quite ordinary, chosen more or less at random, and then given very special training. The fact of the matter is that each of the three individuals – like the eighteenth-century orphan girls of la Pietà whose feats were similarly extraordinary – differed from other people only in the nature of the experiences and the opportunities for learning they had encountered. So far as natural endowments are concerned, we can be virtually certain that not one of them was at all unusual.

The individual who could recall enormous lists of digits happened to be a male student who participated in an experiment in which he was paid to practise recalling digit lists for an hour every day over a two-year period (Chase and Ericsson, 1981). When the experiment commenced, his performance was no better than average. The fact that he eventually became quite exceptional was the consequence of his having received exceptional opportunities to practise the skill, over the two-year duration of the study.

The man who was so remarkably good at identifying briefly presented visual arrays happened to be employed as a technician on a project using visual stimuli to investigate people's cognitive skills (Ceci, Baker, and Bronfenbrenner, 1987). It was his job to prepare the visual arrays that were used in the study. In the course of having to produce the materials that were needed for an experiment, he gained, informally, the equivalent of literally thousands of practice trials at the skill that was to be tested.

And the five-year-old child who was so remarkably competent at swimming and controlling a canoe happened to be a member of the Manu tribe in New Guinea (Mead, 1975). These people live in houses set on stilts above tidal lagoons. All the young children spend much of their time in or near the water, where they are encouraged to play; and they have countless opportunities to watch older children practise their skills. As a result of the children's particular early experiences, by the time they are about three years old virtually all have gained the skills that strike uninformed observers from land-based societies as being so remarkable – so much so that an observer who was unfamiliar with the special features of that culture would assume that special inborn gifts must be involved.

Knowing that feats which are rare in one culture are commonplace in another should help us to resist the tendency to leap to the conclusion that an extraordinary feat, simply because it is unfamiliar, must depend upon special gifts. Some accomplishments that are not at all uncommon in certain cultures are virtually unknown in our own, and vice versa. We are amazed by the ability of aboriginal Australians to follow long complicated routes over trackless and apparently featureless terrains (Lewis, 1976). In many cases the exceptionality of a performance lies in the eyes of the beholder. That is, we attribute to special gifts that which is rare and therefore seems beyond the reach of the average individual. The ability to interpret instantaneously very complex abstract symbols would seem to be an amazing accomplishment in a culture that had not developed written language. Likewise, the ability to navigate across miles of open water during daytime, with no instruments, seems almost miraculous to us but is not regarded as the least bit unusual in the Puluwat culture. (Ericsson and Faivre, 1988, p. 452. See also Feldman, 1980)

Each of the above three examples provides a further contradiction to the belief that only innately extraordinary people can master exceptional feats. It can be noted in passing that the abilities that underlie such feats are often to a considerable extent autonomous. That is, they are independent of and unrelated to the person's other abilities or to their general level of intelligence (except when they depend upon particular kinds of sub-skills, knowledge, or attributes that are inherent in those other abilities) even to the extent of being quite fragmentary. This point will re-emerge in chapter 3, in connection with the acceleration of children's capabilities, in chapter 5, in relation to the abilities of child prodigies, and again in chapter 7, in a discussion of the nature and function of the concept of intelligence.

In conclusion, it is clear that there is no justification at all for thinking that the sheer extraordinariness of what some people can *do* provides firm evidence that there exists inherent extraordinariness in what they *are*. The exceptional skills that certain ordinary people – and, for that matter, a substantial number of mentally handicapped individuals (see Howe and Smith, 1988; Howe, 1989*a*; 1989*b* for reviews of the evidence) – display originate largely in the individuals' experiences. Such people may receive unusual opportunities for learning and practice, and they may be motivated by unusual rewards and forms of encouragement. It makes sense to think along broadly similar lines when we seek to explain the outstanding achievements of those people whom we regard as being exceptional.

## Some Linguistic Obstacles to Thought

Up to this point in the present chapter I have been mainly concerned to show how everyday beliefs about the nature and causes of extraordinary human achievements can bar the way to a fuller understanding.

Another set of barriers that impede understanding is directly rooted in the actual language that we introduce when talking or thinking about extraordinary abilities. As with the obstacles that we create for ourselves as a result of being too preoccupied with the sheer extraordinariness of exceptional individuals, the main outcomes of the language-related barriers are to exaggerate the differences between people and to hide important similarities that can help to reveal causal mechanisms underlying unusual and ordinary feats alike.

## *Reifying everyday Concepts*

The everyday language we habitually use when we are talking about individuals whose achievements are out of the ordinary includes expressions such as 'genius', 'talented', and 'gifted'. On the face of it, there can be no objection to the use of these words: each is legitimate descriptive term. In daily life they are all useful, familiar, and necessary words. But words — or the way we use them — can deceive. Often, they do so by appearing to justify inferences or assumptions that are not strictly valid. And it is all too easy to fall into the trap of taking a word that is actually no more than a solely descriptive term and incorporating it in one's thinking as if it were an explanatory concept, or even a concrete entity or 'thing'.

It is especially easy to slip into the error of 'reifying' concepts. To reify is to make the mistake of assuming that underlying an attribute or quality that we can describe in words there must be some physical object. As John Stuart Mill put it, 'the tendency has always been strong to believe that whatever received a name must be an entity or being, having an independent existence of its own'. Thus, when a person is described as being intelligent it is often assumed that the individual has an unusually large share of a quality called 'intelligence'. Similarly, someone who remembers a large amount of information is regarded as having 'a good memory', and when an individual is described as being talented or gifted it may be inferred that he or she must possess certain 'talents' or 'gifts'.

Once the habit of reifying a term is established, it tends to be taken for granted that the quality that is being described does have the status of a real entity. From then on, that assumption is rarely questioned. Even worse, someone who asserts that a person possesses a talent or a gift may start to believe that an explanation for that person's superior skills is thereby being provided. So a person ends up believing that the reason why, say, a ballet-dancer is especially successful is because she has an unusual gift for dancing. Or a person's success may be attributed to an underlying 'aptitude', or a 'natural ability', or 'the right brains', or to some substance that comes 'in the blood' or 'in her bones'. All too often, we encounter the kind of circular reasoning that permeates the following brief dialogue.

'I wonder why X is such a fine musician.'
'It's because she has a natural talent for it.'
'How do you know she has a natural talent?'
'That's obvious: she's such a good musician!'

In fact, if the question is posed: 'What exactly *is* a talent (or gift, aptitude, or natural ability)?' it quickly becomes apparent that the answer is not at all clear. Whenever one hears someone using one of these terms, it can be informative to try asking them 'precisely what is it?', or 'how do you know it exists?' In my experience the response to the first question is usually silence. The second question almost always elicits answers that simply cite the exceptional performance which the term was introduced in order to explain.

There is certainly no concrete 'thing' to which any of these words unambiguously refers. By way of illustration, take a case in which a particular individual is described as being a talented linguist, and, by implication, as possessing a talent for learning languages. The reasons justifying the assertion that the person has a talent might be ones that have to do with that person's expertise at languages, or they might be based on the ease with which the person acquires new languages, or some other indication of the individual's linguistic capabilities. But in each case the statement that the individual has a talent for languages is purely a linguistic inference: it is nothing more than that. Simply because a person is good at doing something, it is inferred that he or she has some mental quality which we designate a talent. Note that – as in the above dialogue – the sole evidence for the possession of the talent is the performance that the talent is said to have made possible. Even if one is not unhappy about the logic behind the reasoning processes by which the conclusion that a person has a talent is arrived at, it is hard not to baulk at the practice of proceeding to assume that the possession of talents (or gifts) can be an explanation of, or a necessary condition for, superior abilities. The kind of reasoning that leads someone to assume that a concept introduced in order to *describe* superior performance can also provide the *explanation* for that performance ('She's good at music because she has a talent for it') is circular at best, if not entirely nonsensical.

The necessary conditions for making use of a concept such as 'talent' or 'gift' in order to provide a genuine explanation would include the possession of some kind of independent evidence (other than superior performance) of the existence of such a quality. It is quite possible that it does exist, but that possibility does not justify the assumption that it does, in the absence of positive evidence. Later in this chapter I shall raise the question of whether or not any such independent evidence does exist.

## Making Arbitrary Divisions and Typologies

The words 'talented' and 'gifted' are also potentially misleading in another way. Each of them has led users to infer that children and adults can be firmly divided into distinct categories. A person is seen as being either talented (or gifted) or not talented (or not gifted). And if talented (or gifted, or even 'creative') children form a distinct group (or 'type'), one can, it is sometimes assumed, make statements that clearly apply to all individuals within that group and not to others. Similarly, once it has been accepted that it is appropriate to categorize people in this manner, it is often assumed that one can justify according special treatment or special provisions for individuals who are within the group, and regard the members of the group as forming a special and distinct category with special needs or interests (as in, for example, '*The Gifted Child Quarterly*', or '*The National Association for Gifted Children*').

In reality, although it is undoubtedly true that some people are more able than others in various respects (or, if one prefers, 'more talented', or 'more gifted', or 'more creative') there are no clear dividing lines and no natural boundaries of the kind that would make it reasonable to assume, as people so often do, that there exist distinct or homogeneous groups to which terms like these can be applied. Generally speaking, people's ability levels vary along continua: sharp discontinuities are unusual. The fact that individuals differ in their capacity to perform various tasks in no way justifies our inferring that they fall into distinct categories of people, except in the sense that is achieved by inserting an arbitrary line, above and below which there are differing standards of performance. The kind of categorization that is achieved in this way has limited value. It rarely forms a proper basis for making accurate generalizations about the people concerned. Consequently, we ought to be wary of making statements about, say, 'making special provision for gifted children' – as is frequently done – because, appearances notwithstanding, the label 'gifted' does not actually specify any clear grouping of children on the basis of particular characteristics or qualities that might legitimize their receiving special kinds of treatment.

We should be equally wary about assuming that it is necessarily realistic to regard some people as possessing 'traits' of giftedness or creativity. That is not to deny that some children are more able than others: we certainly need to take an individual child's abilities into account when making decisions about that individual's education. However, labelling a person as being gifted or creative is often taken to imply that we are doing something that is both more specific and more explanatory than when we are simply rating or describing someone's abilities. It is assumed that some inner quality is being identified. This assumption is not justified.

In short, although it is true that all children are different, and that their individuality must be taken account of, that is no justification for the common practice of dividing them into what are in effect arbitrarily formed groups, and then assuming that all individuals within each group form a single 'type' and can be expected to be alike in important respects. Unfortunately, the very existence of words like 'talented' and 'gifted' often seems to be taken as providing a justification, both for labelling children in ways that involve making unwarranted and discriminatory classifications, and for assuming that one is identifying underlying qualities that can serve to explain, and not merely describe, the extraordinary feats they perform.

Conceivably, a way to escape from some of these problems might be to avoid linking words like 'gifted' and 'talented' to people as such, and attach them to only to certain *behaviours*, instead. A person would then be described not as being gifted or talented, but as exhibiting gifted or talented behaviours. But this alternative procedure does not genuinely evade the difficulties. It is hard to see what could be meant by 'a gifted behaviour', other than a behaviour that implies the possession of gifts. And that brings us straight back to the initial problem.

But 'talented', 'creative', and 'gifted' are accepted everyday terms in our language. Despite the problems they cause, we cannot legislate them out of existence. We have to live with these commonly-used words, in spite of the fact that they are sometimes introduced in ways that may impede our thinking about the nature of abilities, and despite the obstacles they can cause to the careful investigations that need to be undertaken in order to understand the causes of variability between people in their achievements. Largely for this reason, despite the difficulties associated with these words, I have not entirely avoided using them in this book. All the same, it should be emphasized that when they do occur, no kind of explanatory function is intended. When I write of a person as being talented, my sole intention is to designate the individual as one who has performed exceptional feats or achievements. Similarly, when I write of a 'talent' I am simply referring to an ability, and not trying to account for it. In neither case is there an intention to imply that the qualities that give rise to unusual achievements are being identified.

## Labelling Children in the Classroom

The world of education provides many examples of the misuse of expressions that refer to differences in people's abilities. For instance, children who are not successful in the classroom are frequently labelled 'slow learners', even when there is no real evidence concerning the actual reasons for their failure at school tasks, and when it is plain to all who choose to see that a child's ability to learn skills and acquire kinds of knowledge other than those that are valued by the school is quite unhampered. Worse still is the tendency to believe that it must be possible to firmly identify a child's 'capacity' or even 'potential' for future achievements. The fact of the matter is that it is unwise to presume that it is ever possible to identify or measure an individual's potential psychological qualities.

Of course, it is often possible to make fairly accurate predictions about, say, a child's future academic progress. But when that is the case it is largely so because those circumstances of the child's background that have contributed to the individual having already reached a certain standard will be extended into the future. When abrupt changes occur in a child's life it may become impossible to make accurate predictions about future progress.

## The Concept of Genius

The word 'genius' can hamper our efforts to explain extraordinary achievements, partly for reasons similar to the ones encountered in connection with 'gifted' and 'talented'. It also introduces special difficulties of its own. One particular problem springs from the fact that although we can safely accept that anyone whose achievements are widely enough acknowledged for that epithet 'genius' to be deserved is an individual who has done something exceptional, it is by no means correct to assume that by designating a person as being a genius we are rating that individual's accomplishments in any truly objective sense. What we are actually doing is rather different: we are assessing how those achievements have been judged by other people. To call someone a genius is to bestow an accolade upon them. And whether or not this happens depends on a variety of factors, some of which are matters of luck and chance, and quite outside the individual's control. The difference between being outstandingly able and being called a genius is rather like the difference between being brave and being awarded a medal for heroism. To get the medal you certainly have to be brave, but you also have to be lucky enough to act bravely in the right place at the right time, and be noticed by someone who is in a position to submit a report on your courageous action.

Some of the considerations that determine whether or not a person will be described as being a genius are related to 'the spirit of the times', or to the artistic or scientific climate in which an individual chances to be working. Nobody thought of Mendel as being a genius until many years after his death, partly because his contemporaries, who were ill-placed to perceive the value of his contribution, took no notice of his findings. Our recognition of the genius of Albert Einstein is related to the fact that the particular pattern of striking qualities he possessed was precisely suited for creating important advances at a particular moment in the history of science. Had Einstein reached his peak 30 years earlier or 30 years later, the remarkably happy fit that existed between the skills he had mastered and the qualities that were needed in order to make scientific progress might not have occurred. If the circumstances had been subtly different it is not inevitable that we would now regard him as having been an outstanding genius. Certainly, in Einstein's later years he did not find it easy to come to grips with certain aspects of the quantum approaches to physics which his own discoveries had made possible (Clark, 1979).

For every case in which a person's talents and the needs of the era nicely coincide, there are others where an individual's prodigious abilities fail to make any impact. David Feldman wonders, for instance,

> whether a mind like Einstein's in Galileo's day would have made a contribution to the existing state of knowledge about the physical world. Taking a reverse example, one might speculate whether the twentieth-century mathematician Ramanujan, who independently reinvented much of the mathematics of the past several centuries, might not have changed the course of mathematics had he been Newton's contemporary. (Feldman, 1986, p. 13)

Some of the individuals we now call geniuses were not so regarded until centuries after their deaths. Mihaly Csikszentmihalyi (1988) mentions a number of such instances. For example, not until the mid nineteenth century did Botticelli come to be venerated. He had previously been regarded as a 'coarse' painter. The change in his reputation was largely an outcome of the interpretative writings of John Ruskin and other critics. Even Rembrandt, during his lifetime, was considered a far less important painter than his now-forgotten contemporary Jan Lievens. Composers' reputations have also waxed and waned. J. S. Bach, while he lived, was regarded more highly as an organist than as a composer.

Just occasionally, we glimpse the possibility that awarding the epithet of genius may represent a too-generous estimation of someone's excellence. In the case of Mendel I have already pointed out that his contemporaries were unable to perceive the real value of his work. Csikszentmihalyi mentions an investigation by Augustine Brannigan (1981) which raises the possibility that even Mendel himself was to a marked extent unaware of the real value (as twentieth-century scientists can perceive it) of his famous experiments. Csikszentmihalyi points out that

> [the implications of Mendel's experiments] for the theory of variation and natural selection were discovered only in 1900 by William Bateson and other evolutionists.... Within their theoretical framework, Mendel's work suddenly acquired an importance that it had lacked before, even in the mind of Mendel himself. So where was Mendel's creativity? In his mind, in his experiments, or in the use his results were put to by later science? (Csikszentmihalyi, 1988, p. 328)

So we seem to have a situation that is broadly analogous to one in which it is discovered that the courageous action for which someone has already been awarded a medal might have occurred for partly accidental reasons!

A final complicating factor is that elements of chance or luck are present at a number of the decision points that are important in determining whether the problems on which an individual chooses to work will prove to be tractable or impossible to solve. No one has unlimited foresight: chance always seems to play a hand in deciding which of a large number of equally able and equally skilled people will become the one or two individuals who make achievements that the world judges to be works of genius. Lucky coincidences can sometimes be crucial. I shall return to this point in chapter 8.

## Are Gifts and Talents Concrete Entities?

In discussing the tendency to reify and the other kinds of defective or illogical reasoning that are sometimes encountered in connection with words like 'talent' and 'gift', I stressed that the fact that a word exists does not justify the inference that there necessarily exists any underlying concrete entity. Conversely, however, it is equally true that the fact that reification may take place does not mean that we can assume that there is *not* any corresponding concrete entity. And the fact that a word is a descriptive term does not rule out the possibility that it is also a valid explanatory concept. It is certainly not inconceivable that a person who is described as being gifted or talented may possess some special inherent quality, one that marks out that individual from other people and provides a cause of the individual's exceptional feats. In the above pages I have shown that we cannot assume that this is the case on the basis of our knowledge about a person's achievements alone. I also showed that some outstanding achievements are made by people with no exceptional inherent qualities. But it does still remain possible that some exceptional individuals do have special innate qualities (which we may either choose to call natural talents or gifts or aptitudes, or decide not to do so), and are thereby enabled or predisposed to produce achievements that are beyond the reach of other people.

## *Some Possibilities*

What forms might such qualities take, and how might we detect and measure them? There are a number of possibilities, some more plausible than others. As we shall see, in the case of those candidates that take the form of specific capacities which correspond with most people's idea of what an innate ability might be, convincing evidence for their existence is lacking. On the other hand, there does exist evidence that babies differ, even in the earliest months of life, in ways that in some cases may, albeit indirectly and perhaps via a lengthy chain of causes and effects, exert effects on their patterns of abilities as adults.

In the paragraphs below I only look at those differences which are apparent in the earliest months. Of course, it is quite possible that there are inherited biological differences between people which account for the fact that only a few individuals become outstandingly capable but which do not exert their influence until after the earliest years of life. It is known that certain biologically caused disorders, such as autism (Frith, 1989), do not begin to have noticeable effects until the second or third year of childhood, and it is entirely possible that the appearance of evidence pointing to biological causes of talents could be similarly delayed. If only for that reason, the following suggestions are far from being a complete list of the possible ways in which inherent differences between people could be the causes of differences in their achievements.

On the other hand, it is equally important to recognize that finding that differences between infants that are apparent in the first year or so may predict later differences does not prove that whatever causes the measures to be predictive must necessarily be innate or inherited. For instance, some differences in mothering could have an impact very early in life, although it appears very unlikely that some of the observed early variations in behaviour could be caused by differences in mothering.

1 SPECIAL COGNITIVE MECHANISMS

One possibility, which coincides rather closely with popular beliefs about the nature of an innate gift or talent, is that certain people are born with particular cognitive mechanisms or processes that enable them to do things that other people cannot. For instance, an outstanding musician might be regarded as having possessed since birth a specific neural module that takes the form of a 'music acquisition device' akin to the language acquisition device which, according to Chomsky, largely accounts for the fact that virtually all humans are able to gain language abilities that are denied to other species.

It is not quite inconceivable that some people are born with cognitive processing modules that others simply lack. Yet the available evidence suggests otherwise. It is probably safe to discount that possibility.

2 OTHER STRUCTURAL DIFFERENCES

A less remote possibility is that genetic factors cause fundamental differences in the structure of organs. For example, differences in muscle structure might well account for variability in athletic performance. Conceivably, they might also have an indirect influence on intellectual capacity. For instance, if muscular structure affected the flow of blood to the brain, it is possible that performance at mental tasks could also be affected.

Undoubtedly, certain hereditary differences in anatomical structure do affect athletic capacity. Some kinds of body builds are advantageous for various sports. But a number of research findings challenge the assumption that even those causes of human variability that are apparently most 'fundamental' of all, such as the differences in the physiological structure of people's muscles that undoubtedly exist, are necessarily either innate or wholly genetic in origin. There is absolutely no doubt that the physiological differences are important, but, as Ericsson (1988; 1990) demonstrates, the evidence that they are stable genetic characteristics is remarkably weak. Some of the earlier research studies appeared to provide conclusive proof of this, but recent investigations have failed to replicate the previous findings, and indicate that the extent to which sports performance (and the various factors that underlie it, including proportions of fibre muscle types, aerobic capacity and maximum aerobic power) is determined by genetic factors is smaller than was once believed (Bouchard and Malina, 1986). Such a challenge may have wide implications, because it raises the possibility that any of a variety of other apparently innate differences between people may in fact be caused by alternative factors, such as ones deriving from the differing experiences of individuals' lives.

Ericsson (1988) points out that in order to be successful at long-distance running races it is necessary to have muscles in which an unusually high proportion of the fibres are ones that are known as 'slow-twitch' fibres. So it would appear that individuals who are born with a relatively large proportion of slow-twitch muscle fibres are more likely to become successful long distance runners than other people. Assuming that is correct, it would appear that a genetic determinant of success has been identified. But, as Ericsson notes, recent research findings indicate that the direction of causes and effects may be very different from that implied by the above account. It now seems more likely that the presence in muscles of a high proportion of slow-twitch fibres is largely the *result* of extended practice at running, rather than the initial cause of ability differences. In fact, the proportions can be drastically changed by environmental factors. For instance, cessation of training produces large decreases in the percentage of athletes' slow-twitch fibres (Howald, 1982). Moreover, Ericsson cites research conducted by P. A. Tesch and J. Karlsson showing that the differences between athletes and other people in their relative proportions of fast- and slow-twitch fibres are specific to the particular muscles that are most fully exercised in training for an individual's athletic specialization. For example, compared with non-athletes, experts at the kayak have differences in the proportions of the different fibres in the back muscles, but not in the legs. Conversely, runners' proportions of fibres in their legs differ from those of non-runners, but the composition of their back muscles is no different.

A number of other physiological functions are also affected by practice. For example, Ericsson cites evidence by S. Salmons and J. Hendriksson showing that practice leads to changes in capillaries supplying blood to muscle fibres, converts fast-twitch muscle fibres to slow-twitch muscle fibres, and causes various changes (the form of which depends upon whether practice emphasizes strength or endurance) in the structure of the heart. It is possible that many additional physiological processes are modified by practice, including ones that directly affect the functioning of the brain.

### 3 Innate differences in learning or memory

Another possibility is that a few individuals are born with an advantage over other people in the form of special innate learning abilities, or special powers of memory. These would not make learning unnecessary, but could speed it up or make it easier. The special abilities might be specific to particular forms of competence or they might be of a more general-purpose nature, applicable in any sphere to which the individual chooses to direct them.

Again, however, there is no hard evidence that some individuals are inherently exceptional in this way. It is certainly the case that people who have exceptional abilities are unusually good at learning and remembering anything that is related to their area of special expertise, but their special learning and remembering abilities are acquired skills, not innate qualities. Undoubtedly, individuals' patterns of performance at many learning and memory tasks are related to ability. Yet that is largely because skills that have been learned in the past and previously acquired knowledge largely determine how difficult a new task is perceived to be by the individual who is attempting it. When people are assessed at those kinds of learning tasks that cannot be made easier to perform as a result of a person having previously acquired knowledge or skills that facilitate them, individual differences in learning rate tend to be non-existent (Estes, 1970; Howe, 1975). In these circumstances it is found that young children may do just as well as adults, and that mentally retarded people are as successful as individuals having average or even superior ability (Belmont, 1978). With memory tasks, too, if the nature of the task precludes the possibility of experienced people making use of their existing knowledge or acquired mental strategies in order to improve their rate of success, there will be little, if any, difference in performance between adults and children. In a few circumstances young children actually do better than older people (Ceci and Howe, 1978).

In short, whilst it is quite true to say that individuals who have exceptional abilities are more successful than other people at memory and learning tasks in which the content is related to the person's special expertise, superiority at these tasks is the result of individuals having special skills, rather than the cause. Exceptionally able people are not innately better at learning or remembering; they only become better after they have begun to acquire unusual abilities. In fact, some research that will be described in chapter three shows that in a number of instances the memory feats of 'ordinary' people whose levels of measured intelligence are not above average but who have received intensive memory training, have actually exceeded those very feats of 'outstanding' individuals which have been cited as evidence that the individual concerned must have been born with an inherently exceptional ability to remember.

However, the possibility that innate differences in cognitive processes could be significant for later development has been revived by the finding that early differences in measures of infant looking behaviour are predictors of subsequent differences in intelligence-test scores (Rose,

Slater, and Perry, 1986; Slater, Cooper, Rose, and Morison, 1989). The correlations tend to be small, but this may be due in part to the limited reliability of the infant measures. The results are intriguing, although at this stage it is hard to be certain whether the findings point to the involvement of memory processes or coding mechanisms, or differences in the manner in which babies attend to events, or some combination of these three. Only when more is known about the underlying processes or mechanisms that give rise to the correlations will it possible to know whether or not it is possible to devise appropriate environmental interventions that will improve cognitive functioning in those babies whose cognitive functioning appears to be less than optimal. It is just conceivable that the differences between infants in their behaviour are not inherent but the result of variations in early experiences. (Bornstein, 1985; Tamis-LeMonda and Bornstein, 1989).

4 INHERENT PERCEPTUAL ABILITIES

A fourth category of inborn mechanisms that could conceivably function as gifts or talents, via which early variability might eventually lead to differences in adult achievement, are those underlying particular kinds of perceptual abilities. For instance, it has often been claimed that some exceptional musicians have been born with the capacity for 'perfect' absolute pitch perception. Since such a capacity can be a valuable asset for any musician, someone who was born either possessing it or with qualities that increase the likelihood of it being acquired would have a clear advantage over others, and one that would increase the chance of the person becoming an outstandingly able musical performer. Among musicians themselves, it is widely believed that absolute pitch is inherited (Ericsson, 1988).

But the fact of the matter is that on close investigation perfect pitch perception turns out to be not an innate ability but a learned skill. It is most frequently acquired by children who begin their musical training when they are very young, perhaps because it is easier to give one's full attention to memorizing individual notes before the habit of perceiving notes as part of larger musical structures has been gained (Ericsson and Faivre, 1988). But with careful training it is possible for an adult to acquire the skill (Brady, 1970). Other unusual perceptual accomplishments, such as chicken sexing, certain X-ray diagnostic skills, and abilities based on delicate discriminations between tastes, smells, and colours, have seemed mysterious because so few people have acquired them, and have therefore been thought to be innate and inherited (Ericsson, 1988). But close examinations of these abilities have revealed that they too, like perfect pitch, are in fact learned skills.

## 5 OTHER PERCEPTUAL DIFFERENCES

Although research findings provide no support at all for the suggestion that some people differ innately from others in having certain specific perceptual capacities that make it possible for a person to be exceptionally capable at particular tasks that demand fine perceptual discriminations to be made, it remains possible that there do exist some differences in perceptual sensitivity between young infants. In fact there is some firm evidence that this is the case, and that the differences between infants can affect subsequent development.

Young infants differ in the amount of sensory stimulation they seem to need (Korner, 1971). Some infants like, and appear to require, a large amount of stimulation. Others, who seem to be more sensitive, are overwhelmed and made anxious if stimulation exceeds a certain level. There are a variety of ways in which these early differences could affect infants' later progress, and thereby contribute to differences between individuals in their achievements. For instance, it is known that when babies are picked up they become visually attentive, and thereby gain increased visual stimulation. So when the mother picks up an infant who has an especially strong need to be stimulated via the senses, the effect, from the child's point of view, will be to fill the child's visual field with 'interesting' events, ones that will provide important early learning experiences. For an infant like this, so far as early visual learning is concerned, the more he or she is picked up the better. It will be an advantage for such a baby to have a mother who is unusually attentive and affectionate, and picks her baby up at every opportunity. Conversely, if the baby's mother is less attentive, the acquisition of skills that depend upon visual perception may suffer, and the effect on that baby's perceptual experiences of having a mother who regularly neglects to pick up her infant could be very serious.

But other infants are not like that at all. They are considerably more sensitive to visual stimulation. Too much stimulation will overwhelm these babies and make them anxious. Babies of this kind seem to receive all the visual stimulation they require without being frequently picked up. So, at least so far as providing extra sensory experience is concerned, the effects of being picked up will not be so beneficial for these babies as they are for the others. And for them, the consequences for visual learning of having a mother who does not often pick up and play with the child will be less harmful.

In summary, it is clear that the effects of early differences between babies in their perceptual sensitivity or receptivity may, indirectly, have an influence on later achievements. But note that the long-term effects of such differences are not fixed, or readily predictable, or irreversible.

The actual effects for the child will depend upon a number of additional factors, such as the mother's responsiveness, and her sensitivity to her infant's preferences.

To complicate things even further, the ways in which individual differences between infants help to determine the outcomes of the mother's behaviour towards her child are likely to be considerably more complex than the above account suggests. In that example we only considered those consequences of picking up an infant that specifically affect vision. But a baby may be affected in more than one way by being picked up, and a description that considers only one of the possible outcomes is bound to give a somewhat simplified sketch of the pattern of causes and effects surrounding the child's actual development. All the same, the above account does make it clear that early differences in perceptual sensitivity may have important eventual consequences, even if they are not ones that can be reliably predicted.

6 EARLY DIFFERENCES IN TEMPERAMENT AND ACTIVITY LEVEL

There are various other differences, broadly related to babies' temperaments and activity levels, that are observable within a few months of birth and can have effects on a child's later progress (Thomas and Chess, 1977; Dunn, 1979). As in the case of early differences in perceptual capacities, it is clear from a number of studies that individual differences in temperament which are seen in early infancy have important implications for subsequent development. But, as was also the case with early differences in perceptual responsiveness, the long-term consequences are not straightforwardly predictable, largely because they depend on other factors as well, such as the actions of the child's mother or caretaker. Also, the consequences of having a particular trait to an unusually high or unusually low degree are not irreversible. That is because the child's experiences (the nature of which, especially in the first year or two, will depend very considerably on the manner in which the infant interacts with the mother) may exert either a compensating or an augmenting effect. All the same, continuities are often observed. For instance, most children who are consistently shy and emotionally subdued as toddlers retain these characteristics until at least their eighth year, and a similar continuity of temperament is observed in children who have been sociable and affectively spontaneous toddlers (Kagan, Reznick and Snidman, 1987; Kagan, 1989). However, whereas Kagan believes that the degree of consistency in children's temperament over the years is sufficiently high to form definite evidence of a genetic cause, it is possible that it could result from consistencies in children's experiences.

One important way in which babies differ at birth is in their reaction to being soothed when they are crying. Some remain comforted for longer than others. A reason why such differences may have important consequences for the child is that they may influence the mother's reactions. An inexperienced mother's feelings may be affected by the success or failure of her efforts to comfort the baby, and her self-confidence as a mother may also be affected. This, in turn, will influence her own mothering activities in the future. So even the youngest babies may influence their own environments, via a chain of events that results in the individual characteristics of an infant having an influence on the mother's behaviour towards the child.

There are additional ways in which attributes in which infants differ can affect how their mothers act towards them. For instance, although most infants like to be cuddled, some do not, and they resist their mothers' attempts to hug them. These infants are more restless than others, dislike physical constraints, and consequently have less physical contact with their parents than babies who do enjoy being cuddled (Schaffer and Emerson, 1964). Inevitably, differences between infants in cuddliness have some influence on the form of the mother–infant interactions that take place, with important consequences for the future development of the child.

In all, there exist numerous ways in which a child's development is affected by qualities of temperament that display substantial inter-infant variability in the earliest months of life. Of course, not all early differences are maintained in later years, but some are. For example, Sybile Escalona (1973) found that infants who were unusually active tend to become, when they reach the age of five years, children who do better at tasks measuring their competence at physical skills than at questions assessing verbal achievement. Also, highly sensitive infants tend to become five-year-olds who are unusually good at expressing themselves and articulating their feelings. And even when an early difference is not maintained later, and no trace of it remains, there is still the possibility that it may have had an influence on the child's development, for example through affecting the parent's behaviour towards the child in a way that has been significant in affecting the child's progress.

## 7 Early differences in infants' preferences

It is conceivable that at a very early age babies could develop small differences in their preferences which might trigger off differing responses that eventually lead to major differences in a child's abilities, by a kind of snowballing effect (Renninger and Wozniak, 1985). The initial slight differences in babies' preferences might be caused in any of a number of ways. Early differences in temperament could be a contributing factor, and so could differences in sensitivity to various kinds of sensory inputs. Alternatively, variations in babies' environments might lead to their preferences differing.

How could slight variations in preferences actually produce differences in children's achievements? Here is a possible scenario. At first the tendency of a child to spend slightly more time observing those objects and events that are preferred might gradually lead to those objects and events being remembered more accurately than non-preferred items, and to higher levels of performance at those tasks that involve the preferred objects. Next, these early differences in a child's rate of success, although at this stage probably still very small, may lead to differences in the patterns of reward and encouragment experienced by the child. In consequence, the child may now start to attend more and more selectively to those events which, by this time, have become associated with competence and success as well as high levels of interest. So by the time a child is two or three years old the initial variations in preferences – which might have been quite tiny at first – may have snowballed into large variations in the child's degree of competence at different kinds of task. And by this stage people may begin to notice that the child has special interests and special skills, and start to remark that the child must be 'talented' or 'gifted'. The resulting adult attention and praise may give further encouragement to the child to develop those particular skills that people have remarked upon.

## *Conclusion*

Although there is no firm evidence that some exceptional people possess the kinds of innate mechanisms that come to mind when phrases such as 'natural gift' or 'innate talent' are invoked, there none the less do exist early differences between infants in their psychological characteristics, some of which are probably inborn and possibly inherited, that can have effects of various kinds upon an infant's later development. Newborns are not identical, and their differences have consequences that may influence the likelihood of an individual eventually acquiring exceptional abilities.

# Beliefs about Hereditary Causes

The evidence that was presented in the immediately preceding pages, as well as many findings from entirely different kinds of investigations, points rather firmly to the conclusion that hereditary factors do contribute to exceptional abilities. But efforts to discover exactly how hereditary influences actually affect human abilities are bedevilled by confusions and misunderstandings about genetic causation. Together, these form yet another obstacle that can impede understanding of the causes of excellence. To deny that individuals' inherited characteristics affect their achievements, and argue that all men and women are created not only equal but identical, is to fly in the face of fact and reason. But, on the other hand, some of the assertions about inheritance that have been made by psychologists and other scientists who have been at pains to stress the importance of hereditary influences on abilities have been equally misjudged, largely because they reflect a faulty understanding of genetics. To write of 'genes for high intelligence' as Hans Eysenck (Eysenck *versus* Kamin, 1981, p. 46) does, as if levels of ability were directly and immutably determined by a person's genetic make-up, is inconsistent with an awareness of the true complexity of hereditary influences. Genes do not function as blueprints, and,

> genetic influence does not imply hard-wired circuits that determine a specific response. Consider alcoholism, for example ... Behavioral genetic data suggest genetic influence on alcohol abuse. This does not mean that there is a gene or a set of genes that determines whether an individual will become alcoholic ... Genetic influence is embedded in the complexity of interactions among genes, physiology, and environment. It is probabilistic, not deterministic; it puts no constraints on what could be. (Plomin, 1986, pp. 20–1)

If inherited factors do help determine future achievements, how can environmental influences be equally crucial? It is generally assumed that one of these two sources of influence must be more important than the other, and that the relative strengths of their contributions can be quantified in a straightforward manner. A common assumption is that if genetic factors are important then environmental differences can have only a weak influence on abilities. Another widespread belief is that any outcomes of genetic causes are immutable, irreversible, and cannot be affected by environmental interventions.

But none of these assumptions is actually correct. All of them stem from misunderstandings of the contribution of genes to human abilities (Lewontin, 1982). The fact that it is possible to provide quantitative estimates of the heritability of various traits has misled some psychologists into believing that there are narrow limits on what can be achieved by environmental changes. As Robert Plomin has remarked:

> A spectre that lurks in the shadows is the concern that genetic influence counsels despair: Nothing can be done about genetic effects. As an antidote to this concern, it can be argued that the more that is known about a trait genetically as well as environmentally, the more likely that rational intervention and prevention strategies can be devised. (Plomin, 1986, p. 21)

In fact, measures of heritability do provide an indication of the extent to which a trait has been affected by environmental variability, but typically in circumstances where such variability is very limited, and its effects underestimated because the crucial variables have not been accurately measured, or in some instances not even identified (Lewontin, 1982; Plomin, 1986). Consequently, measures of heritability do not necessarily give a realistic indication of the potential potency of environmental influences.

Contributing to the confusion about genetic and environmental causation is the fact that we are remarkably ignorant concerning the precise nature of genetic influences. Although it is known that genes do have important effects, very little is understood about the mechanisms or processes by which these effects are exerted. This is important because, in the absence of such knowledge, it is difficult to discover whether it is possible to intervene (and how to do so) in ways that provide needed compensations or corrections in circumstances where genetic factors are less than optimal.

Richard Lewontin (1982) has identified some common misconceptions about the effects of inheritance on human capacities. He points out, first, that contrary to common belief, with a few exceptions (such as blood group, for instance) human traits are never fixed by a person's genes. Even body shape and rate of metabolism are partly determined by the environment. So if one member of a pair of identical twins lives at sea level and does light work whilst the other twin has a life working in the mountains as a heavy labourer, the two will develop very different body shapes and metabolic rates.

Secondly, Lewontin notes that the apparently reasonable view that although the environment has important effects, genes do place firm limits on capacities, is incorrect. Certain plausible-seeming metaphors admittedly seem to lend credence to that view. For instance, children's mental capacities have been compared to buckets which can be more or less full (depending on environmental factors) but whose total contents cannot exceed the limitations imposed by the size of the bucket. But in reality, different genotypes, unlike buckets, do not have different fixed capacities. Moreover, there is no ideal environment for each and every genotype. The environment that maximizes the growth of an organism of one genotype will not be the most favourable environment for a genetically different organism.

Thirdly, geneticists insist that it is not even correct to assert that someone has a genetic tendency to exhibit a particular trait. By way of illustration, Lewontin points out that the statement that a person has a genetic tendency to be fat implies that in normal environments that person will be fatter than a person with no such genetic tendency. But this begs the question of what kinds of human environments are 'normal' ones. In practice this may be impossible to specify. Lewontin doubts if there is any basis for saying, for instance, that high or low levels of nutrition are more normal in human life, or the presence or absence of parasites, or individual competitiveness rather than collective sharing. Not only is it true that a person who 'tends to be fat' when there is a high level of nutrition will tend to be considerably thinner when the nutritive input is lower, it is also true that between a pair of people, the one who is thinner than the other when both of them consume a large amount of food may be fatter than the other when the amount each consumes is low.

Similar complications are encountered with respect to the differences in people's abilities. The individual who, after being subjected to one set of environmental circumstances performs better at a test than another person who has experienced the identical environment (so far as that is possible) may perform worse than the second person if the two of them share a different environment. There are many situations in which a particular inherited characteristic may lead to a person doing better than someone else in certain environmental circumstances, but worse than that person in other circumstances.

It is also important to realize that inborn differences between individuals, even when their environments seem to be identical, are not necessarily genetic in origin. Fruit flies (*drosophila*) provide a simple illustration of this point. Their left and right sides are genetically identical but nevertheless differ in the number of bristles that grow on the body. These differences are caused by random phenomena known as 'developmental noise'. Human characteristics too, Lewontin suggests, may well contain inborn individual differences that have nothing at all to do with genetics. In humans, moreover, differences in individuals' prenatal environments affect postnatal development.

Another point to be remembered is that genetic differences are not always inherited. This fact is illustrated by a condition such as Down's Syndrome ('mongolism'). Down's Syndrome is caused by a genetic abnormality, but the abnormality is not present in the genes of either parent.

## Is it possible to compensate for genetic Differences?

It is often assumed that if differences in human genes contribute to differences in people's achievements, they can only do so by operating in a fixed, all-or-none, and unchangeable fashion, leaving no room for experience to modify or compensate for genetic differences. This assumption, which Plomin and other geneticists have shown to be incorrect, leads to the mistaken belief that traits influenced by genetic factors cannot also be affected by environmental ones. Another widespread view that is in fact equally fallacious is that if genetic influences affect human achievements they must do so in a fairly direct manner, for example via physiological processes that affect a person's rate of learning, or accuracy of recall, or the 'power' or capacity of fundamental mental processes.

In fact, there is no valid reason for supposing that the ways in which genetically transmitted qualities exert an influence on psychological processes are either direct or unmodifiable. Nor is there any good reason for assuming that the results of genetic provisions that are less than entirely favourable cannot be compensated for, in many instances, by making appropriate environmental modifications. There is no inevitability about the effects of hereditary influences on psychological characteristics.

A simple example can help to explain the fact that, paradoxical as it may seem, appropriate environmental interventions can have enormous effects on abilities that are partly determined by genetic factors. Imagine that it has just been discovered that a genetic cause underlies differences between children in the ease with which they can learn to read. The precise nature of the genetic mechanism involved remains a mystery, and so does the way in which its effect is exerted. So everyone assumes that there is no way in which the poor readers can be helped. Because the cause is genetic, it appears that their fate is sealed, and nothing can be done about it.

Later, however, it is discovered that the genetic influence is exerted via the visual processes. Quite simply, some children find it easier than others to identify letters of the alphabet. This source of variability leads, in turn, to differences in children's rate of success at learning to read.

In this fictional example there would be no denying that, on the one hand, the cause of the reading differences was genetic. But on the other hand, it is clear that the effects of the genetic difference could, after all, be eliminated with little difficulty, by making an appropriate environmental modification. In this particular instance that might be achieved by providing eye-glasses for those children who have (genetically caused) visual deficits. Spectacles would eliminate the visual disadvantage. Consequently, as a result of the environmental modification (providing spectacles) the (genetically caused) difference between the groups in ability to read would disappear.

In real life the ways in which genetic differences influence human abilities are usually less straightforward than in the above example. All the same, the chances are that in most cases there is an equivalent degree of openness to environmental modification. On the whole, the fact that most genetic influences upon performance work in an indirect rather than a direct fashion increases the scope for introducing environmental changes that have the effect of compensating for genetically-caused disadvantages.

## *The indirect Nature of genetic Causation*

If genes affected human intellectual capacities in a very direct manner, for instance by determining the rate or power or efficiency of basic mental activities, or the rate at which a person can learn, or the capacity to remember, we might be forced to conclude that genetic influences cannot be modified, and that there is no compensating for the absence of a particular genetic endowment. But the evidence points to a different conclusion. So far as it is possible to tell, the way in which most of the genetic differences that can affect human achievements actually make their presence felt is not by directly influencing mental powers or capacities, but by more indirect means. For instance, genetic differences between individuals may affect temperament, motivation, attentiveness, perseverance, concentration, perceptual capacities, or sensitivity. As a result, indirectly and perhaps via a lengthy chain of causes and effects, inherited factors have influences of one kind or other on various aspects of human performance.

One consequence of the indirect nature of the genetic contribution is that there is considerable scope for introducing procedures that effectively compensate for any deficiency that originates in genetically-constrained mechanisms. Another consequence is that, simply because a long chain of processes and events is likely to intervene between genetically-determined differences and their eventual measurable effects on a human ability, it is generally impossible to predict how a particular genetic difference between two individuals will actually affect their lives. At each of the many stages that intervene between genetically determined processes and a person's behaviour the precise effect of an inherited difference will depend on a number of other factors. A result of this is to preclude the kinds of reliable predictions that can be made when a direct link exists between cause and event. Yet it may still be possible to make some predictions about the *average* performance levels of large groups of people. For example, the presence of a high loading of genetic factor X might conceivably be associated with good performance at a skill, so that the average test score of 100 children who are high in genetic factor X is larger than the average score of 100 children who are low in factor X (despite the indirectness of the genetic effects). But so far as our ability to make useful predictions about individuals is concerned, this knowledge may have little or no practical value.

Both of these consequences of the existence of a chain of events between a genetic cause and the distantly related ability on which it may have some effect (namely, first, the scope for intervention, and, second, the impossibility of predicting eventual actual effects on a person's achievements) are illustrated in the following analogy. Consider the proposition that children born in Switzerland are better skiers than children born in England. Assuming it is true, it is only true in the sense that the average skiing skills of a very large sample of Swiss children are somewhat better than the average skills of a comparable sample of children born in England. And the probable reason is that most children born in Switzerland live closer to ski slopes than children born in England. Therefore, other things being equal, Swiss children are more likely to go skiing, and in consequence (again, other things being equal) they will become better skiers. Yet although place of birth does have an effect, on average, there are numerous points at which, in the case of individual children, additional factors can and do override it. These include, for instance, the wealth and the personal circumstances of individual people. In other words, the 'other things' are often far from being equal. In consequence, it is impossible to make predictions about the skiing skills of individuals that are accurate enough to have much practical value. Also, in the case of an individual child, it is possible to provide opportunities that will 'compensate' an English youngster for the disadvantage of not having been born in Switzerland. Likewise, to leave the analogy and return to the broader discussion of hereditary influences on psychological characteristics, it is often impossible, in practice, to predict how a genetically transmitted difference between individuals will actually make its mark on patterns of human achievement. But it is often possible to compensate for unfavourable genetic predispositions.

It is worth emphasizing that the importance of genetic factors is not being challenged here. For many individuals, genetic influences undoubtedly do place constraints on what they can achieve. (I, for instance, would never have made a living as a heavyweight boxer.)

Moreover, the notion that environment determines all, in which case anyone, even a mentally retarded person, could attain the highest levels of intellectual performance if only the right environmental circumstances were provided, is refuted by the evidence. What *is* being challenged is the assumption that genetic mechanisms operate in ways that make it impossible for a person to gain outstanding abilities unless he or she happens to be one of the rare few individuals who happen to possess a particular combination of genetic potentialities. The latter view, that progress is completely mapped out in advance by each individual's genetic make-up, is as wide of the mark as the one that attributes all human differences to variations in people's physical environments.

## Conclusion: Genetics and Inevitability

Even today the opportunities given to many children continue to be restricted, quite unnecessarily, by mistaken beliefs about the genetic causation of human abilities. It is still widely assumed by many people that we have to choose between two simple alternatives: that either human abilities are not affected by hereditary factors, or that inheritance determines people's capacity to learn and achieve in a manner that is direct, irreversible, inevitable, and inescapable. As we have seen, the truth of the matter is that both alternatives are equally wrong. Heredity does have effects that can substantially influence the psychological capabilities of individuals, but inherited influences on people's achievements are not direct, not irreversible or immutable, not inevitable, and not inescapable. The fact that they are not has momentous consequences. The view that most people, however hard they try to succeed at mental activities, are condemned to being mediocre by the lack of the right set of genes, is seen to be a restrictive falsehood. That view, and the accompanying idea that our accomplishments are irreversibly constrained by the particular legacy of genes that we inherit may in reality be no more credible than the astrologists' claim that people's fates are sealed by the movements of heavenly bodies across the sky. It may be comforting for recipients of a privileged upbringing to have chosen to believe that Nature has ordained some people to be born quick-witted and others dull, some to lead and the remainder to follow. But the findings of empirical research contradict this conclusion.

## Environments and Experiences: some Important Distinctions

Psychologists are inclined to speak rather too glibly of 'the environment' as the source of those influences on learning and development that are not directly biological and inherited. Up to a point it is indeed correct to say that the environment provides the circumstances that determine the kinds of information, the opportunities, the encouragements, and the various informative messages, to which an individual is exposed. And it is hardly surprising that efforts to accelerate learning revolve around the manipulation of environmental factors, or that attempts by psychologists to understand the causes of abilities make use of measures of environmental influences. Yet people are only indirectly affected by their environments. The most direct influences upon all of us are our experiences. So instead of measuring and manipulating individuals' environments, why not focus attention directly upon their experiences?

The reason, of course, is that that is far more easily said than done. Of all the difficult problems that are encountered in trying to apply scientific approaches to the task of examining the progress of exceptionally able individuals' lives, perhaps the most awesome of all is that of finding a reliable way to observe the actual experiences of individual people.

To a considerable extent, all individuals are forged by their experiences. How each of us experiences events in the world we inhabit determines how we are influenced by those events, and what we learn from them. It needs to be stressed that experiencing the outside world is far from being a matter of simply absorbing or mirroring it. How a person experiences a situation depends upon how that particular individual perceives and interprets the information that reaches his brain. And that, in turn, depends on a very large number of factors which, taken together, amount to the unique circumstances of that particular person at a particular moment in time. Among those factors which can influence how things are experienced are, for instance, the individual's knowledge, interests, attitudes, personality, self-confidence, temperament, prejudices, mood, and expectations. So if two individuals are placed in what, to an external observer, is an identical environment it is by no means the case that their experiences of the situation will be remotely identical: what that situation signifies to each them as individuals stems from their distinct — and possibly very different — interpretations of it.

Because humans' experiences are entirely personal, subjective, and unique to the individual who has them, we can never directly observe the experiences of another person. But since experiences are all-important causes of the particular route via which each individual progresses from infancy to adulthood, and crucial determinants of the abilities someone comes to possess, it is obviously important to do everything we possibly can to gain evidence about the actual experiences of any individual person whose progress we wish to understand. If we cannot directly observe another person's act of experiencing, we can at least (provided that we know a great deal about that person as an individual) gain various clues and indications that may point us in the right direction. As we shall see, there are procedures and techniques that can help to provide some indication of the experienced worlds of other people.

Unfortunately, however, the direction taken by most psychological research into the causes of human abilities is one that makes no provision for investigating individuals' experiences. In the interest of providing a degree of order and clarity in the face of the numerousness and complexity of influences on human development, the procedure has been adopted of dividing the sources of influence into two categories: first, the hereditarily transmitted biological influences ('nature'), and second, those of the environment ('nurture'). In many respects grouping the numerous and diverse influences in this way is a useful and necessary step: some kind of categorization is necessary and commonplace in the analytic sciences. But in this particular instance categorizing has a disastrous effect: it cuts out experience, which effectively disappears altogether and is subsequently ignored by researchers, simply because experience cannot be placed neatly or exclusively in either the 'nature' or the 'nurture' category.

In reality, the contribution of experience is not simply one aspect of nature, and nor is it a part of nurture: it encompasses both. So the effect of categorizing the various influences on human development into those of nature and nurture has been to exclude from attention the most important influence of all. Investigators who examine the effects of either nature or nurture can never be in a position to perceive, even indirectly, how individual people actually experience their lives. Yet trying to account for a child's progress without taking the experiences of that particular individual into account is an exercise in futility. It is rather like attempting to examine the *Mona Lisa* whilst standing on the canvas, with both feet planted on the lady's face. In each case, the activity of the investigator makes it impossible to observe the true object of the investigation.

Researchers who have investigated the effects of environmental variables have sometimes appeared to believe that environment and experience are synonymous. In fact, as we have seen, that is very far from being true. Environmental measures, however sensitive or accurate, are inevitably ones 'from outside' the experiencing person. They are observations made by persons other than the experiencer, who is the only individual to 'know' or experience the actual impact of perceived environmental information. Since the nature of that impact depends upon interpretative activities that reflect the individual's unique qualities, the kinds of 'objective' environmental measures that an observer can obtain are unlikely to give more than the crudest indication of the actual nature of the direct influences to which the individual is being subjected.

On the whole, from the point of view of the enterprise of trying to explain the origins of exceptional abilities, the closer we can get to being able to perceive how someone is actually experiencing the circumstances of their life, the better. And the more likely it will be that we will gain a more complete understanding of how that individual has become the person he or she now is, and how, over the years, that person has gained a particular collection of capabilities. From a practical point of view, the same argument applies to the task of trying to help individual children to raise the levels of their accomplishments and increase the likelihood of gaining exceptional skills. Here, too, the closer we can approach the goal of being able to see things from another person's perspective, and appreciate how that individual is actually perceiving those events that potentially have educational value, the more likely it will be that we can provide genuinely practical teaching and encouragement.

The following chapters include numerous demonstrations of the practical and explanatory value of being able to get as near as possible to knowing how an individual person is experiencing important events in that person's life. To anticipate a point that will be enlarged upon in chapter four, it is because of the enormous value, so far as teaching and learning is concerned, of having access to the individual experiences of the learner, that those adults who are able to get to know a child really well and can engage in conversations, play activities, and other kinds of dialogue that depend upon intimate knowledge of the other person as an individual, are in an especially powerful position to help the young learner. As a result, the child's own home can be a superb environment for early learning. Parents, who can work and play intensively with their own children, are in many respects far better placed to aid their young children's progress than even the best classroom teachers can ever be. The latter, however skilled and well equipped they may be, have to work with the handicap of having to share their time among a large number of different individuals. Even the most able teacher will fail to get to know all of them well enough to be in a position to provide the kinds of help that depend upon the adult's possessing a good knowledge of how the individual child is actually experiencing the events and the information that provide the ingredients of an education.

# 3

# Accelerating the Acquisition of Abilities

In what circumstances can individuals gain exceptional abilities? The first part of this chapter looks at the findings of research investigations designed to promote superior accomplishments of one kind or another. In the majority of studies the learners have been young children, and the objective has been to ascertain whether or not a programme of relatively intensive training results in the child making accelerated progress, compared with other children of similar age. In most cases it is fairly certain that the children concerned have possessed none of the special innate qualities or 'gifts' that are often assumed to exist in certain individuals and are deemed to be essential in order for extraordinary abilities to be gained. A few studies have involved adult learners. In these investigations the object has been to discover whether or not it is possible for exceptional levels of performance at a learned skill to be achieved by an adult of average ability.

If it is true, as evidence mentioned in the previous chapter suggested, that individuals who acquire exceptional abilities are not extraordinary at the time of their birth, then it could be argued that the simple fact that *some* ordinary people do acquire exceptional skills provides grounds for claiming that in the right circumstances almost *anyone* can do so. The dazzling musical performances of the girls of the la Pietà orphanage in eighteenth-century Venice, which I mentioned in Chapter One, provide firm evidence that individuals whom many people would have regarded as having been unlikely to have inherited special gifts are none the less capable of reaching the heights of virtuosity. Similarly, the present-day feats of thousands of Suzuki-trained young violinists show that with proper training many of today's children can reach extremely high standards of musical performance.

When special training has been given, we need to know whether or not any accelerated learning which may follow it is a direct consequence of the training, rather than the result of chance, or some special quality of the learner, or another cause. The researcher is best placed to be certain about this when it has been possible to exert some control over the conditions in which abilities are learned. Often, it is helpful to compare the performance of someone who has undergone a programme of training with that of individuals who have had no such training. The best way for an investigator to bring about these circumstances is to conduct research that takes the form of controlled experiments. Accordingly, many of the research studies that will be mentioned in the present chapter are broadly experimental in nature. Quite often however, the experimental research that would enable us to give a firm answer to a specific question that has been raised has not yet been undertaken. In these circumstances we have to fall back upon alternative kinds of evidence which have a bearing on the question, but which typically do not yield answers that are quite as direct or as definitive as those that experimental research might have provided.

The first part of this chapter draws heavily upon William Fowler's two-volume *Potentials of Childhood* (Fowler, 1983), which contains a painstaking review of much of the experimental research that psychologists have conducted in order to investigate the effectiveness of attempts to accelerate learning in children. The present chapter does not attempt to provide a comprehensive survey of this research. It merely describes a number of illustrative findings, in order to establish the case that, in some circumstances at least, suitable training reliably leads to young children gaining various key abilities considerably earlier than usual.

In view of the importance of the issues involved, the amount of research that has been conducted is not at all large. Some of the most interesting investigations of the effects of reasonably intensive and long-lasting early childhood educational programmes were published some time ago, well before World War II. Not surprisingly, by modern standards certain methodological aspects of the designs of these investigations are less than adequate. There have been relatively few recent studies measuring the effects of intensive long-term early training programmes designed to accelerate the progress of non-disadvantaged children.

# Broad Attempts to Accelerate Learning in Infancy and Childhood

## Some early Studies

In research examining the effects of special training on children's early progress it is obviously important for the researchers to be reasonably sure that their findings have not been contaminated by the influence of hereditary factors. One approach which seems to eliminate this possibility involves conducting experiments in which genetically identical twins are submitted to varying conditions of training. Under these circumstances, differences that emerge between the twins in their achievements can be attributed to the children's different experiences. Since identical twins do not differ genetically, the possibility of genetic factors being a cause of the differing success in tests designed to measure the effectiveness of training can be ruled out.

## Gesell's Work

Successive generations of psychology students have learned about a series of infant training experiments that were undertaken by Arnold Gesell and his co-researchers between about 1925 and 1945. As usually reported, a major finding of the experiments was that any effects of giving infants special training were very short-lived: the advantages tended to disappear after a matter of weeks. For example, when Gesell and Thompson (1929) gave one member of a pair of identical girl twins six weeks' training in climbing stairs (starting at 46 weeks), they reported that although the specially trained child gained a temporary advantage over the other twin, the advantage was wiped out after the second child had received just two weeks' training, which in her case began seven weeks later.

Gesell saw the finding that a child could catch up fairly easily if training was delayed for a few weeks as providing support for his view of human development as largely an 'unfolding' process. Gesell believed that a person's eventual capabilities are essentially determined before birth. As a child grows, the physical maturation that takes place enables various abilities to unfold. Gesell thought that there was little point in trying to bring forward the development of skills before the point at which the unfolding process makes the child ready to acquire them. At that time, but not before, according to Gesell, they are gained easily and naturally.

Gesell influenced generations of teachers and parents. His belief that it is harmful to teach young children physical skills or intellectual ones (such as reading) until 'readiness' had been achieved, as a result of physical maturation, was widely accepted. According to him, the time at which different abilities appear is 'fundamentally determined by the ripeness of the neural structures' (Gesell and Thompson, 1929, p. 114). His view that the course of human development is largely predetermined led Gesell to assert that attempts to accelerate early progress would have no beneficial long-term effects.

But even Gesell's own findings, when they are carefully examined, do not support this conclusion. In fact, as Fowler (1983) discovered on re-examining Gesell's data, some of the results provide firm evidence that the early training sessions did, after all, have substantial long-term effects. Although Gesell had reported these results he paid little attention to them and failed to draw the obvious conclusions, which would have ended to contradict the nativist beliefs he held.

Fowler noticed that whilst it was true that on tasks at which one twin but not the other received very early training, the initially untrained twin, if taught the skill several months later, did make faster progress than the other twin had done, certain advantages were maintained by the twin who was trained first. For instance, that child's mastery of a manipulation task involving delicate control over toy blocks was never quite matched by the twin who learned the task later. In a later study in which the same twins again participated as experimental subjects, the child who was trained first did better at the vast majority of the skills they were taught. Her advantages were maintained in follow-up tests administered four weeks and 12 weeks after the second twin had received training. Even when the twins were teenagers, the twin who received earlier training in climbing stairs was still superior at a number of motor skills, including running, walking, and tap-dancing. That was so despite the fact that the actual duration of the training was relatively short. (For instance, stair-climbing was taught for only 20 minutes per day, over a six-week period.) Also, even after the twins had entered adolescence, the first child maintained her advantage in important language skills such as pronunciation and sentence construction. She also had a larger vocabulary.

Of course, caution is necessary in drawing conclusions from a study based on only one pair of twins. But the fact that the child who was taught particular skills earliest maintained her superiority at those skills and related abilities for many years, and probably throughout the twins' entire lives, points to the conclusion that accelerated early training can have powerful and long-lasting effects. Yet Gesell was unwilling to admit that the differences between the twins' abilities were caused by their different experiences. Fowler credits Gesell with at least bothering to collect information on children's development, rather than simply making armchair pronouncements in support of predeterminism. But unfortunately, Fowler notes,

> Gesell did look but he did not see. The core of the problem lay in his assumption that a child's behavior consists of underlying traits that evolve in terms of programs prescribed from within, enduring regardless of environmental factors and contexts. He was constantly explaining away various factors without investigating them carefully, for example dismissing the possibility that twin T's superior skill as a teenager in the 50-yard dash could be related to her earlier and longer training in stair climbing. (Fowler, 1983).

Another sign of Gesell's apparent blindness to the influences of early experience was his failure to notice that the progress of *both* twins on the skills at which they had received training was well ahead of developmental norms. Fowler points out that the average American child, according to data collected by Gesell himself, cannot walk up stairs with assistance until around 18 months, and only walks unaided at two years. Yet in the twin study, even the child who was given less training, totalling fewer than five hours over a two-week period, could climb five stairs alone in about ten seconds at the age of one year. Gesell's silence concerning findings such as these leads Fowler to comment,

> Even within the short-term experimental framework of these studies, the investigators in their stress upon maturation all but ignored the substantial gains that both twins invariably made as direct consequence of systematic stimulation. In this way Gesell and his group overlooked many very real specific and cumulative influences that could easily have been explored and analyzed in depth ... (Fowler, 1983, p. 116).

Fowler also suggests that in view of the fact that the training given to the twins was always short in duration and never involved more than a small fraction of the day, the finding that early training did have long-lasting effects provides strong evidence of the importance of early experience. Moreover, as he also notes, it is worth emphasizing that the finding that the twin who had received the earlier training maintained her advantage at a number of skills over a period of years occurred, despite the fact that the other twin had also received special training, albeit briefer and later. In actuality the two children's experiences differed only to a limited extent. The fact that, even so, there were clear differences between the two, makes it fair to suggest that had the studies compared the effects of early training with the outcome of no training at all, and had the training been really lengthy and intensive, the differences in the twins' abilities might have been immense.

## A deprivation Study

In principle, a good way to discover to what extent differences in early experiences can accelerate or retard development would be to undertake long-term twin experiments in which one twin is given unusually intensive early training and the other twin is deprived of potentially valuable experiences. In practice, of course, there are a variety of ethical arguments against undertaking any investigation of this kind. For this reason it is widely assumed that no experimental study has been undertaken that involves deliberately depriving children of early experiences. As it happens, that assumption is wrong. An experimental study carried out in the 1930s examined the effects of deliberately depriving infant girls (Dennis, 1941; Dennis and Dennis, 1951).

Two baby girls, fraternal (i.e., non-identical) twins, were cared for from the age of one month until they were 14 months old in the home of a husband and wife team, the Dennises. The intention was to deprive both infants of any stimulation beyond what was necessary for essential physical care. They were fed, regularly changed, and kept warm, but no further care was given. The room in which they lived contained no toys, no pictures, and very little furniture. The Dennises tried to avoid rewarding or punishing the twins at all, and abstained from actions that could be readily imitated.

At first, the effects of depriving the children in these ways appeared to be fairly small. On most tests administered during their first seven months the twins' scores were within the normal range for babies of comparable age, although they were backward on some items. But their subsequent development was more seriously retarded. On nearly all the tests administered to measure their progress in later months, until the termination of the study when they were 14 months of age, the twins' progress was much below average. This outcome is especially impressive in view of the fact that the deprivation they suffered was not, by some standards, particularly severe. As Fowler points out, the twins were in fact given two hours of undivided attention each day by caring adults – considerably more than many babies experience.

By showing that deprivation can seriously retard children's early development, just as training can accelerate it, the study by the Dennises provides additional evidence of the powerful effects of a child's experiences on progress in the early years. The fact that the twins' performance levels later returned to normal, after they had received extra training following the termination of the main study, gives an extra indication of the potency of early experiences in forming children's abilities.

## McGraw's Research

Many studies of accelerated early learning have been, like the ones in which Gesell was involved, too brief in duration and insufficiently intensive to provide a reliable indication of the likely outcome of a truly massive intervention that greatly increases a child's opportunities for early learning. A study conducted in the 1930s by Myrtle McGraw (1935; 1939) went some distance in that direction. Her subjects were fraternal twin boys. One of them (Johnny) was given training on five days each week between the ages of seven months and 24 months, at a number of physical skills. The other twin (Jimmy) received less than three months' training, and even this was delayed until he reached the age of 22 months. At that time he was given intensive training, lasting for a period of two and a half months, in the same activities in which Johnny had received earlier and more prolonged exercise.

The effects of the long-term early training were dramatic. In all the skills that Johnny was taught, he progressed well beyond the average levels of competence for boys of his age, and he was well ahead of his twin. For instance, by ten months he swam on his own, and he could dive from the side of a swimming-pool at 15 months and from a diving-board at 17 months. Compared with his twin he was bolder and more self-confident, especially when he was faced with a new physical challenge. For instance, when taken to an unfamiliar lake for the first time at the age of 16 months, he immediately dived in and started swimming with obvious enjoyment, although all his previous swimming experience had been in a tiny domestic pool. By this age he was a moderately accomplished roller-skater, and he could also climb up steep slopes.

These findings show that, with appropriate training, a remarkable degree of early acceleration can be achieved. Since the untrained twin did not make any unusual progress at any of the skills, we can be reasonably sure that the accelerated learning was caused by the exceptional learning opportunities that were provided. But did the effects last? McGraw (1939) assessed the twins again when they were six years old. She found that Johnny, the twin who was trained early, was still well ahead of the other boy on all the complex skills that had been taught. He was much better at running, climbing, jumping, walking, swimming, and riding a tricycle. In physical tasks generally, he displayed greater muscular coordination and more daring. The other twin,

Jimmy, was more timid and much more awkward. Even at the age of 22 years, when some of the twins' motor skills were filmed, it was clear that the twin who had been given early training retained some important advantages. For example, when seen climbing a ladder he was clearly more confident and enthusiastic, and also more skilled than his twin.

Since McGraw's classic experiment, other researchers have conducted investigations designed to assess the effects of intensive early training on physical skills. Broadly speaking, their findings provide strong confirmation for those of McGraw. That is to say, well-planned interventions that are reasonably intensive and long-lasting reliably produce substantial early gains in children's abilities. For example, Fowler, Ogston, Roberts, Steane and Swenson, (1983) found that over a period of 15 weeks in which four-year-olds received three 30-minute training sessions each week in gymnastic skills, the children made large improvements in their scores at tests measuring complex movement patterns that were similar to the skills that had been taught. Their gains were no less than five times as large as the progress achieved over the same 15-week period by children who had no special gymnastics training. Yet the gains of the trained children on tests of simple motor abilities that were unrelated to the contents of the training programme were small, and not significantly greater than the improvements made over the same period by those children who were given no training in gymnastics.

## *Compensatory Programmes*

Early childhood education varies in the breadth of its aims. Some programmes are designed to accelerate a wide range of abilities, others aim to extend only a narrow group of skills. A research study is most likely to be successful in establishing what the effects of a particular programme of intervention have been when the design of the research has ensured that

1 the aims of the training are clear,
2 there is a close and direct connection between the form and content of the training and the nature of the desired changes, and
3 there is an equally close relationship between the intended aims of the programme and the skills actually assessed.

Failure to meet the above conditions restricts the relevance, for our present purposes, of many of the numerous research studies that have investigated the effects of early educational interventions designed to remedy the effects of certain kinds of disadvantage in early childhood.

Some of these studies have produced huge gains, but others have been relatively unsuccessful. Whilst the aim of compensating for disadvantages is different from that of promoting acceleration, the two have much in common. We might, therefore, expect to find that research examining investigations designed to achieve the first of those aims would have considerable relevance to the second one. But unfortunately that is not really the case. The main problem is that because of vagueness about the aims (which are typically very broad), and because of the looseness of the connections between the aims of programmes and the criteria actually used for assessing their effectiveness, the findings of studies assessing compensatory educational interventions often leave too much room for them to be interpreted in line with one's existing beliefs or preconceptions.

For example, someone who wants to argue that compensatory education is doomed to failure can dismiss the more successful of these studies by pointing out that in many cases the larger gains have not been permanent, and that few studies have elevated IQ levels to much above average. Conversely, those readers of the reports who do believe in the effectiveness of well-designed compensatory education can discount those findings which show some programmes to have been not particularly effective, by pointing to (1) the fact that they have been too brief and insufficiently intensive, (2) the fact that attending such a programme, however good it is, can hardly be expected to compensate a child fully for the poor subsequent schooling that can be expected by many children living in a disadvantaged community, and (3) the inappropriate uses that have been made of IQ scores as criteria of a programme's success. It is claimed – with some justification – that such scores reflect performance at intellectual skills that are only loosely related to the abilities which most compensatory programmes are designed to teach, and discordant with the values, purposes, and life-styles of the communities for whom compensatory interventions are provided.

All the same, despite the inadequacy of some of the compensatory programmes that have been evaluated, and the inappropriateness of some the measures used to assess their effectiveness, there is firm evidence that well-designed interventions have had substantial and long-lasting positive influences on the intellectual and academic development of children from deprived and poverty-stricken families (Lazar, Darlington, Murray, Royce, and Snipper, 1982; Ramey, Bryant, and Suarez, 1985). Compared with individuals who were otherwise comparable, young people in the United States who had experienced a Headstart preschool programme, designed to compensate for early disadvantages, more frequently completed High School, were more likely to find jobs, and were much less likely to be convicted of delinquent behaviour. They also had higher incomes, were more satisfied with their work, and depended less on public welfare benefits. Fewer of the female students had teenage pregnancies. The Headstart pupils were also more strongly motivated to achieve, gained more satisfaction from educational achievements, and had higher educational aspirations. The quality, duration, and intensity of the intervention are all crucial, but there is evidence that even community day-care programmes which are relatively inexpensive and lack the resources and staff expertise that can be found in the best university-based programmes can be highly effective for arresting the age-related declines in measured intelligence that are normally encountered in disadvantaged children (Burchinal, Lee and Ramey, 1989).

## Accelerating the Acquisition of Language

One fairly common view among parents is that although it may be possible, with intensive early training, to accelerate the acquisition of *some* skills, the development of certain fundamental human abilities simply cannot be accelerated, and attempts to speed up the learning of them are simply a waste of time. Language is one such ability. Children do not seem to need to be taught language: they all learn to talk, even if the parents make no particular efforts to teach them. It has even been observed that deliberate teaching can impede language rather than accelerate it. A research team headed by Katherine Nelson discovered that children whose mothers rewarded them for pronouncing words correctly and punished them for poor pronunciation made less progress than children whose mothers were relatively unconcerned about correct pronunciation (Nelson, Carskaddon, and Bonvillian, 1973). And although numerous studies have found various aspects of child development to be strongly correlated with the child's experience of language, and particularly with the amount, form, and quality of language stimulation provided by the mother (Clarke-Stewart, 1973; Fowler, 1990) or by the staff in day care centres (McCartney, 1984), sceptics have been able to point out that since the evidence is only correlational it does not prove that differences in children's language experiences actually caused the correlated variations in language abilities between children. Chomsky and other theorists have put forward strong arguments for believing that human brains need to be innately wired up in particular ways in order for it to be possible for the young of our species to become competent at using language. This viewpoint has often been taken to imply that the brain's physical development imposes firm limits on the age at which a child's language development can begin.

Nevertheless, a few stubborn researchers have decided to conduct studies designed to evaluate the effectiveness of efforts to accelerate language acquisition in young babies. Their efforts have been surprisingly successful. The main outcome has been to show that despite the assertions that have been made about the pointlessness of trying to encourage faster progress in language without waiting for physical maturation to take place, the linguistic development of babies can indeed be brought forward, and very considerably.

Most of the studies have been relatively narrow in scope and of short duration, and based on infants who were no younger than around nine months of age. In contrast, an interesting set of small-scale experimental studies by William Fowler and his co-researchers (Fowler et al., 1983) examined the progress of 15 infants from the age of around five months. The babies were taught by their parents, in their own homes, and the parents received tuition and guidance from the investigators. The latter had devised a graduated language programme. This began with activities designed to teach single word referents for objects and actions, and gently moved on to more advanced elements of language, including more complex parts of speech and various grammatical forms. Some of the families were from the middle class, and were at least moderately well educated, but other families had little formal education. For instance, there were some Italian-speaking parents in the study who were functionally illiterate.

Broadly speaking, the elements of language training in the programme were not very different from the kinds of activities that many parents spontaneously initiate, except that (1) they took place more regularly and frequently, and (2) involved a larger proportion of the time available; (3) they began when the baby was considerably younger than usual; (4) they were systematic, consistent, and more carefully graduated; and (5) more emphasis was placed on the recording, by the parents, of both the parental training procedures and the babies' early progress at understanding and using language. Much of the language stimulation took place in the context of informal play activities and social interactions that the infants found pleasurable. Parents were encouraged to be consistent with their labelling of word items, to keep play activities simple enough to match their infants' capacities, and to devote time to play that involved social play ('peek-a-boo' for instance), and identifying physical objects and items shown in picture books and magazines. To help the parents, a training manual was distributed and its contents discussed with them. Lists of words were provided, and, for some poorly educated families, picture books.

In order to assess the effects of the programme, some other infants, of similar ages, were allocated to a control condition. These infants, like the ones who did receive training, were given language tests in their sixth month and again in their twelfth month, but unlike the others they did not receive special instruction in the intervening period.

The outcome was impressive, to say the least. After the six-month period the trained infants' language development was well ahead of the norms for babies of equivalent ages. For example, by their twelfth month four of the infants were speaking in sentences, an achievement that is not usually encountered until around the twentieth month. By 20 months three of the infants were using five-word sentences. By 24 months almost all were doing so, although the average age at which that level of language performance is reached is no less than 32 months. They began to use pronouns at 18 months on average (compared with the norm of 23 months), self-referral pronouns such as *I* and *me* at 18 months (compared with 29 months), and plurals before 24 months (compared with the 34-month norm). They first began to comprehend words between five and seven months, and they became able to speak four or more words between eight and 12 months, in both cases well ahead of the age norms. Quantitatively, over the course of the first six months' training they gained just under 40 points in language quotient test scores on the Griffiths language test, rising from an initial mean score of 101 (which indicates that at the time the study began, when they were in their sixth month of age, their scores, as a group, were broadly average for infants of that age) to a mean of 139, after six months' training – an exceptionally high score. In contrast, the scores of infants allocated to the control conditions, who did not receive special language training, were all around 100 or lower at the end of the six-month period. That is, they remained broadly average for infants of their age.

The long-term outcomes were equally striking. Those children whose parents continued to record their progress and to engage in the kinds of language activities used in the programme maintained, and sometimes increased, their superiority at using language, at least until they were five years old, at which time the final occasion on which they were tested occurred. The gains were fully maintained in most of those children who came from families in which language and language-related skills were emphasized and valued.

It is interesting to note that the only middle-class family in which the gains were not maintained was one in which, at the end of the initial six-month study, when the child was 12 months of age, the mother told the researchers that she was discontinuing further stimulation and intended to give only routine care in the future. Her reason was that 'she wanted to be sure that her boy would not be different from other children' (Fowler et al., 1983, p. 105). Her decision had devastating effects. Between the age of 12 months and 18 months (at which time the children were tested again) this child's language quotient score, in sharp contrast with the other children's, dropped from 168 to 134. His IQ score declined even more dramatically, from 149 to 118.

In the less formally educated families, where the parental lifestyle and interests placed little value on the use of highly structured language, the children's language skills tended to regress towards the norm as they got older. Nevertheless, even the children of the least educated Italian-speaking families remained well above average when the final tests were administered.

So after all, intensive language stimulation in early infancy definitely can have large and persisting positive effects. The six-month programme produced greatly accelerated language development in all the children who participated. Despite the relatively short duration of the intervention, the children's progress, by the end of it, was well ahead of the normal. They uttered their first words between two and six months in advance of the average child, their first sentences were produced three to eight months before the normal age, and their vocabularies at the age of 14 months were about ten months ahead of the established norms.

The findings of this early training experiment seem to indicate that the belief that early language development cannot be accelerated is quite wrong. Appropriate stimulation and encouragement does lead to rapid increases in essential language skills. The results of another investigation show that even relatively brief language training can produce substantial and long-lasting advantages. In a study by Whitehurst, Falco, Lonigan, Fischel, DeBaryshe, Valdez-Menchaca and Caulfield (1988) middle-class parents were taught to give their children more encouragement to talk, and better feedback, during the times when parents were reading to the children from picture books. The children's ages ranged from 21 months to 35 months.

The parents were trained to incorporate three principles in their interventions. First, they were shown how to encourage children to talk about the contents of the pictures, rather than passively listening and looking. The parents were told to ask 'what?' questions, (e.g., 'There's Eeyore. What's happening to him?'; or 'Do you think that Kitty will get into trouble?'), designed to get the child to participate actively, rather than questions requiring only a 'yes' or 'no' answer, or ones that focused on names (e.g., 'Who's that?'). Secondly, the parents were encouraged to be as informative as possible in the feedback they provided for their children. They were to expand on their children's answers or demonstrate alternative possibilities. Thirdly, the parents were told to make progressive changes in the form of their interventions and their interactions with the child. For instance, parents were encouraged to make sure that a child knew the names of objects in a book before starting to introduce questions about the attributes and relationships of the characters which a book depicted. The parents taped their home reading sessions with their children. This made it possible for the experimenters to measure the degree to which the planned intervention was actually implemented. The duration of the experimental intervention was only one month, but in order to measure its longer-term effects, the children were tested nine months afterwards, as well as at the end of the one-month period.

The interventions had marked positive effects on the children's use of language. Compared with subjects in a control group, the 30 trained children obtained scores at the end of the one-month training period that were eight months ahead on one test, the Illinois Test of Psycholinguistic Abilities, and six months ahead on another, The Expressive One-Word Picture Vocabulary Test. (On a third test, the Peabody Picture Vocabulary Test – Revised, they scored better than the control-group children, but the difference was not statistically significant.) Nine months later, the children in the experimental group were still six months ahead of the others in each of the first two language tests.

The authors of the study draw attention to the fact that this dramatic improvement occurred despite the fact that the programme was highly economical, requiring only one hour of direct training for the parents, and despite the fact that the children who formed the control group had conscientious and strongly motivated middle-class parents who read to them just as frequently as the parents of the children in the experimental group read to their children. These findings suggest that there is considerable scope for acceleration in most children's language development. As the authors point out,

> Many parents of normal young children spend hours per week reading to them and purchase hundreds of picture books to facilitate that activity. Our research demonstrates that the reading behavior of parents is not optimal, even within a highly select, motivated, affluent sample. The implication is that changes in parental behaviour that are not particularly difficult to obtain could have substantial positive effects on children's language development. (Whitehurst et al., 1988, p. 557)

The findings of other studies investigating the outcomes of language interventions are broadly similar to those obtained by Fowler's and Whitehurst's research teams. For instance, J. McVicker Hunt (1986) observed the effects of intensive special language stimulation by caregivers who had been trained in language acquisition techniques that placed stress on verbal interactions. The special training, which commenced when infants were just four weeks old, had large positive effects on the language development of children in a Teheran orphanage. These children progressed considerably faster than other children brought up in the conditions of the orphanage, and at the age of two years their language achievements were broadly equivalent to those of children brought up in professional families in the United States. In studies by P. W. Drash and A. L. Stolberg (cited by Fowler, 1983) training produced large gains in vocabulary and language use in a small sample of young children. Two-year-olds in another study made substantial gains in grammatical skills following instruction totalling no more than five hours in duration (Nelson, 1977). Hamilton (1977) and Metzl (1980) among others, observed similar improvements in early language skills in considerably younger children as a result of language stimulation. Whitehurst and Valdez-Menchaca (1988) observed that reinforcing children aged two and three years (by complying with their requests for toys) for saying words in a foreign language produced major increases and improvements in language use. Other researchers have noticed similar improvements in language skills following appropriate social or material rewards in normal infants as young as six months (Staats, 1971) and in older mentally handicapped children (Guess, 1969; Guess and Baer, 1973). The latter findings, added to previous evidence that aspects of children's language are correlated to the responsiveness of mothers to children's utterances (Peterson and Sherrod, 1982) and that mothers react differently to their children's word and non-word responses, show that reinforcement is not at all unimportant in children's first-language acquisition.

What seems to be crucial is not the sheer amount of speech that is directed towards the child, but its appropriateness. For example, adult labelling of objects is more likely to result in the child learning the objects' names when the child is already expressing an interest in them than when the mother has to draw the child's attention to the objects (Hart and Risley, 1980; White, 1985; Valdez-Menchaca and Whitehurst, 1988). Research by Paula Menyuk and others has shown that it is extremely important for adults to talk *to* infants and young children, rather than *at* them. Many parents, without being of aware of it, are inclined to do the latter. It is particularly important for an adult who has made a comment or asked a question to pause and give the baby some time to respond. Parents often find it difficult to do this. Even if the infant is too young to make a verbal response it is helpful to communicate an understanding of the concept of a conversation or dialogue, in which each partner takes turns in attending to the other person and in taking a more active role. It is hardly surprising that the kind of 'incidental' language teaching that is most effective is only likely to occur when an adult and a child are together in a one-to-one situation. Only in these circumstances can the adult be in a position to know what is currently engaging the child's attention.

Taken together, the research findings provide conclusive evidence that young children's language skills can be substantially accelerated, to the extent that it would be commonplace for an observer to regard the child's linguistic development as being exceptional. In other words, 'serious attention to the quality of cognitively oriented language stimulation from infancy will enable virtually all children enjoying salutary home environments to surpass cultural norms for language development, often reaching levels historically associated with "giftedness"' (Fowler, 1990).

# Reading

Large numbers of children learn to read early, well before they start attending a school where reading is formally taught. It is difficult to ascertain just how many young children read and how early, because there is no one agreed criterion by which a child can be judged to have learned to read. Reading encompasses a large number of separate sub-skills. (The fact that failure at just one of them can hamper the child's all-round performance as a reader is one of the reasons for so many children experiencing difficulty in reading.) Consequently, it is not possible to state a precise age at which a child has mastered reading, just as it is not possible to say exactly when a person has learned to play the piano. There are, of course, a number of tests designed to measure a child's progress in reading, but comparisons are often difficult because different studies of early reading have tended to use different tests.

## *Avoiding Reading Problems at School*

Accelerated learning aside, there is considerable evidence that the likelihood of a child making even normal progress towards learning to read at school will be impeded if certain skills have not been gained before the beginning of formal instruction. One group of basic skills that appear to be necessary for learning to read involves the ability to be aware of the smallest sound units of language, *phonemes*. A child who does not perceive phonemes accurately or is unable to discriminate between two different phonemes (such as the *b* in *bad* and the *d* in *dad*) will almost certainly find it very difficult to learn to read (Bryant and Bradley, 1985; Coles, 1987). Bradley and Bryant (1983) asked four- and five-year-olds to listen to lists of around three words, in which in every word but one there was a common phoneme. The child's task was to say which was the odd word. The researchers found that the children's performance level at this task was a good predictor of the same children's achievements at reading and spelling four years latter.

This finding shows that there is some connection between phonological skills in early childhood and subsequent progress at learning to read. But does it follow that differences in phonological skills are a cause of variability in children's reading achievements? To investigate this, Bradley and Bryant selected 65 children who did poorly at the above phoneme discrimination task, and who therefore would have been considered 'at risk', so far as success at reading was concerned. These children were divided into four groups. The first two groups were given training in categorizing sounds. The training was not particularly time-consuming or intensive: each child was seen for twenty 10-minute sessions per year, for two years. Group 1 children were taught to discriminate between phoneme sounds and Group 2 were given the same instruction but were also taught to associate letter sounds with actual letters. The children in Group 3 were taught to discriminate between categories, but their training did not include discriminating between sounds, and Group 4 received no instruction at all.

The children in all four groups were tested when they had reached the age of eight years. By this time Group 4, who had not been given any special training, were lagging a year behind the normal standard of achievement at reading, and at spelling they were two whole years behind the average. Group 3, who had received training at making discriminations, but not ones that involved phonemes, were also below average at both the reading and spelling tests. Both of the groups who had been given training at discriminating between phonemes were doing considerably better. The Group 1 children were nevertheless slightly below average at reading, and worse at spelling, but the children who had been in Group 2, and who had been trained to discriminate between phonemes and to make associations between sounds and letters were successfully reading at the level that was expected for children of their age.

Other studies have confirmed that preschool instruction in basic skills involving letters, sounds, and phonemes can lead to big improvements in a child's progress in reading at school and can considerably reduce the likelihood of a child experiencing difficulties in learning to read. For instance, in one study it was found that training young children to blend sounds together, and to break words down into their constituent sounds, produced substantial gains in early reading (Goldstein, 1976). It is possible that many of the problems that lead to a child being diagnosed as having 'learning disabilities' or as being dyslexic have their roots in a failure on the part of adults to appreciate that the child lacks certain fundamental skills that are necessary. And,

> Teachers often erroneously assume that children entering school have 'prerequisite' reading skills developed as part of preschool maturation ... These children have 'deficits' in learning certain reading skills because they simply have no experience with them and because schools, erroneously assuming children should already have these skills, do not teach them. (Coles, 1987, p. 54)

It would be wrong to infer that all parents must provide formal training in either phonological skills or the other abilities that are necessary in order for a child to be able to learn to read. Parents who regularly read to their children, and encourage children to enjoy the kinds of rhyming and other language games that are commonplace in homes in which written materials are regularly used, usually find that children gain the required prerequisite skills in the absence of specific or formal instruction.

## Early Reading

When a young child has learned to read earlier than most, before going to school, a close examination of the circumstances almost always reveals that the child has received considerable assistance from an adult or an older child who has been prepared to spend a good deal of time working with the young learner. The vast majority of children who learn to read early are taught, usually in a fairly informal manner, by their parents. Although it is not uncommon for a biographical or autobiographical account to state that a particular child taught herself (or himself) to read, the fact of the matter is that this simply cannot be done. No child (and no adult, either) can learn to read entirely on his or her own. There must be someone to draw the child's attention to the particular features and associations that reading draws upon. (If you are not convinced, think about it for a moment. How would someone even *start* to learn without assistance?) Learning to read, like a number of other human accomplishments, is only possible if the learner receives a fair amount of help from people who can already do it. Tribespeople in isolated villages where no-one can read do not become literate because there is nobody to teach them the skill.

There is one question which it would be particularly desirable to be able to answer. That is, is *any* normal child capable of learning to read considerably earlier than the usual age? Knowing that many children do learn to read while they are still very young provides a reason for believing that the correct answer may be a positive one, but there is no entirely conclusive evidence on the issue. Undoubtedly, many young children are prevented from learning to read early, for various reasons, including mental retardation, any of a variety of neurological abnormalities, and conditions such as hyperactivity, which can result in a child being too impulsive and too easily distracted to be able to sustain the concentration that reading skills demand. But even if we modify the previous question and ask whether or not early reading is a possibility for any child who is not specifically handicapped and is capable of paying sustained attention to an intellectual task, it has to be admitted that the firm evidence that would make it possible to give a definitive answer does not at present exist. Matters are made more complicated by the fact that even if it is true that all normal children are in principle capable of learning to read much earlier than they actually do, whether or not they do learn early will largely depend on the extent to which their early experiences have given them the kinds of motivations, interests, and curiosity that make them *want* to read. Having opportunities to gain the *desire* to read is just as important as having access to the necessary guidance and tuition.

As early as 1931 Helen Davidson published the findings of a study designed to assess the effects of providing special training in reading to various children, including a group of five bright three-year-olds (Davidson, 1931). Each child had a daily ten-minute individual reading lesson, five days per week, over a four-month period. Davidson reports that on each day there was also a brief group game, based on reading skills, lasting for about five minutes per day. Various reading tests were administered before the programme and at the end of it, and also several months afterwards. The training approach was fairly eclectic. It would have seemed unusually 'child-centred' in the late 1920s, but most of its elements would fit easily into methods of reading instruction that are followed today.

Because some of the periods were taken up with preparatory work, no child actually had more than 61 lessons. Thus the maximum amount of individual instruction received over the total period was no more than just over six hours. Nevertheless, all five of the three-year-olds made very substantial progress. For example, at the end of the study each of them could recognize, on average, 129 words that were shown to them out of context. All of them had reading skills equal to those usually found in children about two years older. Two of the five displayed reading ability equivalent to that of an average seven-year-old who had completed a year's formal schooling, and one was reading as well as a normal eight-year-old.

In her report, Davidson contrasts the rapid progress of the three-year-olds in her study with that of average six-year-olds at school. In about 60 days of ten-minute lessons (plus the five-minute group game) her children progressed further than most six-year-old first-grade children do after having had 85 days of instruction averaging 90 minutes per day. She concludes, 'In view of the results of this experiment, it seems that the great amount of time and energy spent on the teaching of reading in the first grade is unnecessary' (Davidson, 1931, p. 255).

However, Davidson's experiment included ten other children, who were up to two years older than the three-year-olds, but less intelligent, according to their IQ test scores. Although most of these children made satisfactory progress they did not learn so fast. Their reading ability at the end of the experiment was not equivalent to that of normal first-graders. Does this mean that only those young children who are especially bright are capable of profiting from reading instruction at a very early age? That is a possible deduction from Davidson's results. But her descriptions of her child subjects and their family circumstances make it clear that the more and less successful children in her study differed in a number of ways as well as having different IQ scores. For example, the parents of the successful subjects were better educated than the others, read to their children more often, read more themselves, and, in Davidson's words 'read a better type of book than the parents of the other subjects' (Davidson, 1931, p. 252). All but one of the five successful three-year-olds were read to regularly by their parents, but all but one of the ten less successful older children were only read to occasionally.

Thus, despite the fact that the different groups of children received the same amount of formal instruction in Davidson's training programme, the actual quantity of reading activities experienced by the different groups was far from being equivalent. It differed not only during the period of the experiment but before it and afterwards as well. As one might expect, there is firm evidence that children's progress at reading is related to the quality and the quantity of reading experiences at home (Moon and Wells, 1979): there is no better predictor of a child's reading achievement.

It is also significant that some of the less intelligent children in Davidson's investigation had severe problems that were not shared by any of the three-year-olds. For instance, one of the 'dull' pupils is described as 'a very poor pupil in every respect. He is a very trying disciplinary problem both to his foster parents and his teachers. He runs away, is undependable and untruthful' (Davidson, 1931, p. 246).

So although Davidson's findings seem at first to point to the conclusion that young children who possess the mental skills needed for doing well at IQ tests can learn to read much earlier than usual, but that other children cannot, this conclusion is suspect because it fails to take account of the fact that the children in her study whose IQ scores were low were handicapped in a number of additional ways that are likely to have had negative effects on reading. Her findings do not adequately answer the question of whether or not it is possible to teach reading to those very young children who do poorly at intelligence tests. It is quite possible that the reason why the high-IQ children in Davidson's study made more progress than the others was simply that the kinds of family circumstances that lead to a child learning to read early are largely the same as the circumstances that lead to a child doing well at intelligence tests.

The findings of a project carried out by Arthur Staats (1971) provide some useful evidence concerning the possibility of children who do poorly in intelligence tests learning to read unusually early. Staats regarded his project primarily as a test of the effectiveness of certain behaviour modification procedures that were built into his course of instruction. These involved rewarding subjects with tokens that could be exchanged later for a variety of desirable prizes. The length of the instructional sessions totalled around 17 hours, made up of a large number of short trials lasting between five and eight minutes. One subject was a four-year-old boy with an IQ of 89. By the end of the programme he had acquired reading and writing skills that were advanced for his age, despite his low IQ and in spite of the fact that he came from a culturally deprived home environment. Staats draws attention to the finding that when the same training procedure was followed with another child with a much higher IQ, of 130, the rate of progress was not noticeably faster. For Staats, the similar achievements despite the large IQ differences demonstrate that with appropriate teaching most children learn quickly and 'without the large differences we generally attribute to some inner personal quality that we call intelligence' (Staats, 1971, p. 112).

These results seem to rule out the possibility, which Davidson's findings appeared to confirm, that high IQ may be necessary for early reading. But the number of participants in Staats' study was very small, but some results obtained by Durkin (1966), with a larger sample of subjects, provide further evidence that although progress at reading and IQ level tend to be related, reading level does not necessarily depend on a child's level of intelligence. Durkin found that, even when children reached the age of 11, the reading skills of children who had learned to read at three years remained two years in advance of children who learned to read when they were five despite the fact that the two groups did not differ in their IQ scores.

In conclusion, it appears that at least the majority of children are capable of learning to read at least a year or two earlier than the age when this is usually achieved. As well as the findings I have described, additional evidence surveyed by Fowler (1983) supports this view. And it is generally found that early advantages in reading are maintained for at least several years.

The possibility has been raised that early reading could have negative effects on a child. In fact, adverse effects were not seen in any of the studies that compared early readers with other children (Durkin, 1966), and the findings point to a number of positive outcomes. For instance, E. Scott and B. Bryant (cited by Fowler, 1983) found that early readers were more independent than other children, played with their peers just as frequently, were more purposive, and interacted more often with adults. Of course, correlational evidence of this kind can never be entirely conclusive concerning causes and effects. It is quite possible that reading makes children more independent, but it is equally possible that independent children are more likely to read early than others, or that other factors encourage them both to be independent and to learn to read.

## Accelerating Progress at Musical Skills

There is no hiding the fact that evidence concerning the effectiveness of attempts to accelerate young children's progress is somewhat sketchy. Not nearly enough of it has taken the form of experimental studies in which fair-sized samples of children who have had special teaching are compared with otherwise similar children who have not received any exceptional treatment. But, such as they are, the available research findings are definitely consistent with the view that the vast majority of children are capable of acquiring most skills considerably earlier than is usual. As well as movement-based skills, language and reasoning, a variety of other abilities have been found to be amenable to acceleration in young children. These include a number of mathematical skills, memory skills, and abilities underlying Piagetian concepts such as conservation and seriation.

There have been a number of experimental studies of the effects of early training in the realm of music. Shuter-Dyson and Gabriel (1981) provide a useful summary. Generally speaking, attempts to teach musical skills to young children are successful, although the outcomes tend to be specific to the particular abilities that are taught. Moreover, skills acquired unusually early are much more likely to be maintained if the school or home environment provides opportunities to practise them (J. Klemish, 1974, cited by Shuter-Dyson and Gabriel, 1981). By the age of six months infants who receive extensive opportunities to practise (over a 40-day period) can learn to match musical pitches that are produced on a pipe. However, infants aged less than one year do not appear to be capable of imitating melodies (Sloboda, 1985), although, according to Shuter-Dyson and Gabriel (1981) a small-scale study by J. McFie was effective in teaching the investigator's 15-month-old son to sing, 'very accurately', the first four bars of the theme of the Andante of Haydn's Surprise Symphony. Early research by Jersild and Bienstock (1931) established that children as young as two years of age can greatly benefit from instruction in singing, and that early advantages may be maintained for some years.

Young children also profit from aural training that is designed to help them to discriminate between notes, and can learn to recognize musical items even when they are played on new instruments (Fullard, 1967). Shuter-Dyson and Gabriel describe an interesting study by D. Kukenski, who played folk tunes to infants between the ages of three and nine months. During the training sessions a song, lasting 30 seconds, would be repeated ten times, accompanied by a puppet which moved in synchrony. There were also a number of accompanying exercises, designed to encourage the babies to move rhythmically and respond to the tune. Subsequent tests showed that the training had been effective in accelerating the infants' musical responsiveness. Those infants who had been given training over a six-month period performed significantly better than children who only had three months of musical enrichment, and the latter children did better than babies in a control group who received no special musical training at all. As in the case of other abilities, differences in experience lead to differences in coding strategies between children who have had musical training and untrained individuals (Dowling, 1988) and corresponding differences in the ways in which they represent music and communicate musical expressions (Bamberger, 1986; Davidson and Scripp, 1988).

Fowler (1983) points out that the successes of young children who have been exposed to the Suzuki method of musical training demonstrate that far more preschoolers are capable of gaining impressive instrumental skills than anyone would have predicted a generation ago. He notes that one researcher whose efforts to teach three-year-olds to play a tin fife came to nothing reached the conclusion that instrumental abilities are simply too difficult for preschool children to learn. Up to now, there has been little systematic research into the consequences and limitations of the kinds of musical training provided by the Suzuki method, but the achievements of numerous young children who have followed Suzuki procedures prove that in the right circumstances many children, and perhaps most, are indeed capable of impressive musical accomplishments. (That is not to deny that the Suzuki method has its critics: a number of musicians feel that children trained by this approach can become too rigid in their performing skills.) The successes of the Suzuki programme are not unrelated to its child-centred and carefully graduated nature, and its emphasis on engaging the child's interest and motivation, and that of the parent as well. In the early stages much emphasis is placed on developing a proper attitude to the learning task, and the children are required to reaffirm their commitment to the training by respectfully requesting instruction at the beginning of each session. At an early stage they begin to establish a habit of concentrated daily practice, and they are taught a number of routines that are painstakingly practised until they become an automatic and smoothly executed part of the lessons (Peak, 1986; Taniuchi, 1986. Fowler notes,

> The child acquires concepts of musical language functionally in a graduated, extended, contextual manner, the dimensions of pitch, rhythm, tempo, interval phrasing, order, key, and the like, just as the infant becomes familiar with the ordinary dimensions of language ... through daily experiences over many years. The chief difference is the carefully planned, systematic programming of the musical learning experience, usually essential in all except a few already musical families, where music is bread to the daily life, like ordinary language. (Fowler, 1983, p. 288).

# Extraordinary Skills in Ordinary Adults

Studies investigating the possibility of accelerating the progress of young children provide one obvious way, but not the only way, to discover whether or not it is necessary for a person to be inherently extraordinary in order to gain exceptional abilities. An alternative approach to this question is to examine the possibility of 'ordinary' adult people acquiring skills that are usually regarded as demanding innately exceptional capabilities. If it is found to be possible for individuals who, at the beginning of training, have no special abilities or talents to gain a particular skill that has been regarded as impossible to acquire in the absence of appropriate inborn qualities, the case for the necessity of such qualities would be seriously weakened. And if it is discovered that each of a variety of different skills that have been regarded as depending upon the existence of inborn talents can be gained by people who lack any special innate qualities, it would seems appropriate to question the assumption that there exist any mental abilities that can only be acquired by individuals who have been endowed from birth with certain unusual qualities.

In practice, as I mentioned in the previous chapter, many of the exceptional learned achievements that we value particularly highly are ones that demand many thousands of hours of concentrated training. That in turn necessitates a person dedicating most of the waking hours for a period of ten or even 20 years to one particular endeavour. It also involves heavy financial and other costs. Consequently, even if it is essentially true that the acquisition of exceptional human abilities does not depend upon the person possessing inherently special qualities, it would be unreasonable to expect that an ordinary adult, with no previously acquired special skills, could become, say, an outstanding mathematician or an exceptional composer.

## *Memory Skills*

There have been a number of reports of people having an exceptional ability to remember. (A particularly fascinating example is the well-known case study by Luria (1968) of a Russian journalist whose memory for information was so accurate and reliable that he was able to make a living by performing memory feats on the stage.) It has generally been assumed that the memory systems of such individuals must have been fundamentally exceptional from the time of birth. Obviously, such a deduction would be called into question if it were found that their feats were equalled or excelled by ordinary people who, at the start of a period of training, displayed no remarkable ability to remember. As it happens, some investigations by Anders Ericsson and others have demonstrated that with appropriate training ordinary individuals are indeed capable of gaining abilities that are remarkably superior to normal levels of achievement.

In one study, which was briefly mentioned earlier, in chapter 2, Chase and Ericsson (1981) trained a young adult male at a memory feat over a period of more than two years. He was paid to practise for one hour per day at a simple memory task that involved listening to, and then immediately attempting to repeat, lists containing random digits presented at a rate of one item per second. The largest number of randomly ordered digits that most people can recall without error in these conditions is around eight or nine items. Practising the task for up to ten hours or so produces only a small improvement. And because a small amount of practice does not substantially increase the memory span, it has traditionally been assumed that no amount of practice will produce a large improvement (Howe, 1980; 1983a; 1984; 1988d). As a result, psychologists who have conducted research into human memory have agreed that everyone has an essentially unchangeable 'memory span', limited to around eight items, for unrelated verbal items such as digits, letters, or words.

What was new about the approach of Chase and Ericsson is that these researchers questioned the above assumptions. Instead of giving just ten or so hours of practice, like the earlier investigators, they paid their subject to practise for nearer to 1000 hours. This had dramatic consequences. After two years the individual's memory span increased to around 80 items. That is roughly ten times the length of span that had long been regarded as being essentially fixed, and impossible to increase. Without going into details about how the massive increase was achieved, it is enough to say that that particular individual gradually acquired strategies that made it possible for him to group a number of single digits together into larger multi-digit units that could be regarded as being (in many instances) running times for various athletic competitions. For this particular subject these groupings of digits were meaningful, and therefore memorable, because they could be connected to his existing knowledge about one of his main interests, athletics. (Another person might have evolved a strategy based on grouping items in different ways, ones that had meanings that were related to that individual's particular interests.)

Similar improvements in memory span have been reported in a number of ordinary people. One of them is described by Ericsson and Faivre (1988) as having achieved a memory span of over a hundred items, which at the time of writing was said to be still increasing. Ericsson and Faivre describe a number of additional studies which demonstrate that a variety of different memory skills are equally amenable to training. These researchers found that, after training, their own subjects were remarkably similar to individuals who have been described in case histories as having inherently exceptional memory abilities. So far as one can tell, it now seems possible that virtually all those feats of memory displayed by people who are said to have had an innately exceptional memory can be excelled by ordinary people.

It is important to be clear about precisely what is being trained. Practice does not produce 'a better memory'. What it does succeed in doing is to give a person improved memory skills. These skills can be remarkably specific: typically they do not generalize or transfer to any extent to tasks that are different from the one that was practised. Consequently, for example, the individual who achieved a memory span of 80 items in Chase and Ericsson's investigation, remained no better than average at other kinds of memory tasks, despite all the training he had been given. It is true that people who are reported as having an exceptionally good memory may perform extraordinarily well at each of a range of different kinds of memory tasks. But that is because they have been able to acquire a number of memory skills, not because they have 'a good memory'.

In reality, no such thing as 'a good memory' actually exists: the assumption that it does, and that it provides the explanation for someone recalling information unusually accurately, is an instance of the tendency to 'reify' which I discussed in chapter 2. Rather than thinking of a person as having a good (or bad) memory, it is more realistic to think in terms of individuals possessing a number of relatively specific and autonomous memory skills (Hunter, 1984; Ericsson and Crutcher, 1988; Ericsson and Faivre, 1988). If people are given a battery of memory tests, the correlation between an individual's performance at the different tasks is usually near zero (Martin, 1978; Ericsson, 1985; Howe, 1989a). In other words, the chances are that someone who is unusually successful at one test of memory will be no better than average at remembering something else. The commonsense view that there exist broad differences between people in their ability to retain all kinds of information in memory is essentially incorrect.

Generally speaking, people are not invariably successful or always unsuccessful at remembering things, but very good at remembering information which they are interested in and knowledgeable about, and poor at remembering those things which do not interest them. This accounts for a rueful observation by one of the male subjects in Joan Freeman's study of gifted adolescents.

> I could remember all of about sixty-odd totally abstract numbers all in hexadecimal – that's to base 16 – and I could remember pairs of those as operational. I have a good memory like that. I was terribly upset, though, when I had to ask a girl what her name was, and I'd known her for a year. (Freeman, 1990)

Peter Morris and his colleagues have shown that many British soccer enthusiasts can recall lengthy lists of match scores with impressive accuracy. Recall of soccer scores is highly correlated ($r = \cdot 8$) with knowledgeability about soccer, and unrelated to ability to remember other kinds of lists (Morris, Gruneberg, Sykes and Merrick, 1981; Morris, Tweedy and Gruneberg, 1985; Morris, 1988). Many football enthusiasts can recall the scores of all 80-odd major weekend British soccer matches. How is that possible? The main reason is that whereas for someone who is uninterested in the sport a listing of football scores is no more than a list of isolated random digits, for a knowledgeable football enthusiast that same list has many kinds of meanings and implications. Every score is significant, and therefore interesting.

Similarly, someone who is an expert at the game of chess can remember the positions of chess pieces on the board far more accurately than a non-expert. It is not just a matter of being familiar with the individual pieces. Were that the case, chess experts would remember positions more accurately than other people even when chess pieces are placed at random positions on the board. In fact, they only do better when the pieces form legitimate chess positions, indicating that it is the experts' structured knowledge of the game of chess that enables them to remember so well.

## *Perceptual Abilities*

There are certain perceptual skills which, because they are genuinely 'exceptional' in the sense that very few people can do them, may appear to depend upon the performer having inherently special qualities. Once again, however, investigations reveal that such skills can in fact be acquired by virtually any ordinary person who is prepared to put in enough practice. One example is the screen-tracking skill of the video technician mentioned in chapter two. He could identify moving stimuli on a screen far more quickly than anyone else. The mystery of his immense superiority was quickly dispelled when it was discovered that he, unlike the other people, had gained hundreds of hours of experience at the task.

Sometimes the very rarity of skills misleads people into believing that, for ordinary individuals, they must be impossible to acquire. But as Anders Ericsson has demonstrated, given sufficient time and patience, many adults are able to gain perceptual skills that are remarkable enough to have been cited in the past as forming proof that the person seen doing them must have had special innate aptitudes (Ericsson, 1988; Ericsson and Faivre, 1988). There are a number of perceptual abilities that have traditionally been regarded as necessitating the possession of special gifts or talents but which have been shown to be learned skills that can be gained by virtually any person who receives appropriate training. For example, one study revealed that the unusual skill of being able to determine the sex of chickens can be gained without inordinate difficulty, if sufficient training and practice is given (Biederman and Shiffrar, 1987). So, too, can other uncommon perceptual skills such as the ones underlying X-ray diagnosis, identifying heart murmurs, and wine-tasting. In everyday life there are countless instances of people displaying strikingly difficult skills that are quite unrelated to the ones that are taught at school (Laboratory of Comparative Human Cognition, Lave, 1977; 1983; 1984; Lave, 1988; Saxe, 1988; Lave, Murtaugh, and De la Roche). Perfect (absolute) pitch perception is another unusual ability which is often thought to be innate. But that also is an acquired skill. It is difficult to learn, especially after early childhood, but at least one adult has been able to teach himself to do it (Brady, 1970; Costall, 1985; Sloboda, 1985).

Another rare ability is the capacity to make absolute judgements of colour hues. Perhaps surprisingly, a typical adult can identify only five of a set of 21 colours that are only slightly different. But with extended practice, performance improves very substantially. Following 80 training sessions an individual studied by Ericsson and Faivre (1988) increased the number of similar hues he could correctly identify from five to 18 of the 21 differently coloured stimuli. Again, however, as in the case of memory training, the abilities acquired are highly specific ones. People acquire particular perceptual skills, not a generalized ability to make perceptual judgements or discriminations.

## *Some Conclusions*

Taken together, the findings that have been described in this chapter provide a strong case for arguing that, in principle, almost any person of normal intelligence may be capable of gaining virtually any exceptional ability. In practice, there are numerous factors that prevent the majority of individuals from achieving the highest levels of success at difficult skills. Acquiring exceptional capabilities often demands enormous investments of time and concentration, unusual single-mindedness, and exceptionally strong and sustained motivation. At present, the necessary commitment is only likely to be possible for a person whose opportunities and whose experiences of life have been unusual in some respects. Yet the distinction between what someone is unlikely to achieve and what someone simply *cannot* achieve remains a crucial one. Taken as a whole, the evidence that has been presented in this chapter provides no support at all for the view that very high levels of achievement are only possible for a few lucky individuals who have been singled out from birth to be the recipient of special gifts, talents, or aptitudes.

## The Value of Practice

Although few would deny that practice is necessary for the acquisition of any non-trivial skill, the degree to which it is important may have been underestimated. Some studies by Anders Ericsson and his colleagues suggest that differences between people in the amount of time they spend practising are more important than is usually recognized, as causes of variability in performance levels.

Ericsson, Tesch-Römer, and Krampe (1990) describe some research findings which indicate the amount of time that is devoted to practice by various groups of skilled performers. For instance, one study found that amongst athletes who by the age of around 12 years had reached very high levels of ability, those of them who remained at an equally high level (for their age) three years later practised for about 16 hours per week, on average, whilst those who remained active in athletics but failed to continue reaching the highest levels of success practised less, averaging 13 hours per week. The best athletes practised every day of the week, but the others often took a day off. In another investigation the average number of weekly training sessions for runners at national, regional, and local levels were found to be approximately five, four, and three per week, and the most effective predictor of running performance was the frequency with which an athlete trained, the correlation being $r = .56$. Yet another study found the amount of practice during the nine weeks prior to a race to be strongly related to times taken to run a marathon (Hagan, Smith, and Gettman, 1981). In fact, almost half of the variance in race times was accounted for by the length and total distance of training runs in an average week.

Similar relationships between performance and time spent practising are observed in music. In one investigation Ericsson and his co-researchers divided violin students at the music academy in Berlin into three groups: first, the best of all, who were considered by their professors to be potential soloists at international level; second, 'good' violin students at the academy; and third, violin students in a separate department for trainee music teachers in the academy, which has lower admission standards.

There were clear differences between the groups in the amount of time they spent practising. It emerged that the two best groups had practised more than the trainee violin teachers during adolescence, and that in late childhood and adolescence the best students had tended to practise more than the middle ('good') group. There were large differences in the cumulative amounts of time spent practising by the three groups of students prior to the time when they entered the music academy. The best violinists had practised about 7400 hours, the good players had spent an average total of 5300 hours practising, and the trainee teachers had practised, on average, for 3400 hours. In other words, the total amount of time devoted to practising by the best players was considerably more than twice the time spent practising by the less expert third group of young violinists.

The violinists at the academy were asked to keep a detailed diary for a week, in which they recorded, amongst other things, detailed information about the times and durations of their practice sessions. Not surprisingly, it was found that the two better groups practised considerably more than the student teachers. Interestingly, there were other differences as well. For example, the better violinists had a stronger tendency to devote particular times to practising, and they were more likely to practise in the mornings, often soon after waking up. Also, the best violinists were much more likely than students in either of the other groups to report taking naps during the afternoon.

Of course, since the evidence relating practice times to performance is entirely correlational, it is not possible to be at all certain about causes and effects. We clearly cannot be sure that practice is the main cause of the differences between individuals in their performance levels. It is quite likely, for instance, that differences in the time that is devoted to practice reflect differences in opportunities available to performers of different levels. Especially in the case of music, it is also quite possible that the differing practice times may reflect differing expectancies of the teachers who guide performers of varying levels of perceived ability.

Nevertheless, the sheer size of the relationships prompts one to suggest that practice, and the amount of practice, has not been given the attention that it deserves as a crucial determinant of ability to perform difficult skills. The studies mentioned above may well underestimate the actual degree of relationship between practice and performance, because they make no attempt to exclude or control sources of variability which would be expected to reduce the sizes of the correlations. For example, in the above studies it is more than likely that some of the practising was done with enthusiasm and careful concentration, whilst at other times performers were doing no more than going through the motions. Also, some of the practice activities would doubtless have been highly appropriate and well-designed, whereas, others would have been less effective. Had the research studies been able to eliminate these sources of variability, it is quite possible that the relationships between performance and amount of practice would have been even more substantial.

There is clearly a need for experimental studies in which performers are initially matched for level of ability and subsequently required to practise for varying amounts of time over substantial periods. There are obvious practical impediments to undertaking long-term research of that kind, but its potential value would be very considerable.

## Some Consequences of Accelerated Learning

Until now, I have not questioned the desirability of individuals gaining exceptional abilities. There are, of course, a number of matters that may cause concern, especially in connection with the acceleration of capabilities in young children. In practice, the advantages for a child of having the 'good start' in life that results from acquiring certain abilities unusually early have to be balanced against a number of possible disadvantages. The pressures and expectations that over-demanding parents may impose can create serious problems. Also, there may be emotional costs resulting from an unusually specialized way of life during childhood, in which the range of interests that are encouraged may be somewhat narrow, and in which there may be few opportunities to experience some of the activities of a normal childhood. It is quite possible for a childhood regime that is unusually enriched, so far as opportunities to gain exceptional intellectual skills is concerned, to be at the same time one in which there is severe deprivation of other experiences that are equally vital. A comprehensive discussion of all the issues is outside the scope of this book, but they will surface again in later chapters, especially chapter 5.

What is the point of accelerating a child's early progress? What are the advantages for a child of acquiring particular abilities some months earlier than other children do? How are children directly affected by the intellectual skills they acquire? Up to a point, the answers are fairly obvious: children make progress towards gaining various kinds of valued abilities, and such progress helps to open the door to achievements that depend on those abilities. Other things being equal, the greater the early progress, the higher the probability of various peaks of achievement eventually being surmounted.

### *Outcomes of Learning to Read*

Some of the outcomes for a child of gaining particular capabilities deserve closer attention. Take reading, for example. Everybody agrees that being able to read is an invaluable ability, one that is essential for the enjoyment of a full life in a literate culture. Everyone assents to the view that reading provides access to many kinds of information and knowledge, and opens up areas of experience and insight and understanding that are closed to the non-reader. It is universally acknowledged that the skill of reading, if properly exploited, can extend and amplify the intellectual grasp of any human learner. (Olson, 1977; Kress, 1982; Olson, 1986).

Yet I suspect that for all the fulsome assent that greets statements of this kind, the real impact on a young person of learning to read is often underestimated. Most of us, because we have been able to read for as long as we can remember, fail to realize that certain very basic kinds of knowledge about language, which we tend to assume are available to all language users, are in fact the products of literacy, and outside the grasp of illiterate people. For instance, even the concept of a word can have no very precise meaning to anyone who cannot read. Asking an illiterate child or adult to recite a poem 'word for word' or 'line by line' is asking that person to do something that is impossible because it has no clear meaning for them. Similarly, the idea of the 'correct' form of a poem being embodied in a text only makes sense to people in a literate community. Consequently, when people from oral cultures are asked to attempt verbatim reproduction of a song or a passage of poetry, their success, as measured in terms of word to word agreement with a previous version, will be extremely limited (Ong, 1982).

Literate people tend to assume that the flow of heard language divides itself 'naturally' into words. If fact it does no such thing. If you examine a speech spectrogram – essentially a visual record of the sound of a language sequence – you will look in vain for reliable information that specifies where one word ends and the next one begins. That information is not made explicit in the flow of language, a fact that may easily be verified by listening to a sample of speech in an unfamiliar foreign language.

Without literacy, language exists only as sound, and it is difficult to conceive of the possibility that there exists a body of stored knowledge that can be 'looked up'. All thinking will bear the marks of this limitation. For instance, where writing does not exist, the necessity to ensure that what has been thought can later be recalled forces the individual to adopt a number of devices specifically designed to facilitate the accurate retention and retrieval of the information. In oral cultures such devices may involve the use of highly rhymed or rhythmic language, the introduction of balanced language patterns, repetitions, antitheses, assonances, alliterations, and the use of standard, well-remembered language formulas that are easily recalled simply because they are highly familiar. In short, the content of oral reasoning is constrained by the need to take steps that will ensure its memorability.

Within an oral culture it is very difficult to have the kinds of thoughts that we would describe as being abstract or original. What is more,

> to think through something in non-formulaic, non-patterned, non-mnemonic terms, even if it were possible, would be a waste of time, for such thought, once worked through, could never be recovered with any effectiveness, as it could be with the aid of writing. It would not be abiding knowledge but simply a passing thought, however complex. (Ong, 1982, pp. 35–6)

Because reading and writing are now so widespread in developed societies, literate people may fail to realize that a large proportion of the world's population still cannot read. There are at present about 3000 spoken languages. Of these, according to Ong, less than 80 can be said to have a literature. Indeed, as Ong has pointed out, language is so overwhelmingly oral that among all the many languages that have evolved in the course of human history (and these may well have numbered tens of thousands) by far the vast majority have never been committed to writing at all. Amongst all the languages that have ever existed, only a tiny fraction of them have been written down to the extent that they can be said to have produced a literature.

Of course, in thinking about the implications of becoming able to read we need to bear in mind that the experience of a non-literate child living in a literate culture is not the same as that of a person in an oral culture. But they both encounter similar limitations on thinking and understanding. Until a child learns to read, that individual is not simply denied access to the resources of information and knowledge that literacy makes available, but may have limited awareness of the *idea* of accessible stored knowledge. In the absence of such awareness it may be difficult or even impossible to undertake the kinds of symbolic and abstract thinking that take for granted the conceptualization of verbal information as something that can be manipulated, represented, and permanently retained. The non-reader is not just unable to do certain intellectual tasks that depend on having access to information, but is also to a large extent quite unable to grasp what he or she is missing.

## *Effects of early Language Competence*

If it is true that a child is altered, as a result of learning to read, in ways that are more fundamental and far more sweeping than we realize when we consider the effects of reading only in terms of the increased accessibility to knowledge which that skill makes possible, that is doubly true of the acquisition of a child's first language. Language transforms a child's mental capabilities in many ways, most of which, largely because our thinking is so thoroughly infused with and so extensively controlled by language, we find it hard to even think about. It is almost impossible for a person whose thought patterns are based on language to conceive of the ways in which life is experienced by an individual who lacks language. So when we try to describe the effects on our mental capacities of learning to talk or to read extraordinarily early, by words such as accelerating, augmenting, increasing, extending, or magnifying, we fail to do justice to the real nature of the transformation that takes place as a result of these abilities being acquired. They open up, irreversibly, new and previously inconceivable patterns of thinking. Consequently, any one-year-old who gains key language skills several months earlier than is usual thereby gains enormous advantages over other children. Parents who take careful steps to increase their infant's early opportunities to learn language skills can be sure that their patience will be richly rewarded.

# A Concluding Word

Taken as a whole, the research findings give us every reason to suppose that the vast majority of ordinary young children, if they are given sufficient support and encouragement, are capable of reaching standards of achievement at any valued intellectual ability that are far enough ahead of current average levels of performance to be considered quite exceptional. It is worth emphasizing once again that, however widely it is believed, the view that outstanding abilities are beyond the reach of any child who does not have some special genetic advantage is one for which empirical research has failed to produce firm supporting evidence. That is not to say that genetic differences between people never have an influence on their abilities, and it is not to deny the possibility that genetic factors might conceivably impose limits on performance at certain intellectual feats, just as they undoubtedly affect performance at some physical accomplishments. Boxing and weight-lifting are obvious instances. But the idea that genetic factors severely limit the success of individuals at many intellectual skills is false. Until that view is firmly scotched, many young people will continue to be prevented or discouraged from undertaking plans or pursuing ambitions that are in actuality quite realizable, so long as enough opportunities are made available and sufficient support and encouragement are forthcoming.

# 4
# Family Backgrounds

The previous chapter described many different instances of exceptional abilities being gained. In no case did this take place in any kind of vacuum. Always, there existed background circumstances that provided opportunities for learning and encouragement for making progress. In most instances of exceptional early learning the child's home and family provided the necessary source of experiences and opportunities. The family background is the fountainhead of many influential happenings that affect a child's progress. Families contribute in one way or another to virtually all the ingredients of human excellence.

Families differ greatly in the extent to which intellectual activities are valued and encouraged, and in the degree to which pursuits that have a broadly educational function are given priority over other activities. Families also differ in the kinds of role-models they provide, and in the extent to which they expose a child to opportunities to identify with successful individuals. This chapter starts with some research findings that demonstrate just how influential the family background can be.

## How Important *Are* Family Backgrounds?

As an acknowledgement of their excellence a few exceptional people are awarded a Nobel prize. Only the most outstanding contributions are thus honoured. In science, for instance, all Nobel prize-winners have been individuals who have made major achievements in their fields. It would be interesting to know something of their cultural and family backgrounds. For example, have the different individuals' early home lives been similar in any respects? Some useful information about this was obtained in a series of investigations by Colin Berry (1981; 1990), who examined the cultural origins of over 390 prize-winning scientists.

Berry found that the impacts of family backgrounds were not at all hard to detect. He discovered that the families of Nobel scientists have been much more frequently Protestant than Catholic, and that children born in Jewish communities have become Nobel prize-winners far more often than either Protestants or Catholics. National differences as such are relatively unimportant compared with the composition of religous traditions within a nation (Berry, 1990). Also, a disproportionate number of Nobel scientists have come from large metropolitan centres. In the United States, for instance, around 60 per cent were raised either in New York City or one of the Midwestern states. Similarly, more than half of the chess prodigies in the United States come from the metropolitan areas of New York, San Francisco, and Los Angeles (Gardner, 1982). In Germany, children born in Hamburg, Munich, or Stuttgart have been prize-winners ten times more frequently than children born in rural areas. Irrespective of their country of origin, the vast majority of Nobel scientists have come from professional and business families, and within the professions certain occupational groups have contributed out of all proportion to their numbers. For example, the fathers of about 40 per cent of science prize-winners from professional backgrounds have either held university posts or have been doctors.

There are striking differences in the home backgrounds of science and non-science prize-winners. Whilst the children of 'academic' professionals (those concerned with education, research, or scholarship) have contributed the majority of Nobel scientists, very few winners of other Nobel prizes come from home backgrounds of this kind. Individuals whose fathers are non-academic professionals win roughly equal numbers of Nobel prizes for Peace and Literature and for Science. Another point of contrast is that the proportions of Nobel scientists and non-scientists who have experienced family tragedies differ greatly. For example, over thirty per cent of winners of a Nobel Literature Prize experienced loss of a parent in childhood or adolescence, or family bankruptcy or impoverishment, but similar family tragedies in the early lives of prize-winning scientists have been much less common. Generally, the homes of Nobel scientists have been more stable than those of prize-winners in Literature. Berry (1990) points out that in contrast with the popular image of the 'great scientist' as a being a person who has triumphed in spite of poor schooling (like Faraday) or a disrupted education (like Einstein), the majority of eminent scientists have enjoyed childhoods and early careers that were not interrupted by serious disruptions.

Intriguing as these findings are, they are inevitably inconclusive concerning actual causes. More questions are raised than answered. To what extent might the relationships between achievement and home background reflect genetic rather than cultural influences? Is a family's sheer wealth important? Do certain 'elite' schools in large cities have a special importance? A cultured home background may provide successful role-models, access to books, encouragement, good schooling, and high expectations, but are all of these equally advantageous?

## How Families Influence Children

Broadly speaking, there are two main ways in which families can affect the chances of their children excelling at the most demanding human skills. First, families help children to gain essential knowledge, skills, and mental strategies. Laszlo Polgar, the father of three chess-playing daughters who all achieved the quite remarkable feat of gaining Grandmaster status at chess in their teens, is quoted as saying, 'The Jewish religion prescribes for parents to teach their children from an early age. The Talmud provides that the Jewish parents must be the first teachers' (Lennon, 1989).

It is hardly surprising that the ways in which children develop in their early years are affected by the degree to which the parents assume the role of teacher. For instance, as we saw in the previous chapter, a mother who encourages her daughter to read at an early age may thereby be contributing to an explosive growth in the child's capabilities. That is because becoming literate opens up numerous new opportunities for a young person.

Secondly, family members transmit to a child their own values and their attitudes towards those kinds of achievements that depend upon learning and practice. The early experiences of a young person who is exposed to lifestyles in which scholarly activities are enjoyed and respected, and has opportunities to witness the successful outcomes of sustained efforts to learn new skills, will bring advantages that are denied to most children.

The effects of the home background have been seen especially clearly in the achievements of children from Jewish families. In Europe and America Jews have made contributions out of all proportion to their numbers. Before the Second World War, at least 20 per cent of Germany's scientists and mathematicians were Jewish, as were as many as half the mathematicians in Italy, although Jews made up less than two per cent of those countries' populations. In Britain and the Soviet Union Jews have been similarly over-represented in science and the professions. Jewish scholars, artists, and professional people are equally prominent in the United States. The proportion of Jewish children in Lewis Terman's sample of gifted young Californians was twice as high as would have been expected from their numbers in the school population. The fact that Jews, who comprise less than three per cent of the population, have won 27 per cent of the Nobel prizes, is indicative of their high levels of achievement in many fields (Hayes, 1981).

There are a number of contributing factors. One is a respect for scholarly activities, coupled with a keen awareness of the importance of education. There is nothing new about Jewish appreciation of scholarship: in one list of important European scholars that was compiled before the year 1400 the proportion of Jews was three times their numerical frequency. Religious Jews have always held Talmudic scholars in high regard. Even on the Sabbath, when many activities are prohibited or restricted, study has not been discouraged.

Another factor is the traditional importance attached to children in the family. Compared with families from other cultural origins, Jewish families have tended to be small and stable, with relatively few divorces: so most children have benefited from the presence of having two parents at home. Many Jewish families in North America have lived in relatively affluent urban or suburban environments, where schools provide good cultural opportunities and have high expectations. Jewish children have been strongly encouraged to direct their energies towards the kinds of activities that lead to success at school. Other pastimes that children enjoy, such as sporting ones, may receive less encouragement from Jewish than from Gentile parents. In the United States, partly as a result of the importance traditionally attached to education in Jewish families, a much larger proportion of Jews than non-Jews go to college. At college their academic performance is, on average, markedly superior.

Other cultural traditions have features which encourage early learning. In the Orient, for instance, children are taught to be unquestioningly obedient to their parents and to be attentive to teachers and other adults. In consequence, the children of cultured parents often make fast early progress. The effects of combining a cultural tradition of submission to parental demands with expert teaching by an enthusiastic parent can be seen in the achievements of Yo-Yo Ma, a young Chinese cellist of exceptional ability who was also a remarkable prodigy in early childhood. At that time

> Hiao-Tsiun [the father] tutored his children in French history, Chinese history, mythology, and calligraphy ... and Yo-Yo took up the piano and the cello. His cello teacher, Michelle Lepinte, was astonished when the four-year-old,

under his father's guidance, began to play a Bach suite. Hiao-Tsuin had developed a method of teaching young children how to concentrate intensively. No more than a short assignment was given daily, but this was to be thoroughly assimilated. He proceeded systematically and patiently. Each day, Yo-Yo was expected to memorize two measures of Bach; the following day, two more measures. He learned to recognize patterns – their similarities and their differences – and soon developed a feeling for musical structure. By the time he was five, he had learned three Bach suites. (Blum, 1989, p. 48)

The combined effects of parental expectations and encouragement, the presence of scholarly role models, and parents' eagerness to ensure that a child not only has opportunities to learn but also devotes considerable amounts of time to study, can create an emotional and intellectual atmosphere in which it seems difficult *not* to succeed. Sometimes one gains the impression that parents have convinced themselves before their son (but rarely their daughter) is born, that the child will become a genius. Leo Wiener, the father of the great mathematician Norbert Wiener, seems to have had this expectation, which was certainly fulfilled (Wiener, 1953). So, too, did the parents of Yehudi Menuhin. The father gave up his post as a teacher in order to concentrate on helping his children's careers. Both parents firmly believed that every so often a brilliant child would be born into their family, and they seem never to have doubted that their son was destined for greatness (Rolfe, 1978). Prophecies of this kind tend to be self-fulfilling. Many parents would like to believe that their son or daughter is innately gifted, and I suspect that parents sometimes convince themselves that a child really is inherently talented after observing the child respond in a manner which is in fact quite normal but which the parents believe to be an indication of extraordinary early development. And once the parents have got it into their heads that the child is specially talented they start to act differently themselves, thereby making it more likely that the child receives the kinds of experiences and opportunities that do accelerate his or her abilities. The fact that the same 'special' treatment would accelerate the development of virtually *any* child is not sufficiently appreciated.

John Maynard Keynes, who does not seem to have been outstandingly able as a young child, despite the fact that his mother worried about him working his brain too hard even before he reached the age of two, is described by his biographer as having been surrounded by 'the conviction that he was bound to be clever' (Skidelsky, 1983, p. 67) on the part of parents and other relatives: they would have been surprised and disappointed had he turned out not to be. Parental expectations of this kind cannot fail to have some influence on a child, even if the effect is not invariably positive and does not always match the parents' intentions.

Early anticipations of a child's future achievements are not exclusive to Jewish families. Mozart's father had very definite ideas about his son's future career well before the child was weaned. The parents of John Ruskin appear to have decided for themselves very early in his life that their child was going to be a quite exceptional person (Burd, 1973). Frank Lloyd Wright's mother not only decided in advance of his birth that her son was going to be a great architect, but arranged for him to be surrounded by architectural images and pictures almost from the moment he was born. John Stuart Mill could be said to have had genius drummed into his head by the relentless efforts of his ambitious, never-resting parent, James Mill.

So far as the children's achievements were concerned, in each of the above cases the parents' expectations were fulfilled, and their efforts rewarded. But the child may have to pay a cost. The inevitable pressure to succeed, and the emotional intensity of life in the kind of family that has these expectations, can have psychologically crippling effects. This happened to one spectacularly able child prodigy, William Sidis, whose sad life will be described later, in chapter 5.

Of course, not all cultural experiences and opportunities are mediated through the family. Moreover, the influences of historical events may disrupt or outweigh the operation of cultural traditions. The powerful effects of extra-family cultural influences that are brought about by historical changes can be seen in the findings of research by Glenn Elder. He looked at those people in Terman's large sample of unusually intelligent Californians (see chapter 1) who were born at the beginning of the present century, and whose lives were adversely affected at the start of their careers by the Great Depression, and again interrupted in mid-career by the Second World War. Elder found that those individuals were impaired in a number of ways compared with others whose date of birth precluded these events having so great an influence in their lives. Also, not surprisingly, the effects of participation in the armed services for the duration of a war continued to be critical throughout the remainder of a person's life (Elder, 1988; Elder, Hastings, and Pavalko, 1989).

## *The Chicago Studies*

Valuable insights into the ways in which families can help a young person to gain exceptional abilities have been provided by a recent series of large-scale investigations. These examined the early lives of children who, by the time they had become young adults, had already shown themselves to be remarkably accomplished. The investigations were undertaken by a group of researchers at the University of Chicago, headed by Benjamin Bloom (1985). Data were collected in a fairly systematic manner: information about family life and early childhood experiences was obtained directly from interviewing the exceptional young people themselves, and from talking to their parents and the teachers who were involved in their early upbringing. As a result, the descriptions of the individuals' early lives are likely to be fairly accurate. They are appreciably more reliable than most of the (largely anecdotal) accounts that are available about the early lives of most people whose adult achievements have been outstanding. In most other cases, the only source of knowledge about the early circumstances of an exceptionally able or creative person has been biographical or autobiographical material that was collected many years after the subject's childhood.

The Chicago-based investigations included several separate but related studies. Each examined a number of individuals who, as young adults, had become or were beginning to be highly distinguished experts in one field of activity. One investigation looked into the early family lives of distinguished young mathematicians. Other studies investigated concert pianists, tennis champions and Olympic swimmers, sculptors, and neurologists.

What were the characteristics of these individuals' early home lives? The findings showed that in most cases the family was intact throughout the young person's childhood, and the parents were willing to go to enormous lengths to help the individual to do well. The parents often supervised homework, and sometimes checked or inspected it. In most cases, especially when the child was young, they would happily attend any special lessons outside school and be present at practice sessions. As a rule, the parents placed considerable value on success. Most of them were themselves hard-working and energetic people who favoured active over passive pursuits and considered it very important to achieve the very best one could do. Passive interests such as watching television were not much encouraged by these parents. Family life tended to be firmly structured, with the children required to accept responsibilities and share household chores. The children were expected to learn to use their time efficiently enough to fit in a variety of daily activities: in these families time was definitely not to be wasted. The parents were always willing to devote their own time and energy to their children – playing games, reading to them, or teaching them in one way or another.

Obviously, the families interviewed in the Chicago study differed from each other in many ways. In view of the diversity of their interests this was only to be expected. But in some respects there was considerable uniformity. As we have seen, virtually all the families placed a high value on achieving, and they made their children aware of the importance the parents attached to doing one's best. For most of the young people it was the parents who first introduced them to the talent area in which they eventually excelled. Often, although not always, this coincided with a special interest of at least one of the parents. In consequence, the children almost always began developing special skills in the context of home activities, and the parents provided appropriate teaching, usually of an informal kind, whenever a child showed particular interest. In this way, the child was progressively encouraged to participate in activities valued by the parents, and helped to acquire necessary knowledge and skills.

In short, whatever the particular area of expertise, the child's early interest in it came about as a fairly predictable consequence of living in the particular cultural milieu of that individual's everyday family life. And even when learning resources outside the family were called upon, for teaching the piano or giving instruction in swimming or tennis, for example, the parents did not simply leave things to the teacher. Typically, they took on themselves the responsibility to make sure that the child practised regularly (in most cases at least once per day), prepared carefully for lessons, and worked hard at learning new skills. These parents all seem to have realized that young children cannot be expected to practise alone at a repetitive activity. They were willing to spend time with their child, giving help and encouragement in one form or another, or making the practice session into a game. As one mother said, 'I think that helped, especially when they're young. Because it's pretty hard just to sit down and practise without someone there beside you' (Sloane, 1985, p. 456).

The Chicago studies report no evidence of any families of those talented young people either having failed to provide a considerable amount of support or having lacked at least a modicum of interest in the talent area. And all of the parents seem to have been very keen for the child to be successful. In this respect the degree of uniformity appears remarkable. It prompts the question of whether there were any exceptions at all to the above statements. Perhaps surprisingly, there appear not to have been, although it is fair to point out that since the Chicago investigations were planned in such a way as to yield primarily qualitative rather than numerical findings, the data do not provide a basis for an entirely definite answer. But the present findings encourage us to raise another, broader, question, that of whether or not the early development of special talents *ever* takes place in the absence of adult support and encouragement. That question will be examined in chapter 5.

## *The Need to examine individual Lives*

Up to this point in the current chapter the aim has been to find general principles. I have tried to draw generalizations that connect individuals' achievements to the broad characteristics of their home and family backgrounds. But there are limits to the value of this approach. It cannot take us very far towards an understanding of how and why some young people, but not others, become extraordinarily skilled or unusually well informed.

To gain a fuller knowledge of the reasons why certain people are outstandingly successful it is necessary to extend our enquiries in certain directions. We shall have to focus on particular individuals, and recognize that broad statements about influences on the abilities of people in general may tell us little about how and why individuals actually acquire the skills that make exceptional abilities possible. And we must go beyond simply identifying relationships between family background factors and a person's achievements. We also need to look at the mechanisms and processes via which the family's influence is felt.

Many of the questions that arise concerning the acquisition of exceptional human abilities can be placed within one of two complementary groups. First, there are questions about what is possible. What can attempts to accelerate progress actually achieve? The research findings reported in chapter 3 were largely directed to answering questions of that kind. Secondly, and just as important, there are questions about the circumstances of real life in which it actually happens that young people do gain exceptional abilities. For example, what kinds of childhood and what family circumstances tend to produce the most able people? If we are to discover how to increase the numbers of young people who gain high abilities it is important to have answers to questions of the latter type as well as the former. This is one of the reasons for a change in the focus of attention some of the remaining chapters of this book, away from specific abilities as such and towards the individuals who gain them, and the progress of those people's lives.

A glimpse at the early family life of one famous scientist serves to demonstrate why it is necessary to examine reasonably closely the family circumstances of particular individuals. Here are a few facts about the childhood of Charles Darwin. His mother died when he was eight years old. He was the fifth of six children. His elder brother often bossed him about, and so did his three older sisters. His father – a rather overbearing man, of whom Charles was somewhat nervous – had plans for his son to enter the Church of England, and almost forbade him to take part in what turned out to be one of the most momentous journeys in the history of science, the voyage of HMS *Beagle*. Neither his father nor his sisters had great hopes for Charles: a letter from his sister Susan to the 17-year-old Charles combines a nagging reproach ('Remember to write *slow* and then you will form each letter distinctly') with a warning message from the father, saying that 'if you do not discontinue your present indulgent way, your course of study will be utterly useless'.

On this evidence, the circumstances of Darwin's family life do not seem to have been at all well designed for encouraging a young person to become a great scientist. But family activities are private affairs, largely hidden from outsiders. The surface aspects of a family's life – the ones that are on display to the casual observer – may reveal very little about the really crucial influences on a child of being brought up within a particular family. So it was with Darwin. Superficial appearances notwithstanding, Charles Darwin's family background actually gave him a superb start in life, one that was ideally suited to the pursuit of a scientific career in biology.

To begin with, Charles's older sisters made enormous efforts to fill the vacuum left by his mother's death. Compared with most young women at the time, they were remarkably lively and well-informed, and liberal in their attitudes. They read widely, kept abreast of political affairs and current issues, and had a very active interest in pioneering new developments in the education of children. Two sisters, Caroline and Susan, set up a school for infants: they energetically adopted the ideas of recent educational reformers such as Pestalozzi and Guizot. Also, Charles was frequently reminded of the fact that his grandfather, Erasmus Darwin, had been a notable scientific thinker of his time. Erasmus Darwin had speculated about evolutionary matters in *Zoonomia*, a book about the laws of organic life, and in his lengthy scientific poem *The Botanic Garden*. Each made a deep impression on the author's grandson. Erasmus' son Robert, who was Charles Darwin's father, was a successful and well-to-do doctor. He had wide interests and immense curiosity, and encouraged his younger son to accompany him when he visited patients. Caroline Darwin reported,

> My father was very fond of him [Charles] & even when he was a little boy of six or seven, however bustled and overtired, often had Charles with him when he was dressing, to teach him some little thing such as the almanack – and Charles used to be so eager to be down in time. Charles does not seem to have known half how much my father loved him. (Quoted in Brent, 1981, p. 23)

Even from his elder brother, a second Erasmus, set apart by a four-year difference which might have been expected to rule out any common interests, the young Charles learned much that was valuable. Erasmus, yet another member of the family who was an enthusiastic scientist, engaged his younger brother's assistance to help him conduct chemical experiments, aimed at making gases. Charles Darwin said that this experience was 'the best part of my education at school'. From very early in childhood Charles himself was a keen naturalist. At first, this interest took a simple form, in bug-hunting. With his family's encouragement he collected and classified beetles, moths, and butterflies. He also collected minerals with, as he put it, 'much zeal but quite unscientifically' (Brent, 1981).

As he grew older and became more knowledgeable he began to take a more analytic approach to biological things, seeking to explain what he observed, and not just collect and classify. Darwin was no prodigy in his childhood, and nobody at that time considered his abilities to be at all remarkable. But what he learned then, largely thanks to a humane home background that was inhabited by well-informed individuals who cared deeply about each other, were happy to share their knowledge and skills, and who were stimulating, encouraging, demanding, and above all, warmly interested in the activities of all the family, gave him a solid grounding in biological knowledge, skills, techniques, attitudes, and interests. The mature Darwin's scientific activities evolved from and built upon the fruits of his boyhood interests.

It is not possible to be certain, but in all likelihood the early family lives of most people of genius have been just as significant as Darwin's was, in making their achievements possible. But as in Darwin's case, in order to gain any real idea of the ways in which family background and childhood experiences actually exert their influence we have to glimpse behind superficial appearances, and take a closer and more detailed look at the particular circumstances of an individual's childhood.

## *Discovering the underlying Factors*

The fact that someone's achievements are influenced by their family background may not be due entirely to the varying experiences and opportunities made available in different home environments. Hereditary factors may be involved as well. Everyone has heard of musical families such as the Bachs, in which several generations of children have shared a particular exceptional ability. Such a phenomenon does point to the possibility of a hereditary linkage, even if the fact that the vast majority of the parents of great musicians, and the children of great musicians, have not been outstandingly able suggests that genetic influences do not operate by transmitting ready-made talents from one generation to another. In chapter three I demonstrated that the causes of many exceptional abilities lie in special experiences and opportunities, and not in innate aptitudes, gifts, or talents. Yet it remains possible that the relationships that have been observed between exceptional abilities and family backgrounds are caused, at least in part, by hereditary mechanisms, rather than by cultural ones alone.

CULTURAL AND INHERITED INFLUENCES
Converging lines of evidence indicate that cultural and environmental factors do account for at least a large part of the influence of family background upon individual achievements. For example, consider the finding that the number of Jewish people who succeed in intellectual spheres is out of proportion to their absolute numbers. On its own, this outcome may seem as likely to result from genetic as from cultural causes. But a clearer picture emerges when we take account of some other findings as well. Not all Jewish home backgrounds are equally successful in promoting intellectual accomplishments. In the United States, for instance, the average IQ test scores of children brought up in Sephardic Jewish families (descended from immigrants from the Middle East) which do not place a high premium on academic achievements, are considerably lower than those of children in Jewish families originating from Europe. Within a multi-cultured society such as the United States, children's patterns of achievements tend to be closely related to the particular values and cultural priorities of the home background.

SEX DIFFERENCES AS EVIDENCE
Even when finer-toothed comparisons are made the possible influences of hereditary and environmental factors may resist efforts to disentangle them. For example, within the Jewish population of the United States it is conceivable that the above-mentioned differences in intellectual achievements between Sephardic families and families whose ancestors emigrated from Europe, have genetic origins. An approach that avoids some of the problems that are inevitable when both environmental and hereditary sources of influence may have contributed to observed differences in individuals' patterns of accomplishment, is to look at differences *within* families rather than between them. One way of doing this is by examining gender differences in children's patterns of ability. Since there are no overwhelming hereditary reasons for either girls or boys being more able, in general, than children of the opposite sex, we can assume that ability differences between boys and girls within the same

family largely reflect the operation of differing opportunities or expectations.

As is well known, there are few areas of human achievement in which men have not predominated. In a man's world, men have usually held the power to decide which kinds of achievement are to be valued. Males have dominated politics and religion, finance and industry, as well as the arts and the sciences, and men have always taken most of the Nobel prizes. Writing of Einstein, David Feldman has remarked that 'if little Albert had been a girl, I think we would never have heard of her' (Feldman, 1986, p. 172). (But all the same, some women have managed to succeed. Everyone has heard of Marie Curie.)

For most children, even today, the family provides the setting in which boys and girls begin to be treated differently. From a very early age they are encouraged to have contrasting, sex-related, interests. Father Christmas does not hand out guns to little girls or dolls to small boys. Sex-related differences in the activities and behaviours that win parental approval can be seen even in the earliest years. And most girls are still encouraged to take an interest in the skills that make a woman into a good homemaker, whereas very few boys are expected to gain expertise at cleaning, cooking, sewing, knitting, and taking care of babies. In many families a girl's experiences will lead her to see herself as a future wife and mother, who is expected to support her husband's efforts to succeed in his career, but whose own working activities outside the home are confined to jobs that are considered 'suitable' for women. In a study of the early experiences of great mathematicians, Fowler (1986) found that three of the six women in his sample had encountered severe opposition to their careers from their families. Even now it remains true that many jobs held by women are ones that are poorly paid, with limited opportunities for advancement. As Virginia Woolf observed, it is no accident that from well before Jane Austen's time until the present day, the writing of good novels, an enterprise which can, at a pinch, be squeezed in between clearing up after one meal and preparing the next one, has been one of the few areas of creative endeavour at which substantial numbers of women have been highly successful.

The disadvantaged status of women is by no means a thing of the past. Nor is it confined to poorly-educated groups. Even today, many women do not have enough control over their lives to be able to pursue their interests with the single-mindedness and dedication, or the firm sense of direction, that is encountered in men who win Nobel prizes or reach other pinnacles of acknowledged achievement outside the home. The following quotation from a young college woman polled in the 1970s is not entirely untypical.

> My father even has a little bell he rings and my mother comes running and brings him coffee and he will call her from another room to change the television station. And it has been so successful. He is so happy and she is happy doing it. Why not treat him like a king because the male ego is kind of a sensitive thing to go tampering with? My life is probably not going to make that much difference on society, but maybe what my husband and children do will. I don't feel that I am that important. (Hayes, 1981)

Even those women who, unlike the young lady just quoted, do have a serious desire to do well, may find themselves stopped in their tracks by restrictive parental attitudes. David Feldman reports the bitter experience of a young woman who had been a talented young pianist but whose religious parents believed that

> it was a sin for a little girl to have such a passion for mastering the instrument. For several years this woman fought a titanic battle with her parents over her music. She was forbidden to practise and was kept inside to prevent her from finding a piano elsewhere. When her parents were asleep she would sneak out of a window, go down the street to a local church, and practise on the church organ. After several years of this, her endurance waned and she finally gave up ... Now in her fifties, the pain and sadness of her story were still evident. (Feldman, 1986, p. 183)

The outcome of within-family differences in the extent to which boys and girls are encouraged to succeed at non-domestic accomplishments has been to deny certain opportunities to many women. The cultural and environmental factors that lead to between-family differences in the extent to which children are encouraged to succeed are in many respects similar to the within-family sex differences that exist in the way boys and girls are treated. For that reason, the powerful effects on children's achievements of sex differences *within* families serve to illuminate the influence of differences *between* families on the production of exceptional abilities.

## Mechanisms of family influence

A large body of research (much of which is reviewed by Wachs and Gruen, 1982; see also Gottfried, 1984) has examined the relationships between children's development and various aspects of the home background. Apart from some case studies of the home lives of particular individuals few of the investigations have been specifically involved with the early lives of those children who subsequently gain exceptional abilities. Other reasons apart, the impossibility of knowing in advance which children are the ones who will become extraordinarily successful creates practical barriers to any investigation of this kind. By and large, the findings of research that has examined child development in relation to early experience are in line with the results reported in this chapter and the previous one. That is, infants and young children tend to gain basic intellectual and social skills, and communicative abilities especially, earlier than usual if they are raised by parents who are themselves well-educated, and who interact with the child relatively frequently, respond sensitively to the child's activities, and talk to their child more frequently than most parents do, and from an early age.

PATTERNS OF INTERACTION IN THE EARLIEST YEARS
Because infants are not identical, even at birth, it is impossible to prescribe in fine detail the kinds of maternal child-raising practices that are most effective for getting young children started on a path leading towards being highly competent. Much depends upon the needs and temperament of the particular child. Moreover, the parent's effectiveness at aiding a baby's progress depends only to a limited extent on the choice of 'good' child-rearing practices: sensitivity to the particular needs of the individual baby is more crucial. The sensitive mother is good at perceiving her baby's state at a given moment, and discerning the infant's current requirements.

Researchers have collected a very substantial body of factual evidence about the ways in which mothers act towards their infants. Differences in mothering undoubtedly do affect infants' progress, although it is not entirely clear to what extent patterns of early mother–infant interaction influence an individual's eventual competence, as an adult. It is reasonable to suppose that those young infants whose mothers are highly sensitive to their needs are more likely to become intellectually outstanding adults than infants whose mothers are less sensitive. But practical difficulties make it hard to either verify or disprove the assertion that there are inevitable long-term consequences that directly depend upon the mother's degree of sensitivity to the young infant. One problem is that those mothers who are highly sensitive to the needs of their one-year-olds tend also to continue to be sensitive to the needs of the same children when they are three years old, five years old, and so on. In principle, it would be possible to devise a suitable experimental procedure for measuring the effects of early mother–infant patterns of interaction as such, without the confounding effects of subsequent events. This could be achieved by assessing a large sample of individuals whose mothers were induced to act with varying (and carefully measured) sensitivity towards their children in different years. In practice, for obvious ethical reasons it is not possible to do this.

The sensitivity of the mother to her young infant's signals appears to be a crucial factor in determining the infant's progress towards becoming able to communicate effectively with other people. By the end of the first year those infants whose mothers were rated as being highly sensitive to their needs were found to have made more progress than the other babies at acquiring certain other abilities that are essential for intellectual and social development (Ainsworth, Bell, and Stayton, 1974).

It is conceivable that the degree to which the mother is sensitive to her infant during the first year of a child's life may have little direct importance for specifically cognitive aspects of development. However, there are reasons for challenging any such assumption. For example, as was demonstrated in chapter three, the speed and the appropriateness of maternal reactions to infants' vocalizations affect language development. Also, in mothers who are depressed, responses to their children's language utterances tend to be slower and more variable than is normal. For this reason, amongst others, the intellectual development of children whose mothers suffer from depression is likely to be adversely affected.

Most of the findings that emerge from investigations based on observations of interactions between a mother and her child take the form of correlations indicating the size of the relationships between the behaviours of mother and infant. The inevitable limitation of this kind of evidence is that one can rarely be certain that a cause-and-effect influence is involved. The findings indicate that differences in mothers' behaviours *may* affect their babies, but alternative explanations cannot be ruled out. Partly for this reason, and partly because of the uncertainty about the long-term effects of the qualities of child-rearing that are found to affect children's progress in the short term, we would not be justified in making confident predictions about the contributions of someone's experiences in early infancy to that individual's chances of becoming an extraordinarily competent adult. But as we saw in the previous chapter, the studies conducted on twins by McGraw and other researchers have established that at least some of the child-rearing practices that take place in the first year of life can have permanent effects.

## How Crucial are the Earliest Years of Life?

Questions about the long-term psychological effects (if there are any) of a child's upbringing during early infancy lead to queries about the possibility that there are certain 'critical periods' in early life. Underlying the concept of a critical period is the view that if an event does not occur at a particular time in the child's early life, the developmental progress that is normally caused by that event will either never take place at all or be permanently abnormal or incomplete.

From birth onwards, much of what a young child learns is acquired when the child is interacting with an adult. Inevitably, the child's main caretaker – who is usually but not always the biological mother – has a major influence on what a baby learns in the earliest years. But just how important *are* those early years for a child's future achievements? Are the first months and years absolutely critical, in which case a mother's failure to provide an ideal early learning environment will restrict the child's progress in later years, ruling out development beyond a certain level? Or do the mother's activities during her baby's earliest years have a less crucial influence on the child's eventual intellectual development? And, in order to become a person who achieves extraordinary accomplishments, is it essential to have grown up with a caregiver who provided a good environment in the first years of life? Or is it possible to compensate for slow progress in the earliest years?

We are in no position to give really firm answers to the two final questions. The evidence simply is not available. To provide the essential data we would need to have detailed records of the early lives of a substantial number of outstanding people. But since such individuals form a very small minority of the children who are born, in order to obtain records of the earliest years of even a few individuals who are sufficiently exceptional to, say, win a Nobel prize, it would be necessary to collect detailed data on literally thousands of people. Yet, despite the fact that needed evidence is lacking, we can at least take a stab at answering some of the questions. We do know that exceptional individuals have grown up in many different and widely varying historical periods. Between these times the values, customs, practices, habits, and conventions surrounding child-raising have altered enormously. So we can be fairly sure that the early upbringings of exceptional people have not all been similar. And a substantial number of brilliant people have emerged from family backgrounds that have been unhappy, or poverty-stricken, or in other ways far from ideal. Charlie Chaplin had an appalling childhood. His father was a heavy drinker, his mother was mentally unstable, and at the age of five the child was sent to an orphanage, where he stayed for two years. George Bernard Shaw's home background was far from perfect, and he complained (not entirely fairly) that his mother disliked and rejected him. Jack London's home life was particularly grim: and much of his late childhood, in California, was spent in places that were even worse than the blacking factory where the young Charles Dickens was forced to work. Isaac Newton's mother abandoned him when he was a young child, leaving him with his grandmother.

So the possibility that the presence of a very specific pattern of 'ideal' mothering behaviour is an essential feature of the early background of outstanding individuals is definitely ruled out. On the other hand, there are no records of children who have suffered really severe deprivation of caregiving in their earliest years becoming adult geniuses. That is not to say that no outstanding people have been deprived of their biological mothers, but it would appear that in every case the child has had the opportunity to form a secure attachment with one or more caretakers.

Another possibility is that normal development will fail to occur unless learning take place at particular, 'critical' periods during the child's earliest years. There is a substantial amount of empirical evidence on this matter, although as with many other psychological questions, the fact that evidence exists does not always make it easy to give simple answers. (Quite often, increases in knowledge simply heighten our awareness of the multiplicity of influences affecting human development, so that the reply to an apparently straightforward query has to begin with the phrase 'It depends upon ...') One question to which a definite answer can be given is that of whether there are critical periods during babies' first months, when certain things have to be learned if they are to be acquired at all. For example, is a one-year-old who has been visually deprived, or prevented from hearing language, permanently impaired thereby? Here the answer is a definite 'No'. There do not appear to be critical periods for early development of human abilities that are as sharply defined as that. Children have a noteworthy ability to recover from severe early deprivations. But that is not to rule out the possibility of there being permanent retardation if physiological damage occurs, or if the period of deprivation is very lengthy.

In summary, researchers have acquired a substantial body of information concerning the short-term effects of some of the ways in which mothers behave towards their babies. In the short term, maternal behaviours undoubtedly do affect the development of infants and young children. There is much less evidence about the long-term consequences of differences in mothering practices. All the same, and despite the lack of detailed findings concerning the child-rearing practices of the mothers of outstanding individuals, the fact that maternal behaviour is known to affect development in the short term provides a degree of support for the view that the children of mothers who interact sensitively with their babies will eventually be more likely to reach extraordinary levels of achievement than the children of mothers whose child-rearing behaviours are less effective. But the effects of differing standards of mothering are not the all-or-none ones that would be expected if there were firmly defined critical periods for intellectual development. They are not quite so fixed, or irreversible.

Effective mothering in early childhood will usually give a child a good start in life. In most cases that will have beneficial long-term consequences, partly through a kind of snowballing effect. Other things being equal, a child who, as a result of the mother's effectiveness as a teacher, gains useful abilities that facilitate the acquisition of further useful skills, will thereby have a definite advantage over less-favoured children. For example, a child who learns to speak comparatively early will thereby gain communicative skills that open up numerous opportunities to the young learner. Moreover, as I noted in the previous chapter, language, once acquired, encourages thought. As one father observed 150 years ago,

> It is clear that the correct acquisition of his mother tongue makes the child intelligent at an early time, for it puts his attention and his several mental powers continuously in action. He is obliged always to search, distinguish, compare, prefer, report, choose, in short he must work, that is, think.
> (Witte, 1975, p. 75)

If the favourable circumstances are maintained over a long period, the effects will be cumulative. But circumstances can change, and a mother who is unusually effective at providing an optimal environment for her baby's earliest years may be less successful at providing support and encouragement for learning in later childhood.

What is good mothering? For a very sound reason, it is simply not possible to specify the precise mothering activities that will maximize the intellectual development of a child, or any other aspect of early child development. Because young babies vary so much – in temperament, cuddliness, activity level, and perceptual sensitivity, for instance – the kind of mothering activities that are maximally effective differ from one infant to another. So a pattern of mothering behaviours that is ideal for one baby will be much less suitable for a different child. It is largely for this reason that effective mothering is characterized not by particular ways of acting towards babies, but by the capacity to respond with considerable sensitivity to the unique needs of an individual child. There are no grounds for asserting that, to be effective, the mother should always behave in such-and-such a way.

## The Years following Infancy

With studies of the family environments of toddlers and older children we are on much firmer ground. It is clear that a child's progress is strongly influenced by the kinds of activities and interactions that take place within the family. Differences between families in the ways in which language is used are especially crucial. Biographical information about the early lives of outstanding people often points to the parents moving heaven and earth to provide a child with rich early learning experiences. For instance, early in the seventeenth century, at a time when the majority of parents would not have been aware of the potential importance of educational experiences in early childhood, the father of Pascal, the mathematician, went to great lengths to provide intellectual stimulation for his three children. Pascal's father not only spent a large proportion of his own time with his children, but hired a substantial number of tutors to provide advanced instruction in fields outside his competence.

Biographical information about early family backgrounds is often fragmentary, and where it does exist it often takes the form of anecdotes which may be unreliable (Howe, 1982; Wallace, 1986). But the evidence does point to the presence of a parent or other relative who is strongly committed to giving help and encouragement in the early lives of many, and possibly most, of those people who have come to be regarded as being outstanding for their intellectual accomplishments.

### *Feuerstein's Insights*

That 'cultured' homes tend to produce highly educated young people is commonplace knowledge. To be really useful either for practical purposes or for adding to our understanding of the causes of extraordinary achievements, information about the characteristics of effective home environments needs to be more detailed and more precise. For example, how do parents in varying family backgrounds differ in the ways they behave towards their children? How do different parents cope with the task of teaching their sons and daughters new skills? And why is it that even at the time they begin school, some young children are much better equipped than others with mental and social skills that make success likely, and are better at communicating and maintaining concentration? Surprisingly, perhaps, one fruitful source of insights has been the work of a psychologist whose main aim has been to discover why certain schoolchildren have failed to make normal progress.

Reuven Feuerstein, a psychologist working in Israel, was confronted with the learning difficulties experienced by many of the children of recent immigrants to that country. Although these children were in many respects sharp, quick, 'streetwise', and bright, they experienced severe problems with learning at school. However hard they tried, they seemed unable to solve school learning tasks, especially ones in which it was necessary to reflect on a problem before responding, or to categorize items, or keep material in memory. Children like these suffer from what Feuerstein terms 'reduced modifiability'. By this he means a lack of adaptability to new situations, and diminished ability to learn from experience (Feuerstein, Hoffman, Jensen, and Rand, 1985; Howe, 1987a).

Feuerstein (1980) discovered that the root cause of many of the difficulties experienced by the young people who were referred to him lay in their family lives during early childhood. The parents are a child's first guides to an initially unfamiliar world. Most parents spend a great deal of time in various activities that have the effect of passing on to the child a knowledge of the culture into which he or she is born. The precise form of that knowledge, and the way it is communicated, will vary enormously from culture to culture, but in one way or another parents and others act in ways that serve to pass on to the child an awareness of important cultural elements. These include information and activities of various kinds, in the form of customs, conventions, religious beliefs, and ways of behaving in a variety of situations. They also include a number of practical skills.

Teaching seems to be a universal parental activity. Observations of parents and children living together in different societies throughout the world show that the ways in which parents talk to their offspring and interact with them, even in cultures that are technologically very primitive, are often remarkably similar to the patterns of interaction seen in 'advanced' cultures such as ours. And even in the most primitive societies, it is often clear that the parent has a deliberate *intention* to teach. Feuerstein asserts that parental intentionality has important consequences for the child's learning. He suggests that if we were to watch a Bushman training his child to make a spear or a bow and arrow we would see that the parent displays his intentions by requiring the child to follow his actions and by deliberately slowing down his own rhythm of work. Each of these deliberate parental teaching procedures has the effect of increasing the likelihood that the child will be able to perceive how the various activities involved in the construction of a weapon contribute towards the eventual product.

As a result of the instruction received at home, by the end of childhood each individual will have acquired what he or she is expected to know in order to be a fully competent member of the cultural group. Instruction may be formal or informal, and the contexts in which knowledge is transmitted may include any combination of a variety of alternative activities, including story-telling, song, dance, many forms of play and games, other opportunities for imitation, festivities, ceremonies, rituals, and trials of strength. Diverse as human cultures are, they all have mechanisms which ensure that the growing child will interact with other people in ways that result in the child 'learning the culture' in which he or she grows up, and thereby becoming a competent member of the society.

When Feuerstein looked into the backgrounds of the children who were experiencing especially severe difficulties with school learning, he discovered that almost all of them came from families that had failed to provide the cultural learning experiences which form a normal part of the process of growing up. Typically, the parents were recent immigrants to Israel, from very different and technologically unsophisticated societies in the Near East and northern Africa. In Israel they found it difficult to adjust to an unfamiliar and essentially westernized way of life, one which contrasted with the traditional cultures in which they had been raised. As confused newcomers to a strange new society which these parents were trying — with difficulty, and no great success — to understand, they thought that what they had learned in their own childhoods was of no value for life in modern Israel. Most importantly, so far as their children were concerned, the parents felt that they had little that was useful to pass on to the new generation, who would have to make their lives in a westernized modern state. Consequently, believing that what they had learned from their own parents would be useless for their children, these people failed to spend much time with their children or engage with them in the various activities through which, in other circumstances, the children would have learned about the traditional culture. The children were therefore deprived of their parents' teaching and guidance.

A consequence of being deprived of opportunities to interact with their parents in the many learning situations that occur naturally in a society where it is deemed necessary to pass on knowledge to the young, is that children also fail to acquire a number of basic learning and thinking skills, ones that pupils must have if they are to be at all successful at the kinds of learning tasks that are important at school. A child who never acquires these skills, which Feuerstein insists are essential prerequisites for school learning, is very seriously deprived, and can never catch up with others. Feuerstein believes that such a child is 'unmodifiable'. By this he means that the child is closed to the possibility of being altered by new experiences.

The fact that the significant deprivation in these children's lives is not in their lack of culture in its static aspects – knowledge, customs, and so on – but in their failure to experience the cultural processes by which knowledge, values, and beliefs are transmitted from one generation to the next, is illustrated by some apparently paradoxical contrasts in the differing capacities of various cultural groups to adapt to an unfamiliar way of life. Feuerstein compared the experiences of immigrants who came to Israel from the Yemen with those of immigrants from certain regions of northern Africa. Of the two groups, the Yemenites' traditional lives are much more remote from and different to the dominant western culture of modern Israel than are the lifestyles of the North Africans. Yet despite the greater difference between their traditional culture and Israeli culture, the Yemenite immigrants adapted to life in the unfamiliar modern society more rapidly and more effectively.

Feuerstein's explanation stems from his view that what is important, so far as successfully adapting is concerned, is not the degree of similarity between old and new environments but the degree to which the individuals are modifiable. This latter quality depends, as we have seen, upon the extent to which, through the family activities that lead to knowledge of a culture being gained, individuals have acquired the intellectual tools that underlie the capacity of a person to change, to adapt, and also to learn at school. As a consequence of possessing appropriate learning abilities and habits, people who, like the Yemenites, but unlike some of the other immigrants from Northern Africa, have been brought up in highly developed societies – however remote or 'traditional' they may be – are generally able to adapt to the ways of an entirely new way of life.

If Feuerstein is right, an important lesson to be learned is that parents have an essential role as guides and interpreters for their children. They direct children's attention to those aspects of the everyday world that are especially significant. They encourage children to undertake the kinds of mental activities and strategies that will result in skills and knowledge being learned. In the absence of this guidance some forms of learning may be unimpeded, but other kinds of learning, especially those that require the sustained attention and reflective thinking that is often necessary in school learning tasks, will fail to occur.

Feuerstein asserts that children's need for such guidance is often underestimated. Many parents have been encouraged to believe that their children's intellects will develop satisfactorily so long as the environment is sufficiently rich, in the sense of being varied and stimulating. According to this view, all that is necessary is to ensure that there are plenty of interesting events for the child to perceive – for instance, sights and sounds that carry information from which the child can learn. Parents of young babies have been advised to hang mobiles above their infants' cots, and introduce stimuli that provide shapes, colours, and movement. The more lively, varied, and event-filled the child's environment, the more 'enriched' it is thought to be.

Unfortunately, that view is quite wrong. A stimulating physical environment may well be necessary, but this kind of stimulation on its own is very far from being sufficient to ensure that a child gains either knowledge or intellectual skills. As we have seen, it is also essential that the intellectual nourishment which the child's environment provides is channelled and interpreted to the child, or, to use Feuerstein's preferred term, *mediated*, by someone who can explain things, direct attention to what is important, and provide needed feedback for the child's own efforts to cope with various tasks.

One of Feuerstein's own examples provides a neat illustration of the way in which adults can help the child by mediating between him and the physical environment in a way that increases the child's understanding. He asks his readers to consider the difference between the two following instructions, each of which might be given by a parent to a young child:

1 Please buy three bottles of milk.
2 Please buy three bottles of milk so that we will have enough left over for tomorrow when the shops are closed.

Feuerstein points out that in the second instance, as distinct from the first, the child who complies with the instruction is not just carrying out a command. That child will also become involved in the reasoning that lies behind the request. As a result, the kind of understanding that is likely to accompany the action is likely to include anticipating a set of conditions that are likely to occur in the future, and a plan of activities that are designed to lead to the goal that guides the child's behaviour. And consequently, Feuerstein claims, 'the effects of such instructions are not limited to their specific contents but rather produce an orientation that may not be conceivable without exposure to mediation of this nature' (Feuerstein, 1980, p. 21).

With carefully mediated early stimulation children can often acquire difficult skills several years before the age at which they are normally learned. But in the absence of the kinds of guidance and support that a caring parent can provide, the likelihood of a young child gaining certain key skills is minimal. However rich is a young child's environment in interest and variety, stimulation alone is never enough.

## Problems of Family Life

I mentioned earlier that children can suffer as well as profit from being brought up in a family environment where there is intense pressure to do well, or where the emphasis on the training of particular abilities leads to a child being deprived of important childhood experiences. The problems that can be encountered by children whose parents are unusually anxious for them to succeed will receive further attention when child prodigies are discussed. My own reactions to descriptions of the family backgrounds of exceptionally able young people are sometimes mixed. Take, for instance, the people who were studied in the Chicago-based investigations. On the one hand, it seems admirable that families can be so caring, warm, supportive, dedicated, and unselfish, and able to liberate their offspring from the awful scourge of boredom, which spoils many hours for children who are too young to have acquired the inner resources that make life continuously fascinating. (The ten-year-old John Ruskin was expressing a universal loathing of childhood boredom when he wrote to his father, in 1829, 'I do think, indeed am sure, that in common things it's having too much to do which constitutes happiness, and too little, unhappiness.') It seems equally admirable that the parents act towards their children in so constructive and so concerned a way, and are prepared to make sacrifices on their behalf. If only more families could be like the ones described in these studies, the world would surely be a better place, or so it seems.

But this unqualified enthusiasm is clearly naïve. Perhaps it would be more realistic to view these parents, with all their emphasis on success and high achievements, in a more negative light. Some parents seem to be too ambitious for their children, too readily prepared to deprive their sons and daughters of many childhood joys, perhaps too anxious to live their own lives through their children, and uncaring (or unaware) of a young child's emotional requirements. Do some of these parents press their child to succeed in certain narrow areas at the expense of other kinds of growth? Are some parents determined that their children should be seen to achieve at any cost? Are others striving to meet neurotic needs of their own, at their child's expense?

That these fears are not entirely without foundation is confirmed by some of chilling remarks by parents interviewed in a major British study of gifted children undertaken by Joan Freeman (1979). She quotes one parent as saying,

'We don't allow them to watch television at all; they should be doing other things. But sometimes they see it at their friends.' (Said without a glimmer of humour.) (Freeman, 1979, p. 151)

Another parent remarks,

'Of course, he will go to boarding school when he is seven. I can't bear the thought of it, but he has to have the extra tuition which he will get there. The local school is just ordinary.' (Freeman, 1979, p. 151)

It is not difficult to find signs of emotional stress that appears to have originated in the intense family atmospheres that parents who place great store on their children's success are prone to create. As will be seen in the following chapter, Norbert Wiener, the mathematician, found himself over-dependent on his parents and oppressed by the demands of a father who expected too much of his son. John Ruskin's home atmosphere appears to have been equally intense, even claustrophobic. The fact that he was unable to detach himself from his over-controlling mother almost certainly contributed to the mental breakdowns that punctuated his life, and to his appalling behaviour towards his wife, Effie, who finally escaped from their six-year unconsummated marriage by running away with the painter John Everett Millais. And it is more than likely that had James Mill been less harsh and joyless, or a less grimly demanding father, his brilliant son John Stuart Mill would have been a warmer, more engaging, and perhaps happier adult. He might not have experienced the deep depression that almost drove him to suicide at the age of 20. In a number of talented families one gains the firm impression that parents and child have each become too dependent on the other, and at the same time resentful of this situation.

Even so, there are no firm grounds for believing that most parents who give their children unusually rich early learning experiences are either better or worse than other parents at helping their children to become happy and emotionally mature adults. The talented young people interviewed in the Chicago project gave every indication that their childhoods had been at least averagely happy. There is nothing in the interview responses to suggest that, as adults, they are noticeably neurotic or dissatisfied with their adult lives. Certainly, these people do seem to have experienced childhoods that were in some respects unusually intense and demanding, and with a large competitive element. On the other hand, their family backgrounds seem mostly to have been warm and supportive, and parent–child relationships generally appear to have been close and mutually rewarding. It could be objected that the University of Chicago studies of talented young people examined only a particularly successful sample of those children whose parents have made special efforts to provide an enriched early environment. Conceivably, there are other young people who have been stunted or damaged by constant exposure to all the pressures of life in an intense and over-demanding 'hot house' family atmosphere.

A central question that runs through the chapters of this book is that of whether or not the numbers of talented and able people *can* be greatly enlarged. The answer to that question is a clearly positive one: providing better early opportunities for early learning, particularly within the home context, can lead to enormous and permanent increases in achievements of many kinds. But raising the possibility that early family circumstances might also have certain undesirable effects, in addition to the outcomes they are intended to achieve, reminds us that at the same time as we are considering evidence concerning the effectiveness of parental efforts to help their children progress, and examining its implications, we must also keep in mind another question. That question asks whether or not adults *should* take various steps that are designed to increase their children's skills and achievements. It reflects a concern with the matter of whether it is proper for a parent to act in various ways, ones that may not simply affect the child's abilities, but may have other strong influences on the kind of person he or she will turn out to be.

With questions about the desirability of parents acting towards their children in ways that are special or unusual it is often difficult to arrive at the right answer. This is partly because of lack of firm evidence, partly because the desirable states to which the questions implicitly refer are hard to quantify (happiness is not so easily assessed as success at objectively measurable achievements), and partly because they refer to criteria whose importance is debatable, and related to personal values on which there is no universal agreement. (For example, how are we to resolve questions such as, 'Is it better for a person to be a happy 'failure' or a neurotic high-achiever?', and 'Is it better to have interests of many kinds or to be master of one particular field of endeavour?') To complicate matters, even the best of parents may be too closely involved with the lives of their families to be in a position to consider questions about their own children's future happiness in anything like an objective or detached manner.

But, hard as it is to reply to questions like these, we cannot afford to ignore them. They are far too important. As soon as it is apparent that procedures which are intended to extend a child's progress might have additional, conceivably undesirable consequences for the individual, it becomes equally clear that those questions which enquire not what parental intervention *can* achieve but what parents *ought* to do in connection with their early education, must be given very serious consideration indeed. There are always psychological costs to be paid for gaining an extraordinary talent. Unfortunately, some parents are unable or unwilling to recognize that, for some children, the value of a particular achievement may not justify the emotional expense.

## *The different Influences of Family and School*

It may have struck some readers that I have placed too much emphasis on family background as a source of the child's learning experiences and too little on the role of the school. After all, we spend much of our childhood at school, and schools are designed to help children gain important knowledge and skills. Is not the school, as a supplier of educational experiences, more important than the home?

For most children who grow up to be unusually able people, it is definitely not. That is not to deny that parents and their children depend on schools to contribute a substantial proportion of the instruction that is necessary in order for young people to become educated. On the whole, schools do an excellent job with the resources that are available to them. They succeed in ensuring that almost all children become reasonably literate and numerate, with all sorts of knowledge and skills at their disposal.

But, as I mentioned in chapter 2, schools labour under the enormous disadvantage of having a small number of teachers to instruct a large number of children. This does not prevent schools from succeeding at the task of educating vast quantities of children to a level that is usually deemed to be satisfactory, nor does it prevent them from providing the most able children with valuable educational experiences that complement home-based learning. Yet the fact that each teacher has to work with a large number of children does have the effect of making it impossible to give each young child that wealth and intensity of experiences appropriate to the particular individual that the most stimulating home backgrounds can provide. On its own, a school can rarely succeed in giving the intellectual nourishment that results in a child excelling at something, rather than being merely competent.

Schools are undoubtedly essential, and the quality of the schooling they provide is undoubtedly important: the best schools can do a far more effective job than poorer schools (Rutter, 1989). Moreover, many successful people have spoken with warmth about the enormous positive influence of certain outstanding teachers. All the same, when we look for the reasons leading to some children, but not others, becoming extraordinarily able, more of those reasons will be related to differences in home backgrounds than to different experiences at school. Parents who seek to discover what can be done to maximize the likelihood of their child becoming especially able find that most of the best opportunities for taking practical steps towards achieving this aim lie within the home and the family, not the school. Parents get to know their own children really well, as individuals. But for schoolteachers, the practical demands of their job make it impossible to have a comparable knowledge of the individual characteristics of every child they teach. Parents are able to work and play with their children on a one-to-one basis, if necessary for hours at a time. For the classroom teacher this is simply not possible. And for most parents who would like to help their children to become unusually capable adults, the positive effects of sending a child to a good school are far exceeded by those which can be achieved by the parents themselves spending time with the children and encouraging them to learn, and providing an interesting, attentive, and supportive home life.

# 5
# Child Prodigies

> Let those who choose to carve a human soul to their own measure be sure that they have a worthy image after which to carve it, and let them know that the power of molding an emerging intellect is a power of death as well as a power of life. (Norbert Wiener, *Ex-Prodigy: My Childhood and Youth*)

There is no such thing as a disembodied human skill. In the previous chapter I noted that as well as trying to answer questions about the extent to which people who are not inherently extraordinary can gain exceptional abilities it is also important to know more about the circumstances in which people actually gain outstanding abilities in real life. In exploring the reasons for certain individuals becoming extraordinarily accomplished it is necessary to focus on them as individual people, and not just on particular abilities. If we wish to understand why or how it is that a person becomes able to do something which that individual was not previously capable of doing it is important to know something about the life of the particular person.

By and large, the most singular human achievements are made possible by the special circumstances of lifestyles that are highly unusual. Other factors apart, most people have neither the single-minded dedication nor the clear sense of direction that are almost always to be found in those men and women whose achievements are genuinely outstanding. Although it may be wrong to think of exceptionally capable individuals as being people who having been innately set apart from other men and women, it is true that those who are outstandingly competent people do set themselves apart from others. They do so by submitting themselves to the unusual lives and the special experiences that make it possible for stunning accomplishments to be mastered.

Accounts of the lives of child prodigies offer a precious source of insights into the circumstances in which a few children develop into the kinds of adults who are capable of impressive achievements. The evidence helps answer some questions concerning the causes of exceptionality, and raises further queries. This chapter begins by describing the early lives of two child prodigies, with the aim of conveying something of the manner in which progress is made by particular individual children. The two individuals whose childhoods I discuss are an English engineer, George Parker Bidder, and an American mathematician, Norbert Wiener.

## Two Prodigies

### 1 George Bidder

On the edge of Dartmoor in the English county of Devon there is a tiny market town called Moretonhampstead. There, lying in his bed one evening, a small boy overheard his mother and his older brothers arguing about the correct price for a pig of a certain weight. He called down and told them what it should be.

The boy was eventually to become one of the great engineers of Victorian Britain. George Parker Bidder was born in 1806 (coincidentally, within a month of the birth of John Stuart Mill, the best-known of all child prodigies). He was the third son of a stonemason. At the age of six, with the encouragement of his older brother, another mason, George became interested in mental arithmetic. In his own words,

> ... there resided, in a house opposite to my father's, an aged blacksmith, a kind old man ... on winter evenings I was allowed to perch myself on his forge hearth, listening to his stories. On one of these occasions, somebody by chance mentioned a sum; ... I gave the answer correctly. This occasioned some little astonishment; they then asked me other questions, which I answered with equal facility. They then went on to ask me up to two places of figures ... I gave the answer correctly, as was verified by the old gentleman's nephew, who began chalking it up to see if I was right ... this increased my fame still more, and what was better, it eventually caused halfpence to flow into my pocket; which, I need not say, had the effect of attaching me still more to the

science of arithmetic and thus by degrees I got on ... (Clark, 1983, pp. 3–4)

By the time George was nine his fame had spread enormously. He had already acquired a national reputation for his skill at mental calculations, and was known throughout England as 'The Calculating Boy'. He was exhibited up and down the country. A handbill advertising a forthcoming demonstration in Oxford when he was ten boasts that at a previous audience with 'her Majesty [Queen Charlotte, the wife of King George the Third] and the Dukes of Kent and Sussex, Earl Stanhope, Sir Joseph Banks, the Lord Mayor of London, and many other persons of the first distinction in the Kingdom' he had responded to the Duke of Kent's request to multiply 7,953 by 4,648 with the correct answer, 36,965,544. To the Queen's question, 'How many days would a Snail be creeping, at the rate of 8 feet per day, from the Land's End, in Cornwall, to Ferret's Head, in Scotland, the distance by admeasurement being 838 miles?' he again answered correctly, 553,080. And, according to the handbill, he also dealt with 'a variety of others of the same nature', such as:

> Suppose a city to be illuminated by 9,999 lamps, and each lamp to consume one pint of oil in every four hours, how many gallons will they consume in 40 years? – Answer, 109,489,050.
> Suppose an acre of ground to contain 256 trees, each tree with 53 limbs, each limb 196 twigs, each twig 45 leaves, how many leaves are there in all? – Answer, 119,669,760.
> (Clark, 1983, p. 302)

Bidder was fast as well as accurate, although even he needed 13 minutes to do the largest of the mental calculation problems he was asked to solve, such as multiplying 257,689,435 by 356,875,649. It only took him one minute to calculate the answer to the following problem, put to him by the King's astronomer, Sir William Herschel.

> Light travels from the Sun to the Earth in eight minutes and the Sun being 98 million miles off, if Light would take six years and four months travelling at the same rate from the nearest fixed star, how far is that star from the Earth, reckoning 365 days and six hours to each year, and 28 days to each month? (Clark, 1983, p. 304)

George Bidder was unquestionably a child prodigy, a term defined by another ex-prodigy as 'a child who has achieved an appreciable measure of adult intellectual standing before he is out of the years usually devoted to a secondary school education'. As a young child, the only formal education he received was at a small local school where only the most elementary arithmetic would have been taught. At the time he started to become extraordinarily adept at mental arithmetic he had not learned to read and write. Strangely enough, his lack of formal education was in some respects a blessing so far as his career as a boy prodigy was concerned, because a child who had learned mathematics at school would not have hit upon the methods that made it possible for George Bidder to do lengthy mental calculations. These methods are very different from the techniques that are most effective when written calculations are being done. As Bidder himself explained, with mental arithmetic, unlike arithmetic that involves using pencil and paper to retain the outcomes of various steps in a calculation, it is very important to keep the amount of information to be stored (in memory) at any one time to an absolute minimum. So with a calculation like $279 \times 373$ (to use his own example), he would start by multiplying $200 \times 300$ ($= 60,000$), to which he would add $200 \times 70$ ($= 14000$), making 74,000 in all. To that total he would then add, successively, $200 \times 3$ ($= 600$), then $70 \times 300$ ($= 21,000$), $70 \times 70$ ($= 4,900$), $70 \times 3$ ($= 210$), $9 \times 300$ ($= 2,700$), $9 \times 70$ ($= 630$) and, finally, $9 \times 3$ ($= 27$), to give a grand total of 104,067.

Compared with the methods of multiplication that are taught in school this technique may look rather clumsy. But for anyone who is doing calculations mentally it has the huge advantage of greatly reducing the load of data that has to be stored in memory whilst the computation is proceeding. All that needs to be retained is one running total. With the written methods by which children are taught to do long multiplications at school it would be virtually impossible for anyone to do a problem such as this one mentally, without having access to pencil and paper for storing data. That is because the demands for retaining in memory the results of the intermediate steps in calculating would exceed what is humanly possible.

As well as providing a useful income, the exhibitions at which the young George Bidder was paraded as an infant prodigy up and down the country (about 50 years after Mozart had given his more renowned childhood performances) brought him to the attention of people who were willing to pay for him to receive a far better education in mathematics and other school subjects than would normally have been available to the child of an artisan family in rural England. When George was about nine, a group of distinguished scholars at Cambridge University examined him and arranged for him to be sent at their expense to Wilson's Grammar School, in Camberwell, near London. He did not stay there long, and his public tours and exhibitions, which continued for several more years, almost certainly interfered with his education. But by the time he was 13 it had been arranged by a benefactor in the person of a wealthy Scottish lawyer, Henry Jardine, for George to receive private tutoring that would prepare him for entry to Edinburgh University. In those days it was not altogether uncommon for a wealthy individual to pay the costs of educating unusually promising youngsters. John Stuart Mill's father, James Mill, had profited from a similar arrangement. Like Bidder, James Mill attended Edinburgh University.

George Bidder entered that university in 1820 at the age of 14. (At the time this was not unusually young.) He stayed there for five successful years, during which he made a close friendship with a man who was to be very important in his subsequent career, the engineer Robert Stephenson, son of the railway pioneer George Stephenson (who, like Bidder, came from a humble background in which a formal education was not easy to secure). At least one of the lecture courses attended by Bidder at Edinburgh was also to be followed by Charles Darwin, five years later. It was the course on Geology given by Professor Robert Jameson. Bidder's biographer claims that Jameson must have been an inspiring teacher (Clark, 1983), but Darwin reported finding his lectures so 'incredibly dull' that he was almost put off studying geology for ever.

Bidder's subsequent career as an engineer was remarkably busy and successful. His engineering achievements include numerous railways (among them the first railway to be built in the difficult terrain of Norway), large docks (including London's Victoria Docks, constructed on marshland in the Thames estuary), ships, bridges, aqueducts, viaducts, and a number of other large-scale projects including sewerage and water purification systems and telegraph communications works. (He was a founder of the Electric Telegraph Company.) With the Stephensons and Brunel he was one of the great engineers of an age in which engineering was transforming many parts of the world. On Robert Stephenson's death he followed his friend as President of the Institution of Civil Engineers. Bidder died in 1878.

George Bidder was a genuine child prodigy. As we have seen, he was performing calculating feats at the age of seven which astounded spectators at local county fairs, and a year or two later he was able to solve problems that were beyond the powers of any living adult. At that time, of course, the ability to do difficult calculations in one's head had a real utility. His early efforts were powerfully rewarded: in all probability the exhibitions that were organized for him were at first designed simply to make a few shillings for his needy rural family. But as things turned out they did far more than that. As a result of the attention his early achievements attracted, new and previously unthinkable opportunities opened up for him. All kinds of future triumphs were made possible by the fact that he was able to draw to himself the attention of wealthy individuals who were prepared to finance a formal education at school and university. This would otherwise have been entirely outside the aspirations, let alone the means, of a person from his background.

## 2 Norbert Wiener

George Bidder's life highlights the extraordinariness of the feats that certain child prodigies have been capable of, and illustrates the possible consequences of a child's displaying exceptional mental skills at an early age. It would be pleasant to think that George Bidder's case provides a typical example of the life and circumstances of a child prodigy. It would be nice to imagine that many young children from poor families like his, have managed to open up their lives in the way that Bidder was able to by drawing attention to his superior abilities. Sadly, that is not the case. With respect to his family background, George Bidder was not at all typical of child prodigies. As it happens, the vast majority of cases of remarkable childhood precocity are found in educated and relatively wealthy homes.

A more typical child prodigy was Norbert Wiener, who eventually become one of the great mathematicians of the twentieth century. Wiener founded the science of cybernetics, which seeks to understand the principles underlying communication and control in both living and inorganic things. There is one point of similarity in the lives of Bidder and Wiener: in both cases their precocious achievements were partly mathematical. But in other respects the two men were very different. Norbert Wiener was born in 1894, to Jewish parents. His father, Leo Wiener, who had been born in Russia and had emigrated to the United States in 1880 at the age of eighteen (with only 50 cents in his pocket, he told his son), was a very able philologist who was fluent in a number of languages including German, French, Italian, Polish, Serbian, and modern Greek. Leo Wiener was a good classical scholar and an amateur mathematician as well: he wrote a number of articles on that subject. By the time of Norbert's birth Leo Wiener had already established himself as Professor of Modern Languages at the University of Missouri. When Norbert was a young child the family moved to Boston, where his father eventually found a position at Harvard University.

One of Leo Wiener's minor achievements was to translate into English a book which I have mentioned previously, *The Education of Karl Witte*, written by the boy's father (also named Karl), an Austrian cleric who set out to make his son, born in 1800, into 'a superior man' (Witte, 1975). Wiener's views about the education of his children were strongly influenced by this book. The elder Witte's efforts had been remarkably successful, despite the initial doubts of his wife, and the refusal of the teachers to whom Witte confided his plans to believe that intellectual excellence could be created by training. By the time he was 16 the younger Karl had earned two doctoral degrees, and he enjoyed a long life as a productive and distinguished literary scholar. His greatest contribution lay in his analysis and interpretation of the poetry of Dante, a task which he took up in his early twenties, shortly after a scholar of Italian literature had remarked to him,

> There is one Italian writer, the greatest of all, whose books I should advise you to let alone. We Italians sometimes try to persuade ourselves that we understand Dante, but we do not. If a foreigner sets about it, we can scarcely repress a smile. (Quoted by H. Addington Bruce, Introduction to Witte, 1975)

For the young Witte, these words provided a challenge he could not resist. Five years later he completed an important literary essay, entitled 'On misunderstanding Dante'. It had an influence throughout Europe on the appreciation and understanding of Dante's genius.

In Norbert Wiener's autobiography he repeatedly tells the reader that his father was an extremely enthusiastic man. Leo Wiener had a large number of interests, and he was enthusiastic about all of them. Unfortunately, he was also rather overbearing, and too hot-headed and intense for most people's comfort. In a telling sentence Norbert recalls,

> He tended to impose his amusements and preferences on those about him without fully realizing that many of them might have come to a fuller participation in a life together with him if this participation had not been so obviously enforced. (Wiener, 1953, p. 18)

And like James Mill, the father of John Stuart Mill, who was equally precocious in childhood, Leo Wiener was a hard taskmaster to his son. As a young child Norbert was sent to a number of schools, but his parents found them all unsatisfactory. He would have been a difficult child to accommodate at any school: by the age of six Norbert knew far more than most boys about many things. His voracious reading, and a strong interest in all scientific matters, put him well ahead of his age in a number of fields.

When Norbert was seven his father decided to take charge of his education. For the next several years most of the teaching was in the father's hands. Leo Wiener employed one of his own students to teach his son chemistry, and another to help him with Latin. Lessons with Leo Wiener were never exactly relaxed. His son remembered how,

> Every mistake had to be corrected as it was made. He would begin the discussion in an easy, conversational tone. This lasted exactly until I made the first mathematical mistake. Then the gentle and loving father was replaced by the avenger of the blood. The first warning he gave me of my unconscious delinquency was a very sharp and aspirated 'What!' and if I did not follow this by coming to heel at once, he would admonish me, 'Now do this again!' (Wiener, 1953, p. 67)

When he came to read John Stuart Mill's description of his father's teaching, Norbert Wiener was well equipped to recognize the signs of a tyrannous parental regime, beneath the guarded 'proper Victorian' tone of Mill's account. If that account seems to indicate a completely virtuous relationship on both sides, Wiener says,

> I know better, and when I read his few words about his father's irascibility I know just how to interpret these statements. I am certain that even if that irascibility had been more decorous than that of my father, it had probably been no less unremitting. (Wiener, 1953, p. 68)

But if Norbert found his father to be a demanding and domineering teacher, he also saw much to like and admire in him. Leo Wiener had none of the grimness of James Mill, nor the gloomy parental preoccupation with sin and evil that poisoned the Victorian childhood described in Edmund Gosse's *Father and Son*. Nor, unlike the child subjected to an oppressively strict regime in Samuel Butler's semi-autobiographical *The Way of All Flesh*, could Wiener fail to be aware that his own father, for all his faults, was a warm and loving parent with many positive qualities. On the contrary,

> my father was a romanticist ... His righteousness partook of the element of *élan*, of triumph, of glorious and effective effort, of drinking deep of life and the emotions thereof. For me, a boy just starting life, this made him in many ways a noble and uplifting figure, a poet at heart ... It was because of this, because my taskmaster was at the same time my hero, that I was not bent down into sullen ineffectiveness by

the arduous course of discipline through which I went. (Wiener, 1953, p. 74)

From the beginning, Norbert's home life was filled with scholarly and intellectual events. His was a house of learning if ever there was one. His father, as we have seen, was always anxious, even insistent, to share his own interests with his wife and children. 'Ever since I can remember' Norbert recalled, 'the sound of the typewriter and the smell of the paste pot have been familiar to me.' Norbert had every encouragement to read. Although his father was by far the dominant force in his education, Norbert Wiener's earliest memories were of his mother. When he was very young she often read to him: as an adult he remembered how she enjoyed reading aloud in their tiny garden from Kipling's *Jungle Book*. And the child quickly realized that he could learn to read by himself. As soon as he could read he did read, from any book or magazine he could find to interest him.

His parents had a large and catholic collection of books, and the young Norbert read anything he was able to discover on natural history, mathematics, and the physical sciences, as well as more obvious nourishments for a boy's imagination, such as *Treasure Island* and *The Arabian Nights*. Sometimes the father would bring his son books from the Harvard library to help the child extend his knowledge and feed his growing interests. In this way Norbert acquired a book on the physics of light and electricity. This fascinated the child with its description of early efforts to produce television pictures. Norbert Wiener reported that he followed it up by further reading in physics and chemistry. Helpfully, his father was friendly with some of the staff of the Boston Public Library, and one of Norbert's playmates was the daughter of one of the librarians there, whose wife was an author of children's books.

The intellectualism of Norbert's home background was augmented by the fact that many of the family's friends and neighbours were scholars. For example, next door but one there lived an eminent mathematician, a Professor Bocher, whose children regularly played with the young Norbert and his younger sister. The boy also had the run of the house and the library of a distinguished physiological chemist who lived a little further along the road and was married to one of Norbert's mother's closest friends. The numerous other distinguished friends of his parents who influenced Norbert as a young child included the Assyriologist Muss-Arnoldt, whom Norbert Wiener remembered teaching him when he occasionally stayed with the Wiener family, and the brilliant physiologist Walter Cannon. Cannon showed the child the newly-developed X-ray machine with which he was working and explained the basis of the important research he was conducting at that time into the use of X-rays in the study of body tissues. Leo Wiener's own interests included scientific ones. He taught Norbert botany, and talked to him at length about farming, another of his many enthusiasms. He was also a keen mycologist, and took his excited young son on expeditions to collect fungi.

With all the stimulation and encouragement he received from his father, and the many opportunities he had to see for himself how people went about scholarly activities and to learn to regard scholarship and studying as normal elements of everyday living, almost to be taken for granted as a routine part of home life – as they were in his own house and most of the other homes he regularly visited – it is hardly surprising that Norbert Wiener gained the self-confidence to regard the pursuit of acquiring skills and knowledge as an activity that was always useful or necessary, often exciting, and certainly within his grasp. Against his singular intellectual background, even the remarkable autobiographical statement that follows seem less odd than it first appears to anyone who has not experienced a childhood like his. Writing of himself at the age of six or seven, Wiener observes,

> Even in zoology and botany, it was the diagrams of complicated structure and the problems of growth and organization which excited my interest fully as much as the tales of adventure and discovery. Once I had been sensitized to an interest in the scientific ... I became aware of stimulating material all about me. (Wiener, 1953, p. 64)

The outline details of Norbert Wiener's subsequent career are well known. When he was 11 he began an undergraduate course at Tufts College (now Tufts University) in Medford, Massachusetts. He graduated with a bachelor's degree at the age of 14. He was still 14 when he became a graduate student at Harvard, where he gained his doctorate when he was 18. After a period abroad, during which he worked with Bertrand Russell, he returned to the United States. In 1919 he was appointed to a post at the Massachusetts Institute of Technology. He stayed there for 33 years, quickly establishing for himself a reputation as one of the world's leading mathematicians.

The above account may give the impression that Wiener's transition from the young *Wunderkind* into the eminent scientist was smooth and easy, even inevitable. In fact it was none of these. In his adolescence and early adulthood Wiener experienced troubles of many kinds, which left him frustrated, sometimes extremely depressed, and often in a mood of despair. For a start, he was a clumsy, short-sighted child. The early development of his abilities was highly uneven, with his social competence lagging several years behind his purely intellectual skills. He was not at all socially assured. Mixing with his classmates at school and college, most of whom were several years older than him, was never easy for the young Norbert Wiener.

As well as the social difficulties that any child prodigy might be expected to experience, Norbert Wiener had many family problems. As we have seen, his father was a difficult man, demanding and overbearing. He expected a great deal from his son, but neither he nor his wife were prepared to give their son the freedom and independence that a talented youngster needed. Within the family Norbert was for several years in the position of being an intellectual equal to his parents but treated like a child. He was financially, socially, and emotionally dependent on them, with no independent means of his own, and was given plenty of responsibilities but little authority. For example, he was expected to undertake much of the responsibility for educating his younger brother Fritz, although he was never allowed to make any of the decisions about how the child would be taught, or permitted to discipline the spoiled and tiresome (in Norbert's view) younger sibling. Throughout his life he remained bitter about having been saddled with the job of teaching his brother.

Actually, as Wiener must have realized when he read John Stuart Mill's *Autobiography*, compared with Mill he escaped remarkably lightly in this respect. James Mill, although in most respects an unusually prudent man, encumbered himself and his wife (the mother about whom John Stuart Mill's autobiographical account is so conspicuously silent) with no less than six children. They all had to be raised on the tiny income he earned as an author. John Stuart, who was the oldest, was regularly set to teaching the others. He hated the task just as much as Wiener did, and remarked that

> the experience of my boyhood is not favourable to the plan of teaching children by means of one another. The teaching, I am sure, is very inefficient as teaching, and I well know that the relation between teacher and taught is not a good moral discipline to either. (Mill, 1971, p. 13)

But Mill did recognize that having to learn things well enough to teach them could be a useful exercise. He was grateful that, as the eldest son, he had more of his father's teaching than any of the others, and he benefited from it greatly.

At home, the young Norbert Wiener was always expected to help with the garden and the home, but he was always made conscious that it was his parents' house, not his, and he was never allowed to decide matters for himself. As a gloomy teenager he saw himself more and more as the dependent family drudge. It was hardly a state of affairs to make his transition to manhood easy. So far as his career was concerned, too, he felt that his father made all the important decisions for him. Even when Wiener was almost 60, at the time when he wrote his autobiography, he still believed that this deprivation of the right to judge for himself as a young person had not only delayed his maturity but had continued to handicap him throughout his life.

Any young person needs to be given some independence and allowed to make his or her own mistakes, but Norbert's parents found it very difficult to let go of the reins. By his late adolescence it would clearly have been helpful for him to have been able to live on his own, away from the parental home of a family 'living too close together and driven in upon itself' (Wiener, 1953, p. 157). But the parents would hear none of this. His mother made it clear to him that his leaving home 'would be held against me for all eternity, as a sign of my ultimate failure, and would mean the complete and final collapse of family relations' (Wiener, 1953, p. 162). The youthful Norbert Wiener was never allowed to forget how much he depended on his family.

On top of all the other difficulties he had with getting along with his parents, he came seriously into dispute with them on another matter, that of his Jewishness. Although the Wieners were a Jewish family, they not only ignored the Jewish religion and Jewish festivities, preferring to observe Christian rituals, but took a negative, prejudiced, and discriminatory attitude towards Jewish people. His mother tried to keep the family's Jewishness a secret, and constantly belittled Jews and, for that matter, any other minority group she knew about. 'Scarcely one day went by', her son reports, 'in which we did not hear some remark about the gluttony of the Jews or the bigotry of the Irish or the laziness of the Negroes.'

To his credit, Norbert Wiener could not stomach this hypocrisy, which was made particularly unbearable by the fact that it was uttered in the home in which he was obliged to live and by a parent he was forced to obey and be dependent on. The very different attitudes of himself and his parents towards their Jewishness threatened to open up a major rift between parents and son. In later life Norbert Wiener declared himself passionately opposed to any kind of prejudice against a minority, for any reason. Although he came to appreciate that his parents' attitude was not uncommon in recent immigrants, and was to some extent understandable, he never entirely resolved his differences with his parents on this issue. All the same, the relationship that he managed to establish with them later in his life was a reasonably harmonious one.

## Some Questions raised by Child Prodigies

It is not at all easy to decide to what extent the problems with growing up that Norbert Wiener experienced were specifically caused by his being a child prodigy rather than simply by the difficulties that many adolescents have encountered, perhaps especially in close-knit Jewish immigrant families. Nor is it easy to be sure about causes and effects in George Bidder's early life. And if it is hard to answer such questions about individual child prodigies, it is even more difficult to discover general principles concerning important events in the lives of child prodigies in general. Nevertheless, we should make an effort to do so, particularly since it is becoming more and more common for parents nowadays to make enormous efforts to maximize their children's abilities.

With sufficient energy and dedication on the parents' part, it is possible that it may not be all that difficult to produce a child prodigy. What is considerably more difficult for parents to do is to bring up an individual who not only is precocious in childhood, but also grows up to be an adult who possesses personal qualities that enable him or her to make satisfyingly productive use of the special mental resources that an early start in life has made it possible to acquire. If parents have a good understanding of the circumstances that give rise to child prodigies, and are aware of the difficulties that precocious youngsters can encounter in the journey towards adulthood, they ought to be able to avoid at least some of the mistakes that have been made too often in the past by adults striving to maximize their offspring's mental powers.

The lives and achievements of child prodigies such as George Bidder and Norbert Wiener bring to our attention a number of issues concerning the origins of extraordinary human abilities and raise numerous questions, including the following ones.

First, there are questions about the necessity for a person to be a prodigy in childhood if he or she is to become extraordinarily accomplished as a mature person. In order to be a genius, is it always necessary to start as a child prodigy? If not, is it necessary sometimes, and, if so, in what particular kinds of circumstances? In what ways may a person be helped in later life by having been a prodigy in childhood?

Second, in what ways do families contribute to a child's becoming extraordinarily precocious? Is it typically the case that one or more parent is strongly committed to providing an intensive early education, as happened in the childhood of Norbert Wiener? Do child prodigies sometimes emerge in families that are *not* unusually attentive to the child's early education?

Third, what kind of difficulties are child prodigies likely to experience? What unusual personal problems are likely to confront a person who has been a precocious child?

Fourth, what happens to child prodigies? Do most of them become remarkable adults, or do a large proportion 'burn out' or for one reason or another fail to maintain their early promise?

Fifth, at how early a stage in their lives do child prodigies begin to show their exceptionality? Does being seen to be extraordinary usually precede the special attention that is given to their early education, or is the reverse situation more typical, in which children become exceptional only after having already received special attention to their educational needs?

And sixth, how often do parental efforts to accelerate a child's progress actually succeed at all? Is it safe to assume that there are some children who, despite the most strenuous efforts of the parents to provide intense early education, never become at all exceptional? If this kind of failure does occur, in what circumstances is it more or less likely to happen?

These are some of the questions that one would like to see answered, but supplying precise and definitive answers is no easy matter. There is no shortage of evidence: there are published accounts of a number of child prodigies, past and present, and some of these descriptions are highly informative and make fascinating reading. Essentially, there are two reasons why it is so difficult to give firm answers to questions about the lives of child prodigies. The first is that the sheer variety and variability of the many individuals to whom the word prodigy has been assigned restricts the extent to which it is possible to make general statements that apply to all or even the majority of them. The second reason is that the form of the evidence, most of which is to be found in biographical accounts of one kind or another, does not make for precise quantitative statements. There are few of the facts or figures that would make it possible to make the kind of pronouncement which asserts that $x$ per cent of child prodigies are this, or become that, or experience difficulties of such-and-such a kind.

## 1 *To be a Genius, is it necessary to have been a Child Prodigy?*

It is surprisingly hard to think of individuals who were considered to have been great thinkers as adults, but who gave no signs at all of exceptional precocity when they were children. Charles Darwin is one of the few geniuses who would definitely fall into this category. (So, perhaps, would Wordsworth and van Gogh.) But even Darwin, as a child, was never considered to be less than bright. And in his case it would be fair to point out that whilst he never drew attention to himself as being at all exceptional during his childhood, his early experiences and interests did provide a remarkably useful foundation for his later achievements. The fact that he was not considered to be outstanding as a child may have been due in part to his home background being an unusually intellectual one, and one in which the standards by which a child's abilities would have been rated were especially high. For the early development of an eminent biologist, the remarkably felicitous circumstances of Charles Darwin's life as a child and the strong continuities between his childhood interests and his adult preoccupations would have gone a long way to compensate for the absence of strikingly precocious early skills.

In all probability, among the substantial numbers of great scientists, scholars, artists, poets, dramatists, and novelists whose parents and teachers did *not* perceive in them any remarkable qualities when they were children, many did nevertheless possess abilities in childhood which were exceptional, albeit unrecognized. Albert Einstein would appear to belong to this group. The fact that he did not shine at school – perhaps not surprisingly, since the dour and rigid discipline of a German gymnasium would never have suited a sensitive Jewish child – has often been remarked on. It is also true that his parents and teachers did not detect in him any of the signs of immense precocity that lead to a child being called a *Wunderkind* or prodigy. All the same, there is every indication that by the time he was 12 or 13 he had already acquired intellectual interests which reflected and drew upon resources of knowledge and understanding that would have been possessed by very few individuals of his age. At 12, he was reading serious books on the physical sciences and enjoyed talking about physics. He was also an enthusiastic and extremely precocious young mathematician. According to a family friend, Max Talmey,

> He thereupon devoted himself to higher mathematics, studying all by himself Lubsen's excellent works on the subject ... Soon the flight of his mathematical genius was so high that I could no longer follow. Thereafter philosophy was often a subject of our conversations. (Clark, 1979, p. 31)

Much has been made of Einstein's failure to pass the entrance examination to the Swiss Federal Polytechnic School in Zurich, when he was 16. He was in fact two years younger than the normal age for entrance, was unprepared for the examination, and was trying to avoid having to fit in with the career plans his father had mapped out for him, plans which entrance to the Polytechnic at that time would have sealed (Clark, 1979). A better indication of his abilities as a 16-year-old is provided by a brilliant paper on electro-magnetic phenomena which he produced at that age, 'Concerning the investigation of the state of aether in magnetic fields'. This displays the early beginnings of interests that were eventually to lead to massive achievements.

BEING LABELLED AS A PRODIGY
So there is clearly a strong case for arguing that the young Einstein was a child prodigy, even if the majority of teachers and others who knew him at that time were quite unaware of how exceptional he was. And the same may apply to many other individuals who were never, in their childhood, regarded as being prodigies. We certainly cannot assume that the likelihood of a young person having been described as a child prodigy depends on any objective rating of that person's exceptionality. Large elements of arbitrariness are among the factors that determine whether or not the label 'prodigy' happens to be applied to a particular individual. The likelihood of an individual being regarded by others as a child prodigy is almost as poorly related to that person's actual objective qualities as are a person's chances of being called a genius (a matter which I discussed in chapter two). We can be certain that some children who were never regarded by other people as being prodigies have in fact been considerably more exceptional than others who *were* described as child prodigies.

Several factors other than the degree of a child's exceptionality as such have influenced the chances of the label 'prodigy' being applied in particular cases. For example, if the skill that a child excels at is one for which the degree of superiority of a person's performance is easy to demonstrate and quantify – as is the case in, say, chess-playing, performances of instrumental music, and individual sports such as tennis or gymnastics – it is more likely that adults will become aware of the child's exceptionality and start to describe the child as being a prodigy than if that is not the case. Also, if the form of the childhood activity that is exceptional is one that is clearly linked to and ostensibly similar to the adult performance by which mature achievement is judged, it is especially probable that the child's exceptionality will be widely recognized. This provides a further reason for astonishing musical and sporting performances being comparatively likely to receive attention, whereas equally exceptional accomplishments which happen to take the form of abilities that provide the foundations for a successful career in, say, literature or the visual arts, may be less likely to receive a comparable degree of adult recognition. (But there have been a few literary prodigies, including Daisy Ashford, who as a child produced a remarkable novel, Winifred Sackville Stoner, who at the beginning of this century made frequent contributions to the poetry column of a newspaper in Indiana, and Nika Turbina, a Russian girl born in 1974, whose poems have been highly praised, although their subject matter reflects the inevitably limited experience of a young person.)

In addition to all the other reasons that make it difficult to decide whether or not it is appropriate to describe a child as being a prodigy there is the problem of where to draw the line between the individual who is definitely a prodigy and the child who is clearly precocious yet not sufficiently exceptional to be called a prodigy. Some researchers have recommended defining prodigies – and geniuses as well – on the basis of scores measuring performance in IQ tests. But as we shall see in chapter 7, this practice has little to recommend it.

### When is it an advantage to be a prodigy?

For the reasons just mentioned, we should not conclude that an eminent person who is said to have been a child prodigy was necessarily any more exceptional in childhood than another individual to whom that description was not applied. With this reservation in mind, we can return to the broad question of whether or not having been a child prodigy – or a child with unrecognized exceptional abilities – is an essential prerequisite for being an exceptionally accomplished adult. It only takes one firmly contrary example (and as we saw in the previous chapter, Charles Darwin's early life clearly provides this) to justify a negative answer. In that event it becomes more useful to pose a slightly modified question, as follows: 'In what circumstances is it either essential or especially advantageous to have been exceptionally capable in childhood, as a prerequisite for becoming an eminent adult?'

One circumstance in which being a child prodigy is especially likely to have practical utility for the individual is when poverty or other reasons would normally stand between a child and the educational opportunities that are necessary if the young person is to build on early achievements. By being sufficiently remarkable as a child, an individual may be drawn to the attention of those who have the money or the power to ensure that needed educational facilities or tuition are made available. This undoubtedly happened in the case of George Parker Bidder, for example. Nowadays it is considerably more common than it was in Bidder's time, at least in wealthy countries, for children whose parents are poor to receive free or subsidized educational opportunities, but financial restrictions still prevent many young people from having access to advanced education. In the Third World the situation is far worse. Even when a child is clearly recognized to be quite brilliant, there is no guarantee that the resources needed to make proper training possible will actually be provided. For example, in the case of the remarkable Indian mathematician Srinivasa Ramanujan, although he was acknowledged to be a child prodigy of immense ability, he was denied the support that would have made it possible for him to receive higher education. It was not until he was in his twenties, and working as an accounts clerk, that the Cambridge mathematician G. H. Hardy (to whom Ramanujan had sent a portfolio of his work) was able to put into motion the wheels that led to Ramanujan being able to pursue his work on a full-time basis in a university environment. Had the young Ramanujan been given the kind of education that he deserved, his contribution to mathematics would in all probability have been considerably greater than it was. Doubtless there are many thousands of young prodigies who are similarly deprived of opportunities to gain remarkable abilities that could benefit mankind.

If money is short, drawing attention to oneself as a child prodigy can be an effective way of starting a career, even if it does not directly open the way to opportunities for advanced education. As we have seen, one of the immediate consequences of George Bidder's performances was to augment the family's income. In Mozart's time, when good musicians were two-a-penny, it was not at all easy to climb above the ranks of the numerous other ill-paid performers. Mozart's spectacular exhibitions as a child gave him a valuable early advantage over the competition.

In certain fields of human endeavour the training and preparation that are essential for reaching the highest levels of achievement demand resources that are particularly scarce or hard to obtain, or sufficiently expensive to be beyond the means of even those parents whose financial position is relatively sound. For example, to become a top-ranking concert pianist it is essential for the young performer to receive tuition from one of a very small number of distinguished master teachers. But these individuals are prepared to offer their services only to pupils whom they consider to be unusually promising. So, finding such a teacher is a hurdle that a young performer can only surmount if he or she is already extremely accomplished when still quite young. Similarly, in order to become a world-class tennis player it is important to be able to practise all year, and a young player can expect to meet fierce competition for the limited funds that are available to help make this possible. Therefore, only those individuals who have come a long way towards excellence while they are still young will be in a strong position to compete for the funds that are needed in order to gain access to training facilities on which future progress depends.

There is a sense in which the children of rich parents can afford not to be child prodigies. Individuals who are particularly wealthy are to some extent immune from the necessity to draw attention to themselves and make career choices while they are still very young. Tolstoy, for instance, a rich man who was always able to find money to pay his gambling debts, could afford to spend his early years sampling a variety of occupations before settling down in his forties to write novels. William James was able to depend on his father's wealth while he vacillated for several years before deciding to devote his life to the study of philosophy and psychology.

Finally, there are a few fields of scholarship where, in addition to the necessity of maintaining a single-minded commitment over a period of many years in order to reach the highest levels of excellence, circumstances are such that it is unlikely that such a commitment will endure into the middle years of life. From then on, even the most wholeheartedly dedicated of individuals increasingly begin to look outside any particular narrow pursuit, and to take an interest in family matters and wider concerns. Consequently, many of those achievements that depend upon the individual narrowly and single-mindedly concentrating on a particular problem over a period of years are likely to be made fairly early in life. Mathematicians, for example, tend to produce their best and most important work in their twenties and thirties (Roe, 1952; Lehman, 1953). In order to be in a position to reach one's peak by this time it is necessary for an individual already to have reached a high level of expertise by around the late teens. So only if a person has made an early start towards becoming a distinguished mathematician will he or she stand a reasonable chance of being highly successful. As it happens, it is rare nowadays to find very young children who are recognized as being prodigies in the field of mathematics: it is more usual for young mathematicians to begin to show exceptional competence when they are well into their second decade.

## 2 How do Families contribute to Childhood Precocity?

In the previous chapter we discovered that the home backgrounds of the majority of extraordinarily able individuals have been fairly cultured, intellectually stimulating ones. It would be very surprising if that was not equally true of the backgrounds of those extraordinary people who began to exhibit remarkable abilities while they were still children. Indeed, it is true: most child prodigies emerge in circumstances where the parents are educated, concerned about their children's early education, and both willing and able to make a larger-than-average practical contribution towards providing their children with opportunities to learn.

The fairly substantial body of evidence that exists concerning the characteristics of families of children who are intellectually precocious suffers from an important restriction, however. This is that the criterion used for deciding on the degree of childhood precocity is performance at IQ tests. Because these tests only measure performance in a narrow and somewhat arbitrarily chosen range of intellectual skills, it is quite possible for an individual to be a child prodigy and yet not gain a particularly high score in an IQ test. On the other hand, it is not possible for a child to gain a very high score unless he or she has made an unusual degree of progress in acquiring intellectual abilities that are potentially useful. Therefore, as a consequence of intelligence tests being used as the criterion of precocity, some genuine prodigies will fail to be detected. But there will be few 'false positives', in the form of children incorrectly identified as possessing intellectual abilities to an unusual degree.

In his survey of the empirical literature on the contribution of childhood experience to the development of precocity, William Fowler (1981) describes an early study by W. T. Root, who found that 87 per cent of a sample of gifted children aged between six and 13 whose IQ scores averaged 160 had been given an exceptionally large amount of training at home, by the parents. Typically, the mother had devoted a large proportion of her time to preschool education. Some of the mothers in the study are described as exhibiting 'unbounded ambitions and hopes and persistence' concerning their aspirations for their sons and daughters. (The mothers of a number of famous people, including Scott Fitzgerald and F. Lloyd Wright, have been like this.) Eighty per cent of the fathers were in professional or semi-professional occupations. Root's interviews established that virtually all the parents had high expectations for their children. The latter were expected to achieve high standards at intellectual tasks. They were given every encouragement to be successful, at home and at school. The parents displayed considerable pride in their children and made ambitious plans for them. They gave enormous attention to helping their sons and daughters to gain language skills (Fowler, 1990). These parents seem to have had an intuitive understanding of the fact, which is confirmed by the evidence cited in chapter 3, that parents who augment a young child's experiences with language may thereby make an enormous contribution to intellectual development. Such parents were unusually willing to treat the children as intelligent and rational people, rather than talking down to them as many parents do. All the parents seemed to have placed considerable emphasis on the importance of reading, and most of their children had learned to read by the age of three.

By and large, these findings have been repeated in every subsequent investigation of the family circumstances of intellectually precocious children. The most recent investigations, such as the Chicago-based studies of exceptional young people who were making careers in a number of scientific, artistic, and sporting professions, as well as David Feldman's intensive examination of the day-to-day lives of six remarkable child prodigies (Feldman, 1986), agree with the reports produced by Root and other investigators early in the century in finding that most parents of child prodigies are unusually anxious for their children to do well, and able and willing to invest a substantial amount of effort into helping their children to make early progress.

It is interesting to find that essentially similar results were obtained in some research that Lewis Terman conducted in order to examine highly intelligent children's backgrounds, despite the fact that Terman believed environmental influences to be comparatively unimportant. With considerable uniformity, the results of case after case yield clear documentation of the parents having provided unusually intensive intellectual stimulation in early childhood. Even in those few instances where parental responses to interviews or questionnaires provide no direct evidence that exceptional amounts of early childhood training were given, there are usually clues that permit one to infer that, in spite of any denials, the parents nevertheless did devote considerable amounts of time and attention to the child's early education. For instance, several children in a study by Terman are described as having received no instruction in reading, but having learned to read – apparently quite spontaneously – all the same. But as I pointed out earlier, in reality a young child simply *cannot* learn to read without a considerable amount of help from someone who can already read. So, despite what was believed to have been the case by Terman, who may well have been too eager to listen to disclaimers made by parents who were over-anxious to draw attention to their child's exceptionality – which they, like Terman, may have preferred to assume was essentially inherited – it is certain that the children not only received help with reading but were given unusual amounts of early parental training.

As a further indication that parents' denials that their children received any special stimulation cannot always be taken at face value, Fowler (1981) quotes from a mother's account of a child prodigy, who, according to her, developed remarkable abilities quite spontaneously, with virtually no help at all from the parent. This mother claimed to have resisted any temptation to provide teaching, or even encouragement or assistance, to her child, whose accomplishments were, according to the mother, entirely self-initiated. Fowler points out that in spite of all these firm denials the detailed record clearly reveals that this child actually received a great deal of training and stimulation. Belying the impression that the mother acted in a purely passive capacity, content simply to sit back and wonder at the miracle of her child's spontaneously developing powers, Fowler notes that both parents were in fact sufficiently involved in the child's early education to keep an astonishingly detailed record of her achievements. As he tartly notes,

> It needs only to be added that the parents kept an exact record of the child's spoken vocabulary at 16 months (229 words) and at age five, listing and classifying into parts of speech *every* one of her 6,837 words over a six-month period. (Fowler, 1981, p. 355)

A similar example of parents having (in all probability) given their child intensive early stimulation while vehemently denying that they did so, is revealed in another report, by Lewis Terman, of a family who claimed to have first learned of their daughter's ability to read when they discovered her reading *Heidi* at the age of four. The plausibility of this assertion is called into question by the revelation that in fact they too, like the parents of the child just mentioned, kept the most meticulous records of their daughter's accomplishments, such as the exact letters she had learned at particular ages, the age at which she first mastered the alphabet, acquired counting skills, recognized colours, and so on (Fowler, 1981).

There are a number of possible reasons for certain parents having been so reluctant to admit to having taken a major role in training their children. Some of the reasons doubtless reflect a parental belief – shared with Gesell, Terman, and many others – that development consists of the spontaneous unfolding of inherited native endowments. For a few parents, a contributing factor may have been the wish to portray their child's powers as being not simply exceptional but unique, and perhaps miraculous as well, conceivably a sign that the child has been specially 'chosen' by a supernatural deity. Whatever the reasons for parents' reluctance to admit their own role, it is important to be aware that such reluctance is sometimes encountered, and to acknowledge that in child prodigies the absence of a record of intensive early stimulation cannot be taken as positive evidence that no special training was given.

Parents who are similar to one another in the amounts of time they invest in helping and encouraging their children are likely to differ considerably in the actual teaching procedures they adopt. One dimension – to be more accurate, a constellation of related dimensions –

along which equally committed parents may differ concerns the degree to which instruction is structured or formally planned. Certain parents of child prodigies, for instance Pastor Witte, James Mill and (to a lesser extent) Leo Wiener, have clearly planned their children's early education in some detail. They have deliberately provided a regimen of carefully sequenced training and instruction, and have required the child to practise at tasks allotted by the parent. Other parents have been much less systematic, either by accident or design, more inclined to take their cues from the child's own curiosity, and generally more 'child-centred'.

## *Does the Degree of Formality of Parental Training matter?*

Does the degree of formality of parental teaching activities make a difference, so far as the child's learning is concerned? As we saw in the previous chapter, the precise ways in which particular parents and children interact with each other undoubtedly do affect the nature of the child's learning experiences, and thereby influence the child's progress. This is not in doubt, even though for practical purposes the actual consequences of a parent's actions may be impossible to predict. The question that is presently at issue is whether or not there exist grounds for stating that the efforts of parents whose approach to early childhood education is a relatively formal and pre-planned one are either more or less successful than the efforts of parents who do not plan their child's early education so formally or systematically. Are there any research findings that justify advising parents to adopt a particular kind of teaching strategy?

It seems not. William Fowler (1981) carefully sifted the evidence from many investigations in a valiant effort to answer this question, but he encountered a number of difficulties. One problem is that the teaching methods that parents actually use are not uniformly formal or informal across different situations. And even when it is possible for researchers to observe the teaching that is given the approach cannot always be classified as straightforwardly formal or informal. Another problem is that the different approaches adopted by parents do not simply indicate the choice of alternative procedures for reaching identical goals: the varying approaches may also reflect differences in parental attitudes and philosophies, or in their beliefs about the causes of exceptional human abilities. So it would be naïve to assume that in looking at the progress of children whose parents have taken different approaches to early childhood education one is observing the effects of a natural experiment that provides a straightforward comparison between like and like, one in which the instructional method is the only parameter that varies.

Still, we can look to see whether or not there do exist any dissimilarities in young people's progress that are reliably associated with disparities in parental approaches, even if the above-mentioned complications dictate that we would not be justified in inferring that any observed contrasts in children's cognitive growth would supply proof of the differing effectiveness of alternative methods. But as it happens we are spared the agony of trying to decide on the reasons underlying such variations in early progress, because Fowler found no evidence that there are any of the latter. That is, there appear to be no differences in children's abilities that are systematically related in any way at all to dissimilarities in the particular teaching methods adopted by parents who are equally committed to the early education of their children.

IS IT POSSIBLE TO BECOME A CHILD PRODIGY WITHOUT PARENTAL INVOLVEMENT?

The fact that there is evidence of an unusual degree of parental involvement in the early training of the vast majority of child prodigies and other children whose intelligence test scores indicate precocious early intellectual development prompts the following question. Is it possible to be a child prodigy in the absence of considerable involvement on the part of parents or other adults? Are there any child prodigies whose education in early childhood has *not* been unusually intense?

It is certainly difficult, if not impossible, to locate such cases, especially if one is careful to avoid being misled by unreliable parental disclaimers. None of the many case histories reported in Fowler's survey provides convincing evidence of extraordinary precocity in the absence of adult involvement. Nor do any of the reports concerning the many subjects interviewed by the Chicago team. Nor do any of Feldman's reports. In searching for exceptions, two possible directions seem especially promising. First, there have been a few eminent individuals who, according to biographical evidence that is readily available, experienced remarkably bleak and unstimulating childhoods. The case of the writer H. G. Wells, who is nowadays best known for his prophetic novels such as *The Time Machine*, but also made important contributions as a social thinker and an influential popularizer of scientific knowledge, seems to fit into this category. The second promising direction in which to look for possible cases of child prodigies who have received no intensive education in early childhood is among the ranks of mathematical child prodigies. In at least some respects, the young mathematician can be considerably more self-sufficient than a child whose talents lie in other fields. Compared with, say, either a would-be young reader, or a musical child prodigy, whose early progress depends to a very considerable extent on the teaching that is available, a child who has become interested in numbers can forge ahead with a considerable degree of independence and autonomy.

## THE YOUNG H. G. WELLS

Wells's childhood is particularly interesting. He was a remarkably precocious child despite the fact that he was brought up in conditions of considerable penury. His parents were unhappy, unsuccessful, and not well educated. Their relationship was somewhat rancorous and bitter. His mother had been a lady's maid until she married his father, an under-gardener who worked on a country estate. During Wells's early childhood they struggled, with very little success, to make more than a bare living (MacKenzie and MacKenzie, 1973). Wells tells us that he spent his early years in a damp, cold, bug-infested, and thoroughly squalid little house, where 'there was not a scrap of faded carpet or worn oil-cloth in the house that had not lived a full life of usefulness before it came into our household. Everything was frayed, discoloured and patched' (Wells, 1966, p. 40). The house, much of which was below ground level, was squeezed between a haberdasher's shop and a tailor's workshop, and also adjoined (across a soggy yard) the local butcher's, where 'pigs, sheep and horned cattle were harboured violently, and protested plaintively through the night before they were slaughtered' (Wells, 1966, p. 40).

But, as in the case of Charles Darwin's early circumstances, a closer look at the actual details of H. G. Wells's childhood reveals a portrait that is subtly different from the picture that we see at first glance, and in Wells's case not nearly so bleak. And the differences are ones that would have been crucial for a child's early intellectual development. Examining Wells's – or any other individual's – childhood in greater depth serves to illuminate how very greatly our understanding of someone's early progress can be changed by switching from a relatively superficial observation of the individual's first years to a deeper examination of them. This insight provides a necessary warning-bell, giving a useful reminder of the need to be wary about taking at face value the kinds of biographical information about people's childhood years that are most readily available and most easily quantified. Since it is just these kinds of data that are most likely to be collected in attempts to apply 'scientific' or 'objective' approaches to the study of individual people's achievements, it is only too likely that those approaches will fail to detect factors that are extremely important in actual human lives. Investigations that neglect to make proper use of those pieces of evidence about individuals that are too subtle, either to be readily quantified or to be detected by relatively coarse-netted techniques of observation and measurement, may produce highly distorted accounts of the true state of affairs.

In Wells's case, a closer look at his family life reveals that his father, Joseph Wells, although a bit of a dreamer, never very successful at the jobs he took on, and too restless to be other than dissatisfied with his lot, was nevertheless a thoughtful and intelligent man who had made considerable efforts to extend his knowledge. Throughout his life he was a keen reader. (He had his moments of glory. He sometimes played cricket for Kent, and on 26 June, 1862, four years before his famous son's birth, 'he cleaned bowled four Sussex batsmen in four successive balls, a feat not hitherto recorded in county cricket' (Wells, 1966, p. 62). Joseph Wells had an attractive personality and considerable charm. His feats at cricket made him a local celebrity and brought him regular employment in a coaching job at a nearby school.

However penurious the family background, by the standards of its time it was not entirely lacking in intellectual stimulation for a young child. For a woman of her social background Wells's mother was most unusual in that she kept a daily diary. She taught her son to count when he was quite small. She also pasted up large letters from the alphabet in the kitchen, and the child was sent to school from the age of five. And when, at seven, he was laid up for some weeks with a broken leg, he discovered to his joy that 'I could demand and have a fair chance of getting anything that came into my head, books, paper, pencils and toys – and particularly books' (Wells, 1966, p. 76).

The accident was well timed. The boy had just begun to enjoy reading, and his parents kept him supplied with all the books he could have wished for. He reports,

> And now my father went round to the Literary Institute in Market Square and got one or two books for me, and Mrs. Sutton [a local publican's wife, whose son's clumsiness had contributed to Wells's accident] sent some books, and there was always a fresh book to read. My world began to expand very rapidly, and when presently I could put my foot to the ground, the reading habit had got me securely. (Wells, 1966, p. 77).

Details like these give us a fresh and very different perspective on Wells's early life. We can see that despite the penury, the rancour, and the smelly, bug-infested house, Wells's background was not, after all, quite such a barren environment for a child's first years. Also, Wells was lucky with his schools. A number of the teachers he encountered were astute enough to spot his early promise. For instance, at the age of nine Wells was enrolled in a small local school run by a Scotsman named Thomas Morley. Morley had already taught Wells's two older brothers, although without enormous success, but quickly saw that this child was eager to learn, and gave him all the help and encouragement he could. At the same school Wells made a long-lasting friendship with Sydney Bowkett, who later became a playwright. This offered the young Wells, as Wells's son was later to perceive, 'a world of companionship and interest unclouded by family tension and sibling rivalry' (West, 1985).

MATHEMATICAL PRODIGIES

I mentioned earlier that a second promising direction in which it might be possible to detect cases of child prodigies who are exceptions to the general finding that extraordinary childhood precocity is only found when there is marked adult involvement in the child's intellectual development, is among the ranks of mathematicians who were known to be prodigies when they were children. Although they are rare nowadays, mathematical child prodigies were less unusual in the past, largely because it has always been possible for children to acquire impressive mental calculating skills, if they are willing to practise enough. In previous centuries a considerable number of mathematicians have been highly skilled at doing mental calculations, and have acquired that ability when they were children. Gauss and Leibnitz are examples of such individuals. In the present century the incentives for a child acquiring skills of that kind have lessened. This is partly because — especially since the advent of, first, mechanical calculators and, more recently, electronic ones — the practical value of possessing calculating skills has diminished, and partly because, as the nature of mathematics has changed over the years, the importance of mental calculating abilities as a stepping-stone to more advanced aspects of mathematics has diminished. (The modern-day equivalent to a nineteenth-century calculating prodigy might be one of the young wizards who create intricate computer games.)

A reason for believing that the field of mathematics might be a promising area in which to look for possible cases of child prodigies who have received little adult help or encouragement at home (in previous centuries, if not in the current one) is that in many respects the individual who is making progress at learning to be a mathematician can be more independent and self-sufficient than is possible for learners who are working in other fields of knowledge (Stanley, George, and Solano, 1977; Marjoram and Nelson, 1985). Thus we read of Jacques Inaudi sharpening his mathematical abilities (aided, it must be noted, by his elder brother) as he worked as an illiterate shepherd boy (Smith, 1983), and of Ramanujan rediscovering on his own large segments of the mathematical knowledge that has been acquired in recent centuries. We also encounter an individual such as George Bidder who, despite coming from a home background in which the parents' level of education must have been low, was nevertheless able to gain mental calculating skills that were sufficiently impressive to open up educational opportunities that made it possible for him to become a great engineer. But in Bidder's case we do not know nearly enough about the actual circumstances of the family background to be able to say with any certainty that he did not receive a fair amount of intellectual stimulation when he was a child. Appearances do point to a degree of intellectual deprivation, but the discussion of H. G. Wells's childhood serves as a warning against reaching conclusions about this on the basis of limited information.

The home backgrounds of the vast majority of great mathematicians have been ones in which either there exists direct evidence that special early stimulation was provided or there are strong reasons for our inferring that the individual did receive an unusual amount of early training or encouragement. For instance, evidence collected by William Fowler (1986) shows that among a sample of 25 'historically recognized great mathematicians' there was firm evidence of 21 of them having been given special early stimulation. Facts about the early lives of the other four are too sparse to allow definite conclusions, but it is known that three of them were brought up in cultured families. The one possible exception is Fourier, whose father was a master tailor. Very little is known about Fourier's early childhood.

Contradictory accounts have appeared of the childhood of Carl Friedrich Gauss, who was one of the greatest mathematicians of all time. The contradictions draw attention to one of the problems encountered with biographical evidence. It is has been claimed by one recent author, Amy Wallace, that Gauss's father was 'a poor, uncouth laborer' and was reluctant to allow his son to be educated (Wallace, 1986). But in an article published in the year in which Wallace's book appeared, another author describes Gauss's father as having been an accountant, and a fine calculator and a good writer (Fowler, 1986). As a child Gauss was a brilliant prodigy, and his mental calculating was quite remarkable. Despite the father's apparent lack of enthusiasm about his son's education, the circumstances of Gauss's early home life may not have been at all unstimulating or unsupportive. It is known that Gauss had an uncle who probably made a large contribution to the child's early education, and did a great deal to encourage him. It is also clear that Gauss's mother took great pride in her son.

I suspect that in most (and possibly all) of the cases where first appearances suggest that a child prodigy has emerged in the absence of any stimulation or encouragement at all, a closer examination of the child's circumstances would reveal – as in Wells' case – that one or more individuals have in fact given the child a substantial amount of help. There are occasional reports of young mentally retarded 'idiots savants' gaining remarkable skills in spite of being deprived of intellectual stimulation in their childhood years, but to the best of my knowledge there is no clear case of an intelligent child prodigy coming from a totally unstimulating early intellectual environment.

## 3 What special Difficulties and Problems do Child Prodigies experience?

By definition, child prodigies are unusual children. If only because of this, it would be surprising if they experienced no unusual difficulties at all. But it would be wrong to say that growing up is always more difficult for a child prodigy than for an 'ordinary' child. In fact, the evidence indicates that children who gain unusually high scores on intelligence tests, such as the participants in Terman's large-scale Californian study, are on the whole less, rather than more, likely than others to experience severe personal problems in childhood and adolescence. But most of the children in Terman's sample, although they were undoubtedly intellectually precocious, would not have been nearly so extraordinary as those rarer children who have been described as prodigies. It may well be that being very exceptional creates problems that do not arise for the child who is merely fairly exceptional. So we cannot assume that what was true for Terman's large sample of able children is necessarily also true for the smaller numbers of (more clearly remarkable) children who can be described as being prodigies. And the previously mentioned difficulty of objectively deciding exactly who is a prodigy and who is not precludes the kind of quantitative examination that would be necessary in order to produce a direct answer to the question of whether or not child prodigies have more problems with growing up than other children.

Nevertheless, there are certain kinds of childhood difficulties to which child prodigies are particularly prone, including those described below.

PARENTAL PRESSURES
First, many child prodigies have had to cope with unusual parental pressures of one kind or another. That is not to say that all parents of child prodigies have placed unreasonable demands on their children,

nor to deny that many children who have not been prodigies have had very demanding parents. Nor is it to pretend that it is easy to draw a line between the conscientious parent who is understandably determined to do everything to encourage his child to do well, and the parent whose determination that his child will be successful is communicated in ways that make a reasonably carefree childhood impossible, and threaten the child's future happiness. All the same, there is no denying that the parents, especially the fathers, of child prodigies have often been people who have not only expected a great deal of their children, but have made that quite obvious to the children concerned, to the extent that the children have been aware that failure to fulfil their early promise and reach the highest standards of excellence would lead to strong reactions of disapproval as well as disappointment on the parents' part.

Norbert Wiener was one child prodigy who saw his father as a demanding taskmaster. In his different way, James Mill made his son's childhood difficult and stressful. Mozart and his talented older sister Nannerl were almost certainly subjected to a good deal of pressure from their father, who was excessively anxious to display their exceptionality to the world. It is possible that contemporary child prodigies are less likely to experience unreasonable parental demands to excel than prodigies in previous generations, if only because there is widespread agreement nowadays about the undesirability of 'pressurizing' young children. Certainly, in none of the detailed case histories provided by David Feldman (1986) is there evidence of excessive parental pressure, and the same is generally true of the much larger sample of highly successful young adults examined in the Chicago studies. (Many of them, but not all, could be said to have been prodigies when they were children.) Although it is clear that many of the parents studied by the Chicago-based authors were very keen for their children to do well and strongly encouraged them to set high standards for themselves, the investigations unearthed few obvious signs of parents making unreasonable demands.

On the other hand, some descriptions of contemporary ex-prodigies do point to the likelihood of there having been sufficient parental pressure during childhood to have had adverse effects on the individual. For example, newspaper reports of Edith Stern, whose father, having emigrated to the United States after being a prisoner in a concentration camp during the Second World War, announced to the press that he was going to make her into a genius and 'a perfect person', suggest that although she was as strikingly precocious a child as any father could have hoped for, she never quite managed to fulfil his ambitions for her. He has not tried to hide his disappointment at the fact that she now prefers to work at a fairly ordinary job (developing computer software) rather than aspiring to be the outstanding scientist dedicated to the pursuit of improving human life that her father had wanted her to become (Walmsley and Margolis, 1987).

As we saw earlier, Norbert Wiener's autobiography makes it clear that as well as the 'pressure to succeed' imposed by some anxious parents, families may inflict other kinds of pressures that can be equally oppressive to a young prodigy. These can take a number of forms, but more often than not their effect is to make it very difficult for the young person to enjoy an independent and self-directed life. The words that describe the less attractive aspects of the Wiener family – close, claustrophobic, demanding, intense, judgemental, inward-looking – hint at some of the negative qualities that are not uncommon in parents of child prodigies. These parents invariably identify somewhat closely with their children and take the keenest interest in their progress. Difficulties arise when the degree of identification is such that parents start to live their own lives through the child, to the extent that the child's successes are vicariously experienced as victories for the parent. This is especially likely to happen if the parents' own early hopes have been frustrated. For a parent who is trying too hard to shape a child's destiny, the growing child's natural desire to become more independent and free from parental control may be seen as a kind of rejection, which threatens to destroy the desired state of affairs in which the parent's own needs (ones that are no less intense for being neurotic ones) are being met by the child's activities. As I hinted earlier, the kinds of family circumstances in which children appear to be over-dependent on their parents are in fact almost invariably ones in which strong dependencies operate in more than one direction: parents and children are each unhealthily dependent on the other. The parents' unwillingness to 'let go' of their children, and permit them to live their own lives, is a sign of the parents' own abnormal dependence on the children.

BEING DIFFERENT

Especially amongst children, an individual who is very unusual may be seen as freakish and alien. Exceptionally able children are likely to be different from others in a number of ways, if only because their values and interests are not those of an ordinary child (Fox, 1976; Keating, 1976; Freeman, 1985). David Feldman quotes the remark by an ex-prodigy, Hans Eberstark, that 'We are an odd lot, often at odds with the society we were born into. We are out of context. Few, if any ... were socially adapted conformists. Some were slandered and ridiculed' (quoted in Feldman, 1986, p. 5).

Most children like to have friends of their own age. They want to feel that they are accepted by their peers. It is a harsh fact of life that ordinary children tend to be intolerant of other children whom they perceive as being odd or peculiar. Of course, some child prodigies get on very well with their schoolmates. Prodigies who have well-developed social skills and are unusual only in being exceptionally able do not find that precocity on its own produces crushing difficulties for them.

Typically, however, the very circumstances that make a child exceptionally precocious lead to the child being unusual in other respects. One contributing factor arises from the parents' values and interests. These may contrast with those of the families of a prodigy's peers and have the effect of restricting the extent to which the child can enjoy interests that are shared with others, shared knowledge of the world outside school, shared attitudes, and shared values. All of these serve to oil the wheels of social intercourse and make it easy to form friendships. Consequently, a child who rarely watches television will lack one useful point of contact for casual social encounters and easy interactions with classmates. On its own, the effects of being different in a small way like this are relatively trivial and form no major obstacle, but the combined effect of being unlike one's peers in a number of ways, even small ones, may be to make it quite hard for a young prodigy to form comfortable social relationships with other children.

At school, the fact that an intellectually precocious child may be placed in a class in which most of the pupils are considerably older can lead to further difficulties. It is never easy for a young person to be fully accepted by others who are more socially mature. Life at school may be especially hard for an individual who is smaller than most classmates and relatively incompetent at some valued activities, such as sports and games.

Obviously, not every child prodigy will experience all of the problems I have mentioned, but biographical accounts show that these kinds of difficulty are not at all uncommon. For instance, a number of the many problems that Norbert Wiener experienced during childhood and adolescence stemmed from the fact that others regarded him as being different from themselves, and he was not helped by being a shortsighted and clumsy child. His contemporary, William Sidis, an acquaintance of Wiener who attended Harvard at the same time but was never able to make the transition from being a brilliant child prodigy to becoming an adult capable of making productive use of his talents, was similarly harassed by problems that were rooted in the fact that he was so very different from other young people of a similar age. For Sidis, unlike Wiener, these and other personal difficulties prevented him from enjoying the successful career that his early promise appeared to portend.

## Specializing

Most people underestimate the extent to which it is possible for an individual to possess particular skills in isolation from other abilities. It is quite possible, for instance, for someone to be a brilliant chess player, or a superb musician, or an excellent mathematician, while having less than average ability at other intellectual skills, including ones that might appear to be quite closely related to the field in which he or she excels. The expectation that a person who is competent in one area of expertise will also be competent in a similar area is not altogether unreasonable, since in the majority of people who are not child prodigies there does exist a positive relationship in their degree of success at different intellectual tasks. But it would be wrong to infer from this that one person's different skills are necessarily interdependent. To a surprising degree they are quite autonomous.

The abilities of child prodigies are often highly specialized. Prodigies' intellectual development, compared with that of most ordinary people, can be highly uneven in ways that confound the expectations that people may have formed on the basis of a child's superior abilities in one area. It can be rather disconcerting to find that a ten-year-old whose mathematical expertise is on a par with that of an exceptionally able adult may have the social maturity of an eight-year-old or the sense of humour of a six-year-old. Quite a number of child prodigies have run into troubles that have been caused by their failure to live up to people's unrealistic expectations that their special abilities would be matched by comparable superiority in quite different areas of competence.

The fact that child prodigies do tend to specialize can also produce consequences that follow directly from the fact that specializing at one activity inevitably limits the time available for other potentially valuable activities. A child who is practising at the piano for eight hours a day cannot simultaneously be learning biology or mathematics. In reality, it is probably true to say that, for most child prodigies, concentrating on one area of expertise restricts opportunities for other kinds of learning only to a limited extent. It is unlikely that if a child who regularly practised at the piano stopped doing so he or she would start to devote the equivalent amount of time to valuable learning experiences of a different kind. For most young people, the majority of leisure hours are not filled with activities that have enormous educational value. For this reason, the price to be paid by a child whose leisure time is restricted as a result of having specialized interests may be a relatively small one.

Nevertheless, that price is not entirely negligible. As we have seen, children do learn from watching television, reading novels, taking an interest in sports, enjoying leisurely conversations with their friends, social activities of one kind or another, and other kinds of relaxed spare-time occupations. So it would be wrong to assume that an individual whose time-filling specialized interests seriously curtail these alternative kinds of activities will be at no disadvantage at all. The responses of children to a number of interview and questionnaire studies have shown that among the reasons for children choosing to watch particular television programmes is the fact that they often provide useful information. Television also supplies practical demonstrations that show young people how to act in significant but unfamiliar social situations that they are likely to encounter (Howe, 1977; 1983b).

Although the benefits to be gained from enjoying literature may be difficult to measure, they are none the less important. Reading novels can help a child to gain wisdom, humility, a sense of humour, awareness of the needs and feelings of other people, and many varieties of insights into the human condition. In the following account by a journalist of his frustrated efforts to interview a child prodigy it is conceivable that the uncooperativeness he experienced may simply have been an expression of irritation with the continued intrusions of reporters. Yet it seems more likely that the unsympathetic responses reflect a negative consequence of a highly specialized education – a failure to perceive the need to react with good grace in a situation in which the real purpose of initial questions is not so much to elicit information as to make human contact and establish the common ground that makes mutual understanding possible.

> I asked, for example if there had ever been a subject that she had found difficult. It provoked hours of discussion. 'What sort of question is that? I can't possibly answer it.'... I said it was a perfectly simple question of the kind asked every day by non-geniuses. 'No question is ever simple,' came the triumphant, if rather pat, chorus from father and daughter ... It was the most taxing conversation I have ever had, and also among the least interesting, like a football match that is constantly stopped by the referee for technical infringements.
> (Stephen Pile, quoted in Walmsley and Margolis, 1987, p. 54)

THE ATTENTION OF THE PRESS

For some child prodigies, the attention of media journalists and the resulting publicity can create real difficulties. Some contemporary and recent prodigies have been clearly upset by the attention they have received, and previous generations have also suffered. Norbert Wiener certainly did. As he recounts,

> I was pestered by a swarm of reporters who were eager to sell my birthright at a penny a line ... Finally I learned that reporters were on the whole to be avoided, and I ultimately developed enough fleetness of foot and ability at dodging to conduct a reporter across the college campus ... without giving his partner a chance to take a usable photograph.
>
> Most of these articles ... belonged to a class of ephemeral literature which has long since returned to the gutters from which it emanated. While they flattered my childish desire for attention, both my parents and I recognized this for the sickly narcissism which it was ... Besides the direct damage to me, these articles could only have accentuated that feeling of isolation forced on the prodigy by the hostility latent in the community round him. (Wiener, 1953, p. 118)

Adding to Norbert Wiener's problems with the press was the fact that his own father seemed to welcome all this attention. Leo Wiener liked to sound off at length, either in interviews or articles, in which he expounded his educational theories and was at pains to emphasize, to his son's embarrassment, that Norbert was just a quite ordinary boy whose successes were entirely due to the superlative education his father was giving him. The young Norbert was understandably piqued by these unflattering accounts, although, as the middle-aged Norbert recognized,

> I suppose that this was in part to prevent me from being conceited, and that it was no more than a half-representation of my father's true belief. Nevertheless, it rendered me more diffident as to my own ability than I would have otherwise been even under my father's scolding. In short, I had the worst of both worlds. (Wiener, 1953, p. 119)

But the troubles Norbert Wiener experienced in connection with the attention of the press were trivial compared with those which assaulted his acquaintance and contemporary, William Sidis. Sidis was often hounded by reporters, and ridiculed in cruelly hostile newspaper articles. In Sidis's case it would be fair to say that the unhappiness caused to him by the unwelcome attentions of the press was one reason for Sidis, who was just as brilliant an adolescent as Norbert Wiener, failing to follow up his early promise with a productive and successful adult career. Frequent newspaper reports on him appeared throughout his childhood. He was described as 'the most remarkable boy in the United States' (A. Wallace, 1986, p. 47). When Sidis was eleven, several large articles about him appeared in the *New York Times* and the *Boston Sunday Herald*. The tone of these articles was generally friendly, despite the fact that Sidis's parents were even keener than Leo Wiener to fuel the discussion by holding forth about their views on the education of children. But as time went on the press coverage of William Sidis became increasingly hostile. At the age of 11, a few days after he had given a brilliant two-hour lecture on 'Four-dimensional bodies' at Harvard University, Sidis had a bad attack of influenza. The *New York Times* was quick to assume the worst. Describing his illness as 'a breakdown', the paper reported:

> ... young Sidis, the marvellous boy of Harvard, the astonishing product of a new and better system of education, has broken down from overwork and is now in a state of nervous prostration seriously alarming his family and friends ... [the method of his education] is fatally bad and the inventor stands condemned of something worse than failure. (Quoted in A. Wallace, 1986, p. 69)

There was a continuing chorus of similar reports, all homing in on the child's weaknesses and eccentricities. All conveyed the message 'I told you so' with gloating satisfaction. The hounding and ridicule continued throughout William Sidis's adolescence. When he was thirteen his father added to the public's interest in William, and to its hostility towards him, by producing a book entitled *Philistine and Genius*. This scathingly attacked conventional educational practices and proclaimed the superiority of Boris Sidis's own ideas and methods. The fact that William at that time was an awkward and unhappy child, socially backward and decidedly odd in a number of ways, made it inevitable that journalists would leap to gloat on the son's failures, as an easy way to attack the father's ideas. Sadly, William Sidis continued to be a target for hostile journalism even when his days of early promise were long past and he was living a quiet life of simple poverty and wanted only to be left alone. In a *New Yorker* article, as Norbert Wiener recounts, 'Sidis, who through his later life was a defeated – and honorably defeated – combatant in the battle for existence, was pilloried like a side-show freak for fools to gape at.' Wiener reproachfully adds, 'The gentlemen who were responsible for this article overlooked the fact that W. J. Sidis was alive and could be hurt very deeply' (Wiener, 1953, pp. 134–5).

## 4 What happens to Child Prodigies when they become Adults?

The majority of child prodigies do become unusually capable adults who enjoy productive and successful lives. Of course, the prodigies whose feats are most spectacular do not necessarily eventually achieve the highest levels of eminence. To take the case of two brothers, for instance, the sons of James Thomson (a teacher of mathematics and a writer of textbooks who became a professor at Glasgow University) were both child prodigies. But whilst the older brother, James, had the most glittering childhood, won several prizes at the University when he was still in his early teens, and died with the reputation of being a highly distinguished engineer, his minor fame was eclipsed by that of his younger brother, William. The latter's less dazzling childhood was followed by a brilliant scientific career, as a result of which he became Lord Kelvin, and was one of the greatest of nineteenth-century physicists.

Norbert Wiener once remarked that the prodigies who most readily come to people's minds are those who have been either hugely successful in adulthood (he mentions John Stuart Mill and Blaise Pascal) or spectacularly unsuccessful. William Sidis clearly belongs in this latter category, as does the brilliant young Hungarian pianist Erwin Nyiregyhazi (Revesz, 1925). Well-known recent cases of prodigies who have failed to enjoy successful adult careers include Chrisien Kiens, a brilliant young Dutchman, who composed music, conducted, and was also a talented pianist and violinist, but killed himself in his early twenties, at a time when he was working as a disc jockey, as well as Lilit Gampel, another musician, who dropped out of sight following a remarkable childhood career (Elkind, 1981). As Wiener put it, the ex-prodigies we hear about are those who 'point a moral or adorn a tale'. Wiener pointed out that it is perfectly reasonable and desirable for an individual who has been a prodigy in childhood to live a modest life of unspectacular success. Wiener felt that it was most unfortunate that people tend to believe that a prodigy's childhood must be followed by 'immense failure or immense success'. His objection stemmed partly from the fact that the assumption is simply not true, and partly from his awareness that the expectation of great success in the young prodigy's future, which can rarely be fulfilled, puts unfair pressure on the ex-prodigy, who may feel himself or herself to be a failure as an adult, through being unable or disinclined to meet other people's unrealistic expectations.

Of course, as we have seen, although a substantial number of child prodigies have gone on to highly distinguished adult careers, and a few, like William Sidis and Erwin Nyiregyhazi, have dramatically failed to live up to their early promise, the vast majority of ex-prodigies are moderately successful and happy enough, but are neither outstandingly successful nor sufficiently extraordinary in other ways to draw much attention to themselves. This state of affairs may be inevitable, if only because the numbers of children who are described as being prodigies are simply larger, as a proportion of the population as a whole, than the numbers of adults who become famed or well known by virtue of their outstanding intellectual qualities. After all, there are only so many Nobel prizes and Olympic gold medals to go around, and the public's appetite for names on whom to bestow the reputation of being famous is not unlimited. So it comes as no surprise to find that investigations which have examined the subsequent lives of large samples of intellectually precocious or 'gifted' children, such as the Californian individuals whose lives were followed in the large-scale research study initiated by Lewis Terman, have found that the majority of gifted children enjoy careers that are reasonably successful but not earth-shattering. None of the 1500 children who participated in that study became a Nobel prize winner. But there were some prominent scientists among them, and several judges, a distinguished film director, at least one well-known writer, and substantial numbers of scholars, doctors, and lawyers.

## WHY ARE SOME PRODIGIES MORE SUCCESSFUL THAN OTHERS?

Why are some ex-prodigies, in adulthood, more successful than others? There are numerous possible reasons, and it is not always easy to say just why things turn out better for some individuals than for others. Although a child's cleverness or the brilliance of his or her intellectual powers may be enough to ensure that the child is labelled as a prodigy, the success of an adult career never depends on these qualities alone. Among the other determinants of later success are factors such as temperament, personality, self-confidence, strength of commitment to a goal, social skills, and the ability to communicate with other people. And luck can also play a part. So the attributes that may suffice to ensure that a child is regarded as a prodigy are not, on their own, sufficient to guarantee that the same individual will prove to be an unusually capable adult. Also, as I mentioned in chapter 2, in discussing the influences that determine whether or not a talented individual comes to be regarded as a genius, some of the crucial factors are external to the objectively measurable qualities of the particular person, and have less to do with the individual's abilities as such, than with events in the outside world that determine how they will be received by other people.

### Comparing Bidder and Colburn

The difficulty of explaining just why one prodigy becomes an eminent adult and another does not is illustrated by comparing two individuals who in some respects were remarkably similar to each other. Two years before the birth of George Bidder, a child named Zerah Colburn was born in the American state of Vermont. Like Bidder, Colburn was a remarkable juvenile calculating prodigy (Smith, 1983). Like Bidder (whom he met on one occasion, when Colburn was probably 14 and Bidder 12, and discovered that Bidder 'could answer some questions which [Colburn] would not like to undertake, but he was unable to extract the roots, and find the factors of numbers' (quoted in Smith, 1983, p. 205), Colburn first drew the attention of adults to his talent when he was about six years of age. At that time his father heard him repeating multiplication tables to himself, although the child had only attended the local school for a few weeks. When the father asked his son to multiply 13 × 97 he was immediately given the correct answer, 1,261. Like Bidder, the young Colburn travelled round the country giving public demonstrations of his abilities. (These earned him considerably more than Bidder received.)

Like Bidder, Colburn came to the attention of wealthy individuals who were willing to pay for his education. He was offered a number of opportunities that would have made it possible for him to make himself into a highly educated young person. His early precocity was even more marked than Bidder's. When he was still only six he could solve problems requiring him to state the number of seconds in 2000 years, to give the product of 12,225 multiplied by 1,223, and the square of 1,449. A year later it took him precisely six seconds to state the number of hours in 38 years, two months and seven days. At the age of only nine he became one of the first mathematicians to establish whether or not certain very large numbers were primes, and his ability to factorize considerably surpassed Bidder's.

Yet, unlike George Bidder, the adult Zerah Colburn never came to much in the world's eyes. It is not easy see why, with such similar abilities, the two men should have enjoyed such contrasting degrees of success. By all accounts Colburn was an outgoing man, and personable enough. He was clearly intelligent. At different times in his short life he was a mathematician employed to make astronomical calculations, a teacher of literature and modern and classical languages, an actor, and a minister of religion. In 1833, at the age of 28, he wrote a perceptive autobiography, *A Memoir of Zerah Colburn, written by Himself*. Yet most of his adult life was unhappy, and he lived in poverty. When he died at the age of 35 there was none of the acclaim and praise which followed Bidder's death.

Granted that riches and material success are not the only measures of a life's worth, and that Colburn could hardly have accomplished in 35 years achievements equal to those of Bidder's 72-year life span, it still remains a puzzle why the two men, of seemingly equal talents, should have had such different fortunes. Perhaps it was largely a matter of chance favouring the one and not the other. Bidder's remarkable energy and vitality may have made a difference, or perhaps his greater worldliness was a significant factor in his greater success, compared with Colburn's. Despite being a bold and outspoken individual, Bidder appears to have had a good eye for the main chance and a willingness to conform when doing so was in his interest. His temperament and his abilities seem to have been well matched. Compared with him, Colburn seems to have been something of a lonely wanderer, perhaps rather a lost soul after his father's death in 1824, and with little of the dynamism and panache that Bidder employed in the management of his own career.

FIVE HARVARD CONTEMPORARIES
One factor that makes it difficult to explain why some ex-prodigies have much more success in their adult lives than others is that making comparisons between individuals generally involves comparing people who have been born in different places, at different times, and whose cultural backgrounds have been different in a number of respects. When there are a large number of dimensions on which people differ from one another, it may be impossible to discover which of those dimensions are most crucial. For this reason it would be helpful to have an opportunity to compare a number of prodigies who have been brought up in circumstances which, in some respects at least, are not dissimilar.

Fortunately, some relevant information became available as a result of a situation which came about in the Boston area, early in the present century. In the year 1909 no less than five child prodigies were enrolled at Harvard. Norbert Wiener was one. William Sidis was another. The third was Adolf Berle, a more outgoing and socially accomplished child than either Wiener or Sidis. Berle, whose brother and two sisters were also exceptionally able (one sister, Lina, learned to speak several languages by the age of three), had a dazzling career as a lawyer, becoming Assistant Secretary of State under Franklin D. Roosevelt (A. Wallace, 1986). The fourth child prodigy was Roger Sessions, who became a well-known composer, and lived until 1985. Cedrick Wing Houghton, the fifth, died before graduating.

Of the five, except for Sidis, all those who lived into adulthood had highly productive lives. William Sidis, as we have seen, was never able to make use of his remarkable abilities. According to Norbert Wiener, Sidis developed a resentment against science, mathematics, and all that his family stood for, as well as 'a hatred for anything that might put him in a position of responsibility and give him the need to make decisions' (Wiener, 1953, p. 132).

It is not difficult to find reasons for Sidis' failure to enjoy a happy and productive adulthood. His childhood would have been difficult enough even without the press attention that, as I have already said, helped to destroy his self-confidence. His dependence on his parents was even greater than Wiener's. As we saw earlier, Wiener only just managed to detach himself sufficiently from his parents' control to create a life for himself: some brilliant young prodigies have failed to make the necessary break. For example, even when he was 18, Erwin Nyiregyhazi, the dazzling Hungarian pianist, could not feed or dress himself properly, or tie his own shoes (Feldman, 1986). Sidis was equally unable to look after himself properly. With his appalling lack of social skills and his inability to keep himself clean or dress himself, he was ill-equipped for a fully independent life. Yet he resented his dependence on his parents, and the resentment grew to hatred. He refused to attend his father's funeral. Towards his mother, a domineering and by all accounts appalling woman in some ways, he developed an intense loathing.

The comparison between Wiener and Sidis is interesting because their backgrounds were remarkably similar. The parents of both of them were ambitious and successful recent Jewish immigrants to the United States. Both fathers were Russian, were themselves intellectually precocious, and both arrived in America in the 1880s. Both men were fiery, energetic, dominating, and somewhat overbearing. In photographs they even look alike. Both had strong (and similar) ideas about the education of children. Strangely, however, whilst Leo Wiener put almost as much energy into the education of his daughter, Sarah – who developed into an extremely capable person – and the youngest child, Fritz, as he did into his elder son's, Boris Sidis paid remarkably little attention to the early education of his daughter, Helena.

Boris Sidis was no ogre. He was not knowingly cruel to his son and his teaching methods seem to have been less harsh than those of either James Mill or Leo Wiener. And the education he gave his son was neither narrow nor unenlightened. In theory at least, he strongly opposed the use of any compulsion or pressure, and was in favour of taking cues from the child's own curiosity. In his provocative book on education, *Philistine and Genius*, which produced considerable controversy at the time of its publication in 1911 (largely because it was extremely critical of current educational practices), Boris Sidis wrote:

> If, however, you do not neglect the child between the second and third years, and see to it that the brain should not be

starved, should have its proper function, like the rest of the bodily organs, by developing an interest in intellectual activity and love of knowledge, no forcing of the child to study is afterward requisite. The child will go on by himself, – he will derive intense enjoyment from his intellectual activity, as he does from his games and physical exercise. The child will be stronger, healthier, sturdier than the present average child, with its purely animal activities and total neglect of brain-function. He will not be a barbarian with animal proclivities and a strong distaste for knowledge and mental enjoyment, but he will be a strong, healthy, thinking man. (The passage is quoted in the Introduction to Witte, 1975)

Intellectually, the training that William Sidis gained from his parents was magnificent, but for a number of reasons he never achieved what had been expected of him. One reason was that his parents were too concerned with their educational theories to pay sufficient attention to the emotional, non-intellectual needs of their growing son. Although they gave him plenty of their time and showed him off at every opportunity, they failed to see just how uneven his development was. They also neglected to make sure that he was properly equipped with the personal and social skills that are necessary for survival in the harsh world outside the protected environment of home. And whereas Norbert Wiener learned in childhood to enjoy a number of healthy outdoor interests, and went on long nature walks and hiking expeditions with his father, Boris Sidis was so opposed to all non-intellectual pursuits (he talked of 'meaningless games and silly, objectless sports') that the young William never had a chance to acquire the kinds of habits and interests that most well-rounded people depend upon for relaxing the mind and fortifying the body. Most importantly, his parents completely failed to equip him to deal with all the public attention that came his way. That the attention of the press came his way was largely the result of the parents' frequent proclamations to the effect that William was a superior individual (as a consequence of the superior education that the parents were giving him).

Even more damaging to William Sidis' sense of ease and self-confidence was the fact that his parents' marriage, unlike that of the Wieners, was not at all happy. For this there were a number of causes. Neither Boris Sidis nor his wife can have been easy to live with, although it was the mother, who appears to have been bad-tempered, humourless, and domineering, always nagging and criticizing her son, whom William grew to dislike the most strongly, and who did most to undermine his fragile confidence in himself.

The adult William Sidis failed to make real use of his abilities because, although there was little wrong with his intellect, his childhood left him frightened and unhappy, neither self-confident enough nor sufficiently at peace with himself to rely on his intellectual powers. They stayed largely unused until his death in 1944 at the age of 46. With hindsight, is easy to say that Sidis might have made an enormous contribution if only his parents had done more to make him self-sufficient and independent, instead of concentrating on his intellect to the neglect of matters that are equally important. Any parents of a prodigy might do well to keep in mind the words of an earlier prodigy's father, the elder Karl Witte. He wrote,

> But let me tell what I wanted to make of him; then it will appear of itself what I did not want him to become. I wanted to educate him to be a man in the noblest sense of the word. So far as I in my circumstances could do so and was aided in this matter by my knowledge and experience, he was first of all to be a healthy, strong, active, and happy young man, and in this, as everybody knows, I have succeeded. He was to enter manhood with this invaluable equipment. He was to develop his bodily powers to the utmost extent and yet harmoniously, even as he should do with his intellectual powers. (Witte, 1975, pp. 63–4)

Norbert Wiener only just learned to stand on his own feet. William Sidis never did. Some of the greatest of ex-prodigies – Wiener himself, for example, and John Ruskin and John Stuart Mill as well – bore throughout their lives the scars of having been too dependent on overdemanding parents. The parents of today's prodigies would do well to take note of Witte's good sense.

## 5 At how early a Stage do Prodigies begin to display their Exceptionality?

According to the accounts that are available, most of those individuals who have been recognized as being prodigies in childhood and have also been exceptionally accomplished people when they became adults did not display any unusual precocity in their earliest months. On the contrary, with remarkable uniformity the parents of a number of the most impressive child prodigies of all, including Karl Witte, John Stuart Mill, Norbert Wiener, and William Sidis, have insisted on the sheer ordinariness of their infants. For instance, the elder Witte described his son as being inherently ordinary, and lacking any unusual basic aptitudes. He quotes, as a testimony to the accuracy of his assertions, a letter from Pastor Glaubitz, a long-time friend of the elder Witte:

> I am convinced that Karl has no extraordinary aptitudes, and I am not one of those who marvel at his progress as at a miracle. On the contrary, I tell myself, you, and all who wish to hear it, that his aptitudes are only mediocre, but that his progress could not help being what it is, and the results of your education will one time appear even more brilliant. I know your educational plans and your way of doing things. They must succeed, unless God wants to hinder them. (Witte, 1975)

James Mill regarded his son's ability to learn as no better than average. As the latter recorded in his *Autobiography*,

> From his own intercourse with me I could derive none but a very humble opinion of myself ... I was not at all aware that my attainments were anything unusual at my age ... if I thought anything about myself, it was that I was rather backward in my studies, since I always found myself so, in comparison with what my father expected from me. (Mill, 1971, p. 35)

Leo Wiener, as we have seen, repeatedly emphasized that he regarded his son as an essentially average boy whose unusual abilities were the result of exceptional training. And Boris Sidis was adamant that William's remarkable early accomplishments were the inevitable outcome of the equally remarkable early education the boy had been given.

Of course, we cannot accept these accounts entirely at face value. Just as we previously found it necessary to treat with some scepticism the assertions made by parents anxious to convince themselves and others that the remarkable abilities of their offspring could only be attributed to miraculous powers, or divine selection, or parental genes, we ought to be no less wary about accepting the equally confident opposing statements of those parents have wanted all the world to appreciate the effectiveness of the training procedures they have devised, with their own children used as guinea pigs. Nevertheless, it is true that there are no strong reasons for believing that children such as Karl Witte, John Stuart Mill, Leo Wiener, or William Sidis would have been in any way exceptional had it not been for the very exceptional childhoods that their parents arranged for them.

The fact that children such as Helena Sidis, who were not submitted by their parents to any unusually intensive early educational regime, did *not* develop any abilities that were at all precocious or exceptional, despite being brought up by the same biological parents, and in the same family home, as siblings who were exceptionally brilliant child prodigies, provides some support for the assertion that the extraordinariness of child prodigies' early backgrounds does account, at least in part, for their remarkable early development. And that conclusion gains additional support from the finding that in cases where a number of children in the same family have each received intense and prolonged early education from the parents – as in the Thomson, Berle, and Mozart families, for example, or, more recently, the Menuhins - more than one child has gained exceptional abilities. Interestingly, that does not seem to happen in those families in which the youngest siblings have been subjected to a second-hand or diluted version of the parental teaching methods, administered by a less-than-enthusiastic older brother, even if that brother is as exceptionally able a person as John Stuart Mill or Norbert Wiener.

From the interview findings obtained in the Chicago studies it is clear that the evidence that is available about contemporary child prodigies paints a highly similar picture. Many of these children talked fairly early. A substantial number learned to read early, but not spectacularly so. Yet the majority of those of the children examined by the Chicago-based researchers who could safely be labelled as being prodigies by middle childhood did *not* appear to have been remarkable right from the very beginning of their lives. It was not until after they had begun to receive considerable amounts of training or special encouragement from their parents (or another adult) that they started to display abilities that were strikingly advanced for children of their age. This tended to happen after, rather than before, these children had become unusually interested in an activity, and after they had begun to channel their energies in that particular direction. Typically, by this time the child had been encouraged to regard himself or herself as having already gained some degree of competence at his (or her) own special skill. Usually, it was not until after a degree of self-identification with a skilled activity or an area of knowledge had been achieved, and the child had acquired the habit of practising the activity frequently and enthusiastically, that really exceptional achievements began to be displayed.

For instance, Lauren Sosniak (1990) points out that among the young concert pianists whose childhoods she investigated, the majority did not show any unusual promise at the start of their training. Even after seven years of study and practice, when they began to play in local competitions, they were frequently far from being successful. Sosniak reports

> We began our study with the question of how individuals were discovered and then helped to develop their talents; we found the reverse. The youngsters spent several years acquiring knowledge and developing skills and dispositions appropriate for their fields before they were 'discovered' as the most talented in their family or in their neighborhood and accorded the status of biggest fish in their small ponds. In turn, a discovery of this sort, by a parent or teacher, typically led to increased opportunities for development. (Sosniak, 1990)

Yet there are occasional reports of children who have made extraordinary progress at a very early age, sometimes even in the first six months of life. In most of these cases it is clear that their home backgrounds have been unusually stimulating and encouraging. One report by H. B. Robinson describes a boy who began speaking when he was five months old. A month later he had a 50-word vocabulary. At 13 months he started to read. By the time his age was two years and three months he knew five languages and could read in three of them, and had a good understanding of basic arithmetic.

Even more remarkable is a young boy named Adam, who was aged three and a half when David Feldman (1986) began to investigate his early life. By that time he had already learned to read and write, spoke several languages, studied mathematics and composed music for the guitar. According to his parents, Adam had begun to speak not only in words but in grammatically correct sentences at three months of age. The parents reported that Adam engaged in complex conversations by six months, and that by his first birthday he could read simple books.

I know of no other case of very early precocity quite so extraordinary as this one. There are a substantial number of reports of children who say words before they are six months of age. Some of them have begun to speak in sentences in the third quarter of their first year. And there are occasional reports of a child who reads before the age of two. But Adam seems to have been the most remarkable of all. Feldman reports that Adam's paediatrician noted that he was 'exceedingly mature neurologically at birth'. Apart from the information about Adam's (very unusual) early home circumstances that Feldman was able to obtain, there were few other clues to the possible causes of Adam's extreme precocity. The parents were understandably taken aback by Adam at first. As Feldman observes, 'They were not prepared, however, for a child who challenged their parenting resources and stamina – and their fundamental notions of ability and development – before they had even become used to their new parental roles and responsibilities' (Feldman, 1986, p. 35).

Yet it must be said that Adam's home life was quite extraordinary in the extent to which it was deliberately arranged to cater to the needs of a young child. Feldman points out that his was an exceptionally child-orientated environment, and that the rooms were arranged to give Adam space to explore and experiment. His parents – a science professor and a psychotherapist – had hoped for a bright child who 'would approach learning with joy, spontaneity, and excitement' (Feldman, 1986, p. 35), and had decided well before Adam was born that they would do all they could to give careful attention to the child's intellectual, social, and emotional needs. Adam's parents took their responsibilities towards him very seriously indeed. They spent a large proportion of their time with Adam. Feldman says that when he first visited their house he found that it was crammed full of Adam's toys, educational materials of many kinds, and large numbers of books. The parents seem to have done as much as was humanly possible to provide a stimulating and encouraging environment for their child. David Feldman, who was no newcomer to witnessing the often unusual family backgrounds of child prodigies, was taken aback by the parents' absolute dedication and their 'unending quest for stimulating and supportive environments' (Feldman, 1986, p. 36). He reached the conclusion that, as a trio, they were the most intellectually active people he had ever had the opportunity to observe.

What should we make of a child like Adam? In his first year he was already quite exceptionally precocious, even if we allow for possible exaggeration by his justifiably proud parents, who clearly shared an intense emotional involvement in their child's remarkable early progress. (Unfortunately, there are very few cases in which detailed 'objective' observations by an unbiased examiner have been made during the first year of the life of a remarkably precocious infant.) As we have seen, Adam's early environment was also exceptional. It would be fascinating to know how Adam would have developed had his early background been quite ordinary. Unfortunately, of course, there is simply no way of telling. It would also be fascinating to know how another child – an adopted infant, perhaps – would have developed in the identical home environment provided by Adam's parents. Again, sadly, there is no way to know. Although there does exist a substantial research literature on the effects of adoption on young children's intelligence, there are no studies in which adoptive parents have shown a degree of intense dedication to a child's early progress that was remotely comparable to that demonstrated by Adam's parents.

It is frustratingly difficult to provide firm statements about the extent, frequency, or magnitude of intellectual precocity in the first year of life. Uncovering the causes is even more difficult. Even when it is clear that an infant has been remarkably precocious, it is generally impossible to disentangle, retrospectively, the possible influences. On the one hand there are environmental factors that help determine a child's earliest experiences. On the other hand there are other possible causes of exceptional early development, such as genetic ones. Ascertaining the causes is not helped by the fact that most of the available evidence is in the form of parental reports, often made years after the events they describe. There are inevitable questions about the objectivity of the data.

There exist a few snippets of autobiographical data which on first inspection seem to provide confirmatory evidence of the spontaneous or 'natural' appearance of already formed skills in the first year or two of a child's life, apparently in the absence of any instruction being received by the child. For example, In his book *Frames of Mind*, Howard Gardner (1984) quotes Aaron Copland saying about composing, 'it is something that the composer happens to have been born to do'. Gardner also reports Saint Saens' statement that the process of composing is like an apple tree producing apples. He refers to a claim by Artur Rubinstein, the pianist, that as a child he would refuse to speak but was always willing to sing, and that although nobody in his family had any interest in music he quickly mastered the piano with very little effort. Gardner also quotes an unnamed composer as saying, 'I can never understand how anyone could have difficulty recognizing tones and deciphering musical patterns. It's something I've been doing since the age of three at least' (Gardner, 1984, p. 121). He also relates Stravinsky's story of how, at the age of two, he astonished his parents by skilfully imitating some local people whom he had heard singing on their way home from work.

Unfortunately, autobiographical reports of early childhood are notoriously unreliable. Even when a person genuinely and strongly believes that what is being remembered about events in early life is taken from an unadorned record of those events, as laid down in childhood, it is almost always the case that adults' childhood memories have suffered from substantial distortions over the intervening years (Howe, 1982). For this reason, however convinced someone may be that a clear and uncontaminated memory for early childhood events is being drawn upon, the wisest course is to assume that considerable alterations to the original record have taken place, albeit without any awareness on the part of the person concerned.

## 6 Do parental Efforts to accelerate a Child's early Progress sometimes fail entirely?

A number of questions concerning the possibility of accelerating skills in infants were addressed in chapter 3. Here is another one. Do some young children fail to be affected at all by the kinds of strenuous parental efforts that (as we have repeatedly seen in this chapter) are usually to be seen whenever the home circumstances of a child prodigy have been examined? Up to now we have only encountered cases in which, whether or not the child eventually developed into a happy and fulfilled adult, the parents' efforts did at least have enough initial success to ensure that their child, at some stage, was unusually precocious.

There may well have been many cases in which the parents, however dedicated and however skilled they were at teaching, were denied even that success. Yet the record is mute: one does not come across case-histories describing the failed attempts of parents who have striven, but with no success at all, to give their children a remarkable early start. Of course, the lack of evidence of such failures cannot be taken as proof that they have not occurred: in the absence of published findings there is no way of telling. People are understandably more likely to report on their successful than on their unsuccessful efforts. Even when reports are written, ones that describe positive findings are more likely to see publication than those describing interventions that have had no apparent effects. Unhappily, this issue belongs to the category of subjects which, as Stephen Jay Gould remarks, 'are invested with enormous social importance but blessed with very little reliable information' (Gould, 1984, p. 22).

Granted that trying to answer hypothetical questions can be a frustratingly unproductive enterprise, it is tempting, all the same, to enquire why some parental efforts to stimulate their children's progress fail completely, assuming that it is safe to assume that this does sometimes happen. If it does, it would not necessarily be right to conclude that such failures indicate that a child is 'slow' or 'born dull', or reflect any simple limitation in ability to learn, or even a lack of 'cleverness' or intelligence. As I have mentioned earlier, many learning difficulties are caused not by limitations that are narrowly intellectual in form, but by features of temperament or cognitive style that happen to be incompatible with the demands of a particular learning task. For this reason, a failure is just as likely to be caused by a child's being impulsive or distractible, or the absence of a habit of reflecting on things, as by slowness or inadequacy of learning processes. 'Slow learning' is often given as the main cause of learning failures, but it may be instructive to repeat an experience described by one psychologist, Dennis Stott. He spent much of his life investigating the causes of children's learning difficulties. Stott was struck by the fact that when he examined a large number of children who had learning difficulties he never seemed to encounter a child who was 'just dull'. He found that,

> In every case that I examined there was a mixture of temperamental handicaps, emotional stresses arising from severe family anxieties, social disadvantages, erratic schooling, long-standing ill health, any of which would have been sufficient to account for the academic failure. Surely, I thought, there must be some dull children. So I asked the teachers ... to go carefully through their class registers and pick out for me those whom they regarded as simply of low intelligence, without behavioural, emotional, social or health handicaps. They readily agreed, thinking they had plenty of them. When I asked for the lists they told me rather apologetically that they could find fewer than they thought ... In not one case did I have to conclude that the child must have been genetically dull. (Stott, 1974, p. 68)

So even if it does turn out that some parents' efforts to advance their children's progress are totally unsuccessful, we shall need to be very cautious about forming conclusions concerning the reasons for such failures. It would certainly be unwise to leap to the conclusion that some children are simply 'too dull' or 'too slow' to profit from early stimulation.

# 6

# Motivation and Temperament

Most people, if asked what are the special qualities possessed by the kinds of individuals who are regarded as being geniuses, or win Nobel prizes, will readily come up with terms such as intelligent, cerebral, clever, quick, brilliant, or knowledgeable – adjectives that pinpoint the specifically intellectual attributes of eminent individuals. All of these terms are apt ones: the chances are that such a person will be highly intelligent, for instance, by any definition of that term. But it is all too easy to jump to the conclusion that the distinguishing attributes of those who make outstanding intellectual achievements must be exclusively cognitive ones. That is by no means true. In a number of the extraordinary individuals I have mentioned it was clear that the main reason for the person's superiority over others lay in that individual's being, not more intelligent or cleverer than everyone else, but more curious, more keenly interested, more dogged, more determined, or more strongly driven to succeed.

That is not to say that such people are not intelligent: of course they are. But their cleverness may be as much an outcome of an unusual way of life as it is a source of it. What is being challenged here is the view that the root causes of extraordinary abilities must lie in specifically intellectual exceptionality alone. There are strong grounds for believing that motivation, temperament, and personality are equally crucial. On its own, intellectual prowess produces few remarkable achievements.

Many outstanding people are as extraordinary in the degree to which they possess qualities that are not exclusively intellectual – independence, self-directedness, and doggedness, for instance – as they are in their mastery of cognitive skills and abilities (Baltes et al., 1980; Radford, 1990). Moreover, even in people who are not exceptional, measures of adult success, including occupational status, are as highly correlated with indications of personality and temperament in childhood as they are with childhood measures of intelligence (Rutter, 1989). It follows that no explanation of the sources of exceptional abilities will be complete unless it examines both the origins and the outcomes of those qualities of motivation and personality that underlie outstanding achievements.

The ways in which motivational factors contribute to individuals' achievements are not at all simple, and nor are they uni-directional. The manner in which they operate at a given time largely depends on the particular individual concerned and the specific circumstances of that person's life. Consequently, the scope for making broad generalizations about the effects of motivational influences on human abilities is somewhat restricted. Much depends upon the precise significance of those influences for the individual.

## Motivation in one Man's Life: Sir Richard Burton

A brief account of one outstanding person will serve to illustrate the sheer importance, as well as the complexity, of the motivational factors that contribute to exceptional human accomplishments. Sir Richard Burton, who was born in 1821 and died in 1890, is best known today as the scholar who translated the *Arabian Nights* into English. But his other achievements were prodigious. If he is less famous than some other intellectual giants of recent centuries, it is largely because compared with, say, Darwin or Einstein, his interests were not nearly so specialized. His attainments, unlike theirs, were not concentrated in one particular area.

Nevertheless, the sum total of Burton's accomplishments is breathtaking. He was a distinguished explorer who led more than one expedition searching for the origins of the Nile, and he was one of the first Britons to enter the forbidden holy city of Mecca (having painstakingly established a false identity as a Pathan physician). In addition to the 16 volumes of the *Arabian Nights*, he also translated into English a very substantial amount of Portuguese, Persian, and Indian literature, Latin poetry, and folklore from Europe and Africa: he was undoubtedly one of the great linguists of his time. Burton also wrote poetry of his own, and two volumes of it were published in his lifetime.

Early in his life he spent some time as a soldier, and wrote a short book on sword exercises for infantrymen. Having an erudite knowledge of swordsmanship (and he was an outstanding swordsman himself), he also produced a scholarly history of the use and significance of that weapon, entitled *The Book of the Sword*. And on top of all he accomplished as a soldier, poet, explorer, and linguist, he made contributions to archaeology and ethnology, was a distinguished early anthropologist, and was sufficiently knowledgeable about botany, zoology, and geology to make useful discoveries in those fields. In addition to the books I have mentioned Burton published no fewer than 43 other volumes describing the insights he gained in the course of his exploration and travels in many parts of the world. Many of his achievements were only possible because he had a quite remarkable command of languages. In all, he mastered about 30 separate foreign languages, as well as a substantial number of related dialects.

How could any person accomplish so much in one lifetime? It is not an easy question to answer, but, as a brief sketch of his early life reveals, the motives and interests that directed many of Burton's activities played a big part in helping him to acquire the exceptional skills that made his most dazzling accomplishments possible. Burton was the son of high-born but impecunious parents who left England in the year of his birth and chose to live on the Continent. Consequently, most of his childhood years were spent in France and Italy, with a short interlude in England when he was nine. He was an outgoing child, lively and gregarious, and from his earliest years he was frequently in the position of wanting to mix with people who spoke different languages from his. He soon discovered that the ability to communicate in other people's languages could be extremely useful. The particular circumstances of Burton's life dictated that any efforts he made to acquire expertise in a foreign language were quickly and amply rewarded.

So by an early age he was fluent in French and Italian. He had also gained some knowledge of Spanish and German, some Greek (learned from Greek-speaking inhabitants of Marseilles), Béarnais (a language spoken in south-west France) and some Portuguese. By the time he reached adulthood learning new languages was a habitual activity for Burton, one which had become a regular element of his way of life. His childhood experiences had proved to him that all the effort was worth while. His early successes demonstrated to him that the task of acquiring any new language was one he was capable of mastering. So he had gained the confidence in himself to take on linguistic tasks that most people would have found too arduous, too daunting, and with insufficient likelihood of eventual success to justify the huge effort they demanded.

It is important to realize that, so far as it is possible to tell, Burton did not begin his career with any special facility for learning languages. He never claimed that he found it easy to master a new language: it was always a long, hard slog. By present-day standards, there was nothing particularly unusual about the learning techniques he followed. He complained that he would forget the most recently learned language whenever he attacked a new one. What was most unusual about Burton as a linguist was his sheer dedication to the task. He would maintain a dogged determination to keep on struggling until he succeeded, however long that required and however much effort it took. When he was learning Hindustani, he complained of having to give 'some twelve hours a day to a desperate struggle' (Brodie, 1971, p. 56). But he persisted all the same, long after most people would have succumbed to the temptation to give up. Burton would keep up such a regime for many months at a time.

The self-confidence that came from past successes, buttressed by the linguistic knowledge and skills gained from previous achievements of language mastery, contributed to Burton's exceptional dedication to learning foreign languages. So, too, did the fact that the particular circumstances of Burton's life, interests, and personality made linguistic achievements particularly rewarding for him. As an outgoing individual for whom travel and exploration were ruling passions, Burton was well placed to take advantage of his linguistic accomplishments, and to see the rewards to be gained by extending them. When he was a young man in his first post as an army officer in India, he quickly became aware of the value of becoming competent at certain languages as a means of gaining promotion to the kind of staff position he aspired to. At a later stage of his career he wrote that in India there were three ways for a young officer to get ahead. The first was by doing something sufficiently heroic, eccentric, or outrageous to draw attention to oneself. The second was by currying favour or exploiting the influence of social connections. But Burton claimed to prefer a third route. As he put it, 'The other path, study of languages, is a rugged and tortuous one, still you have only to plod steadily along its length, and, sooner or later, you must come to a "staff appointment"' (Brodie, 1971, p. 54).

As well as bringing these practical rewards, Burton's linguistic feats nourished other appetites, including ones buried deep within his psyche. He was exhilarated by the experience of mastering each new language, and enjoyed the insights languages gave him into exotic peoples whose lives and thoughts seemed mysterious – and inexplicable – to most Europeans. His relish of language mastery is apparent in the words he uses to describe his approach to learning. He writes, for instance, of being delighted with the most difficult Chinese characters because of their striking visual appearance. Certain languages were especially seductive for him. Arabic, which he loved best of all, he called 'a faithful wife following the mind and giving birth to its offspring' (Brodie, 1971, p. 57). At Oxford University, where he was bitterly disappointed when he failed to gain a fellowship which he felt that he clearly deserved, the act of taking on yet another language was not only a new challenge to his ambition, but also, according to his biographer Fawn Brodie, a way to heal the wounds which his self-esteem had suffered. Brodie writes of him dreaming that one day he would outshine the Oxford scholars who had scorned him.

Despite the brevity of this description of Burton's early life, one point keeps recurring. We are repeatedly made aware that the influences that led to him achieving his phenomenal accomplishments were not, in the main, specifically intellectual ones. Quite the reverse: again and again we find his intellectual activities being dictated by drives, aspirations, needs and motives that have much more to do with his career, his temperament, his personality, and his emotional life than with his intellectual powers as such (Howe, 1980; 1982; 1987b). Burton's needs were constantly goading him into new achievements. Those needs were varied. They included, at one time or another, his desire to communicate with others, his wish to prove himself, to gain promotion, and to boost his self-esteem.

## The Fuelling of Achievements by Non-Intellectual Qualities

In Burton's case the degree to which the man's needs and motives fuelled his intellectual achievements is revealed unusually clearly. But there is no reason to suppose that the effects on an individual's accomplishments of those influences that are not specifically intellectual ones – a sense of direction, drives of one kind or another, determination, patience, doggedness, self-confidence, curiosity, various interests and needs, and so on – have been less potent in other successful people's lives than they were in his.

I do not know of any single person who has made striking intellectual achievements without having had strong reasons for doing so. Whenever we examine the life of an individual whose accomplishments have been outstanding, it soon becomes clear that there have been powerful reasons for the person submitting herself or himself to the kinds of learning experiences that are necessary in order to gain the expertise which made that achievements possible. Motivational factors are always heavily involved. Of course, the particular motives vary enormously. In some people overwhelming curiosity seems to be the only spur required to lead a person to great discoveries; in others the desire for glory, fame, or riches may be an important incentive. But without strong motivation in one form or another, little is ever achieved.

So, whilst it is undoubtedly true that people who are described as being geniuses are also clever and intelligent, that fact does not justify the assumption that the essential qualities possessed by people of genius are exclusively intellectual ones such as cleverness and mental agility. To a large extent, the motives, interests, and inclinations that fuel a person's daily activities are also the forces that determine the same individual's long-term achievements. The human intellect is neither autonomous nor self-sufficient. There is a sense in which it has to be driven into action.

People of genius are not noteworthy for being falsely modest, but the statements they make when they are asked to account for their own success rarely give any indication that the individual perceived himself or herself as having had fundamentally special mental powers that would have made the task of acquiring complex skills seem unusually easy. Einstein, for instance, insisted 'I have no special gift – I am only passionately curious' (Gruber, 1982). But in many cases autobiographical reports make it clear that although most exceptionally successful individuals have not regarded themselves as being outstandingly intelligent, they have often perceived themselves as being unusual in other ways that would have added to the likelihood of their making extraordinary achievements. For instance, in describing themselves and their approaches to their fields of accomplishment, such people typically introduce terms such as dogged, persistent, unusually curious (in Einstein's case), hardworking, attentive, strong-willed, self-directed, independent, enthusiastic, energetic, self-confident, assured, and determined.

Some of these individuals describe themselves as having a thirst for knowledge or an exceptional sense of direction, or as being very keenly – even obsessively – interested in the problems they have pursued. They often have an unusual ability to resist the distractions of everyday life, to ignore discouragement or ridicule, or to persist in working towards their goals in the face of repeated failures. One author writes about exceptionally curious young people 'keeping alive the capacity to wonder, to ask strange questions about ordinary things when other children have settled matters and laid them to rest' (Gruber, 1982, p. 17). Rosamund Shuter-Dyson reports the statement of a headmaster of the Yehudi Menuhin School for young musicians, that in trying to select the most promising individuals what was sought, above all, was evidence of an appetite for music that was insatiable, and so strong that without music the child would feel deprived.

## The Importance of 'Sheer Industry' and Concentration

Charles Darwin complained about his inability to remember things. He insisted that 'my power to follow a long and purely abstract train of thought is very limited' (Darwin, 1958, p. 140). He was equally convinced that 'I have no great quickness of apprehension or wit which is so remarkable in some clever men'. He attributed his success to curiosity, determination, a capacity for careful observation, and sheer industry. The latter, he admitted,

> has been nearly as great as it could have been in the observation and collection of facts ... From my early youth I have had the strongest desire to understand or explain whatever I observed, – that is, to group all facts under some general laws. These causes combined have given me the patience to reflect or ponder for any number of years over any unexplained problem. (Darwin, 1958, p. 140)

Mozart had a stunning ability to give total concentration to what he was doing, even when he was a young child. In a letter to the composer's sister, one of his contemporaries, Schachter (the Court Trumpeter at Salzburg), wrote that 'whatever he was set to learn he gave himself to so completely that he put aside everything else'. Also, Schachter noted, once Mozart gave his attention to music he was quite unaware of anything else, and even in childhood, games and other activities only amused him if they were accompanied by music (Schenck, 1960, p. 29). This observer recalled how

> As soon as he began to give himself to music, all his senses were as good as dead to other occupations, and even his childish foolery and games with toys had to be accompanied by music if they were to interest him ... Whatever he was set to learn he gave himself to it so completely that he put aside everything else. (Schenk, 1960, p. 29)

Similarly, Isaac Newton, asked how he had discovered the law of universal gravitation, answered, 'By thinking upon it continually' (Westfall, 1980, p. 110). Einstein's biographer Ronald Clark, writes of that scientist's 'ferocious concentration on the task to be done and his determination that nothing should be allowed to divert him from it' (Clark, 1979, p. 115). Clark describes a meal at which Einstein, insulated as he was from many of the day-to-day realities of most people's lives 'began to cover a much-prized "party" tablecloth with equations' as he sat talking with his host. Moreover, one observer reported, 'I have seen him in his keenness, when no table was handy, kneel down on the floor and scribble diagrams and equations on a scrap of paper on a chair' (Clark, 1979, p. 176).

Isaac Newton could be just as oblivious as Einstein to the social niceties and the culinary demands of mealtimes: he frequently neglected his meals, forgot to sleep, and became totally absorbed in the problems he worked on. For long periods a particular interest would completely dominate his mind. He worked so hard that, according to one contemporary, if he 'had not wrought with his hands in making experiments, he had killed himself with study'. Even Albert Einstein could not match Newton's phenomenal determination and sheer doggedness. These qualities can be seen in the following account of Newton's attempt to teach himself mathematics from Descartes's *Geometry*. Newton, apparently,

> read it by himself when he was got over 2 or 3 pages he could understand no farther than he began again & got 3 or 4 pages farther till he came to another difficult place, than he began again & advanced farther and continued so doing till he had made himself Master of the whole without having the least light or instruction from any body. (John Conduit, quoted in Westfall, 1980, p. 111)

Having the ability to concentrate effectively for long periods is equally advantageous for many capable individuals whose achievements fall far short of those of geniuses like Newton, Darwin, and Einstein. Joan Freeman (1979) observed that the highly intelligent young people whom she studied in her investigation of gifted children displayed unusual feats of concentration about three times as often as children of average ability. As was noted in chapter 4, there are substantial differences between cultural traditions in the extent to which experiences at home and school encourage children to attend to and concentrate on information that can facilitate learning. Children who are brought up in oriental cultures often owe much of their success at mastering difficult achievements to having had the habit of carefully attending to instruction successfully instilled during early childhood.

## *Blocking unpleasant Thoughts*

The fact that Newton was an isolated and socially withdrawn child, and probably an unhappy one, may have contributed to the fact that he gained some remarkable abilities at an early age. To acquire a difficult skill necessitates close concentration and focused attention being maintained for lengthy periods of time. Most people, children especially, find it very difficult to keep concentrating on one area of interest for long periods: they tend to get tired or bored, but there are some individuals for whom lengthy concentration seems to be more rewarding than it is for others. In some cases a reason for this is that doing so blocks out unpleasant thoughts. Ericsson and Faivre (1988) suggest that whilst most people are happy enough to concentrate for brief periods but find it very difficult to attend to something for a long time,

> there might be situations in which the opposite becomes true. Under normal conditions daydreaming and nondirected thinking might be pleasant and rewarding. However, in fearful situations, with the intrusion of anxiety-provoking thoughts, such relaxed states would be aversive. Focussing attention as required in the practice of a mental skill would serve to block out such thoughts ... As a result, an impressive skill would develop, given sufficient time. (Ericsson and Faivre, 1988, p. 455)

It is more than likely that motives of this kind play a part in the acquisition of some of the very striking skills that are seen in 'idiots savants'. These mentally retarded individuals, some of whom are autistic, can perform extremely impressive feats at one or more areas of expertise (Smith and Howe, 1985; Howe and Smith, 1988; Howe, 1988a; 1989a; 1989b; 1989c). For at least some of these people, it is likely that

> a reason for specializing in memory tasks is that concentrating one's energies in the direction of a particular narrow interest can serve to keep threatening thoughts and anxieties out of mind. By directing all one's attention to calendar dates, for example, a person may be able to block out certain unbearable ideas. In some respects the device of channelling mental activities as a means to escape thoughts that a person needs to avoid is similar to the strategy of concentrating on solitary tasks as a means of avoiding the need for social interactions. But whereas the latter may be a realistic or practical response for certain mentally retarded people, there is something more decidedly pathological about having a desperate need to shut out unpleasant thoughts. (Howe, 1989a, ch. 3, p. 22)

## Isolation

The experience of being isolated from others may provide another set of circumstances that can make it easier to sustain one's concentration on a particular topic for lengthy periods, even when the isolation is involuntary. A number of autobiographical accounts have drawn attention to the positive effects of the intensive reading that a child has done when confined to bed because of illness. It is also significant that some of those individuals who have become extremely skilled at the kinds of 'lightning calculating' problems of mental arithmetic that George Bidder and Zerah Colburn were able to solve (see chapter 5), acquired their abilities when they were working as shepherds, with much time on their hands, and no human company. Inaudi was employed as a shepherd when he was a child, and according to F. D. Mitchell (1907), so also were a number of other exceptionally skilled mental calculators.

# The Developmental Origins of Drive and Determination

Today, drive, determination, and commitment are just as evident in the kinds of individuals who are described as being exceptionally talented as they were for previous generations of extraordinarily able young people. A number of writers have commented on the passion that many able children direct towards their activities, and on their persistence, perseverance, and the intensity of their efforts. Having abundant energy is clearly important (Hershman and Lieb, 1988), as is the ability to engage in solitary activities for lengthy periods (Storr, 1988; also see Gardner, 1988). Talented teenagers often spend several hours each day on activities related to their field of expertise – even longer than the considerable lengths of time that many young people devote to watching television.

## How young Musicians learn to Persist

How does a young child gain the personal qualities that underlie perseverance and persistence at a difficult activity? The teachers of unusually successful young children have almost always given particular attention to maintaining the child's interest. In music, the crucial importance of motivation is continuously stressed, perhaps most explicitly by followers of the Suzuki method (Peak, 1986; Taniuchi, 1986), in which strenuous efforts are made to ensure, not only that the child is highly motivated to learn, but that at least one parent is also highly enthusiastic.

As Lauren Sosniak has remarked, although children are curious and eager to explore their environment, gaining a long-term commitment to learning is a different matter. She notes,

> But studying something spontaneously, with a teacher, at a set time and place, and practising daily in preparation for lessons, are not activities arising spontaneously from normal physiological or psychological development. Years of persistent work at one type of activity is rather unusual in today's society, especially for people between the ages of five and twenty-two (Sosniak, 1985, p. 478)

Sosniak, who points out that it is unusual for young people to work persistently for years at one type of activity, discovered that all the successful young pianists she studied had received a great deal of encouragement for their efforts. She remarks that when one listens to successful young players talking about what kept them at the piano, one is immediately struck by the multitude of motives and rewards for their efforts, an observation that I can confirm from my own conversations with young musicians. The form and nature of the rewards which Sosniak found to be most important depended on a child's age. In the youngest children, parents helped to make the learning experience enjoyable by finding a teacher whom their child would like, and by being willing to change to a new teacher if the child was not getting along well with the first one. Typically, the teachers and the parents made a big effort to help the child enjoy the lesson, making it an event to be looked forward to. The parents did their best to ensure that practice sessions were frequent and also enjoyable. As a result, the children tended to progress faster than most, and they also acquired a strong habit of practising, which made further progress easier.

For the older children too, playing the piano brought many rewards, but they were different ones. The children were encouraged by the progress they had already made, by the knowledge that playing the piano was an opportunity to be special, and to do something that others of their age could not achieve, and by the attention and applause they were given. By this time a child might be regarded by others as being specially talented. Such a judgement would have important consequences for the child. In music, and indeed in many other fields, the reactions of teachers and adults usually ensure that 'those who are initially successful have greater opportunities for future success' (Cole and Cole, 1973, p. 119). The sheer belief that a child is talented conveys large advantages. For children so designated,

> Figuratively, and sometimes quite literally, they moved to the head of the class. The flow of resources important for musical development, from parents and teachers, grew stronger... Parents became more convinced of their child's potential with each recital or comment from a teacher or neighbor. Teachers joined in 'recognizing' the student. A concerted effort was made to find a better teacher for the child, ... (Sosniak, 1985, pp. 493–4)

But determination to succeed can sometimes be counter-productive. Too much striving can destroy enjoyment, prevent spontaneity, and create pressures that raise anxiety to intolerable levels. Lauren Sosniak (1987) suggests that had the young pianists she studied (and their parents) striven for exceptional success right from the start they might well have eventually been considerably less successful than they were. She draws attention to the value of the parents' and the teachers' responses of delight at the children's accomplishments, and the excitement and enjoyment that even the smallest early achievements produced. Each sign of progress was valued for itself, and the pleasure that greeted it was accompanied by small alterations in aspirations and expectations. No-one was too preoccupied with far-off goals, or too anxious about the overwhelming task of progressing all the way to distant standards of perfection. The small day-to-day gains and victories were quite enough to keep teachers and learners occupied and engaged. Everyone was too interested in daily progress to have much time to be worried or overawed about what was yet to be achieved if the child was to proceed to the highest levels of accomplishment. For most parents, teachers, and children, that was not a matter of great day-to-day concern.

## Motivation in Success and Failure

It is not easy to see how it might be possible to chart the effects of each of the many influences upon a person's intellectual development that are not, in themselves, specifically intellectual in form. Each of the factors that I have listed is undoubtedly influential, but how can we know in advance how a particular motivational influence, or an unusual trait of temperament or personality, will actually affect a person's achievements at a particular time in their life? The exact influence of a potentially important factor may depend upon the precise circumstances of the situation. One woman's doggedness helps her to persevere with a dauntingly difficult task in the face of failure and discouragement until her endeavours are finally rewarded with success and approbation, whilst a similar trait of doggedness in another person prevents him from seeing that he is in a blind alley, and makes him too rigid, too resistant to new ideas, to enjoy real success. The same early success which encourages one timid adolescent to buckle down to the rigorous demands of a difficult course of instruction will tempt another young person, already confident and self-assured, to set himself unrealistic aspirations, and eventually become the elderly victim of too much early promise.

Many people's lives might have turned out entirely differently had they persevered a little more at one period of their life, or been slightly less curious at another, or if their early efforts in a new area of interest had met with just a little more success, or a little less. We are dealing here with a confusing host of influences that can have huge effects upon people, but the effects are always hard to predict, sometimes impossibly so. We may be tempted simply to bow our heads in wonder at the complexity of the forces that mould a human life, or fall into the temptation of investigating only those influences which offer the convenience of being easily measurable and readily manipulable, and pretend to ourselves that those influential factors that resist that treatment are not that so important after all. Psychology is not the only science in which some researchers have dodged important questions and turned to more tractable ones, choosing not to notice that the latter may be somewhat trivial.

Up to a point it can be helpful to regard the factors that motivate a person as being forces that fuel or direct the kinds of mental activities which result in learning and intellectual development. But it will never be easy to arrive at a detailed description of the ways in which the many different motivational influences that contribute to the development of a person actually operate. The events that can motivate achievements are numerous and sometimes unexpected: for instance there is abundant evidence from many sources that even personal loss can fuel creative advances (Albert, 1971). To complicate matters, motivational variables operate as both causes and effects. Yesterday's outcome can be today's cause, last week's metaphorical chicken producing today's egg, and today's egg becomes tomorrow's chicken. Moreover, intellectual and non-intellectual determinants can each influence and also be influenced by one another. The fact that they interact in complicated ways makes it impossible to examine their effects separately, and also makes it doubtful whether any kind of account in which the two are conceptually kept apart can do full justice to the complex states of affairs that actually occur. Scientists who have used broadly scientific approaches for investigating intellectual development have tended to neglect those influences on development that are not specifically intellectual. In view of the problems I have been discussing, it is not hard to see why. One additional source of difficulty is that whilst it may be not too difficult to demonstrate how needs and motives and personality variables may have contributed to the growth of the intellect in the life of any *individual* person, it is harder to see how it might be possible to formulate *general* principles that specify how people's needs are translated into human achievements. Here, as elsewhere, we are confronted with the sheer uniqueness of individuals.

The difficulties are daunting ones. A possible response to them is to concede that it may be unrealistic, at least for the present, to search for general rules and principles that underlie the operation of motivational influences and fall back on a strategy of gathering descriptive information which could be expected to yield the kinds of insights that were gained from examing Sir Richard Burton's early life. Such a strategy can at least provide hints and pointers concerning some of the the ways in which motivational influences can operate. But despite all the difficulties, abandoning the search for explanatory principles and becoming resigned to pursuing a purely descriptive and idiographic approach seems an unduly pessimistic and defeatist response. But there is no escaping the fact that the influences that have shaped one person's accomplishments are very different from those that have affected someone else.

## *Some unexpected Findings*

Although the mechanisms by which motivational and related determinants of success exert their effects have not been fully explored, their importance has long been recognized. Even the founder of eugenics, Darwin's cousin Francis Galton, appreciated this, despite his belief in the view that superior abilities are inherited. He acknowledged that renowned scholars also profit from being unusually energetic and dedicated in the pursuit of their interests, and exceptionally independent and purposeful as well. And Lewis Terman, following an investigation comparing the 150 most successful and the 150 least successful of his (intellectually) gifted subjects (Renzulli, 1986) in which he was eventually forced to conclude that the two groups did not differ to any extent in measured intelligence, found that the four traits on which the two groups were most different were of personality and temperament, and not intellectual ones at all. The four traits were: persistence in the accomplishment of ends, integration towards goals, self-confidence, and freedom from feelings of inferiority. Essentially, the reasons underlying the much greater success of the people in one group, compared with the other people, lay in their drive to achieve and their emotional and social adjustment. Although both groups were highly intelligent, differences in intellectual ability were not among the causes contributing to the two groups' differing degrees of success. This finding sharply contradicts a number of the beliefs which Terman had spent much of his life persuading other people to accept. The evidence, combined with the fact that humanly valued skills virtually never depend on just one intellectual competence, points to the conclusion that, in most spheres of human endeavour, an individual who lacks certain non-intellectual attributes will be very unlikely to be successful, however impressive that person's intellectual qualities.

How do characteristics of temperament and personality, and motivational state, work together to influence a person's capabilities? Rewards and incentives, and parental encouragement, were discussed at some length in chapters 4 and 5. It was evident there that the vast majority of extraordinarily capable young people have come from family backgrounds in which at least one parent or relative has gone to some lengths to make sure that the individual engaged in learning activities and gained some real benefit from doing so. But although the giving of rewards and encouragement goes some way towards helping to account for someone becoming unusually capable or knowledgeable, it does not seem to offer much assistance towards explaining how some people, but not others, acquire the relatively enduring traits of character that highly capable people need to depend on, such as persistence, single-mindedness, independence, a sense of direction, and the like. How do these qualities arise?

## *A Sense of Mastery*

One potentially fruitful approach starts with the assumption that people differ in the extent to which early learning teaches them that they can exert control over their own lives. Even in early childhood, learning activities may be influenced by the extent to which an individual experiences a sense of having some mastery over the environment. From infancy onwards, the fact that there are predictable outcomes to the individual's own actions contributes to the beginnings of an awareness that some control over events is possible. One psychologist, Martin Seligman, recorded some of his infant son's opportunities to perceive synchronies between responses and their outcomes:

He sucks, the world responds with warm milk. He pats the breast, his mother tenderly squeezes him back. He takes a break and coos, his mother coos back. He gives a happy chirp, his mother attempts to chirp back. Each step he takes is synchronized with a response from the world. (Seligman, 1975, p. 139)

As they get older most children discover that their own actions are influential in a gradually increasing range of circumstances: they learn that their activities have predictable results. But a child who does not regularly or reliably experience the kind of feedback that attentive caregivers usually provide may fail to learn that her actions have reliable consequences. This may be a consequence of parental neglect, or a result of having overprotective caregivers whose responses to the child take no account of the child's own actions. In the latter case a child may fail to experience regularities between her own actions and the events that follow them, not because the actions are ignored, but because the caregiver does not respond selectively, in ways that discriminate between different activities.

The claim is that children who are deprived of opportunities to experience regularities between their own actions and subsequent events will eventually differ markedly from others in the extent to which they perceive themselves as having control over important aspects of their lives. One young woman may come to believe that the important events in her life largely depend upon chance, fate, and the influence of other people, whereas another young woman learns to perceive that whatever happens to her depends to a considerable extent upon her own activities. Of course, because of the varying circumstances of their lives, people will differ in the extent to which each of these alternative perceptions is accurate. But it is certain that those who (whatever the reasons) perceive that they exert a considerable degree of control over their own destinies will be more likely than others to engage in the kinds of learning activities – especially ones that are time-consuming, prolonged, or stressful – from which substantial achievements are forged.

Although there is a plausible case for the existence of links between experiences of childhood and the acquisition of powers of independence and self-directedness that are characteristic of outstandingly successful adults, solid evidence is lacking. But various items of information are consistent with the suggestion that there do exist such links between childhood experiences and the characteristics of the mature person. Martin Seligman, who coined the term *learned helplessness* to describe the result of having a lack of experiences of control over one's own life, has drawn attention to findings from experiments on human and animal subjects which demonstrate that when an organism learns that it has no control over what happens to it, it becomes unusually passive and unresponsive, fails to learn, and does not acquire normal social behaviours. Seligman (1975) advanced the theory that learned helplessness contributes to a number of the symptoms of adult depression. He drew attention to a number of similarities between the withdrawn, isolated, and indecisive kinds of behaviours that are characteristic of depressed patients and the responses of animals in which learned helplessness had been induced by their being placed in circumstances in which their actions had no predictable outcomes.

The related concept of *locus of control* has been introduced in studies examining individual variability in the extent to which people believe that events which affect them are controlled by factors that are internal or external to the person (Rotter, 1975). People who tend to think that events depend to a considerable extent upon their own attributes (such as ability) or their behaviour are said to perceive control to be internal. People are regarded as perceiving events as being externally controlled if they believe them to be caused by factors beyond their control, such as fate, or luck, or other people's actions.

A child's (or an adult's) perceptions about locus of control may have a marked influence upon the individual's approach to the kinds of situations that challenge the individual to engage in learning and studying. Someone who thinks that the possibility of a successful outcome depends upon his or her own actions is likely to engage in appropriate study activities, and persist with them. An individual who believes that outcomes largely depend upon external factors will be much less likely to devote his or her full attention to the task.

Measures of individuals' perceptions of locus of control correlate positively with indications of people's success, for instance at school achievements, a fact which is clearly consistent with the view that perceived locus of control is an important influence. But we cannot take it for granted that this is the case, because it is conceivable that the correlations reflect the influence of a third factor on both achievement and perceived locus of control. In that event, there might not exist any cause-and-effect relationship between the two. Yet the findings of some experiments seem to indicate that perceptions of locus of control do affect individuals' achievements. For instance, in one study a number of classroom teachers followed detailed instructions that were designed to give young children greater responsibility for arranging their own learning and study activities. Subsequently, a marked improvement was seen in the children's performance at reading skills, with progress being greatest in those classrooms where the teachers were judged to have been most successful in following the instructions (Matheny and Edwards, 1974). Essentially similar findings have emerged from other studies in which children have been encouraged to take more control of their own studying routines (see Howe, 1984).

Alterations in young people's perceptions of locus of control appear to have had a key influence in a number of other situations in which sudden improvements in learning have been observed. One example is an American project in which high school students who were poor at reading were paid to teach young children who were also backward readers (Cloward, 1967). The experiment was a successful one so far as the young children's progress was concerned, but the most dramatic improvements occurred in the reading skills of their tutors. Over the seven-month period during which they participated in the study, tutoring the younger children for an average of four hours per week, the high school students' reading skill levels rose by an average of 3·4 years. That was twice the gain that took place during the same period in students who were allocated to a control condition. There are a number of possible reasons for the large improvement, but it seems more than likely that a shift towards feeling in greater control of reading activities was an important contributing factor.

Sheer self-confidence is a necessary element of success. It is, said the poet Alexander Pope, 'the first requisite to great undertakings'. Above all, it is important for a learner not to be frightened of failing. The very fear of failure forms a major obstacle to learning in the lives of many schoolchildren, largely because for those individuals who are fearful that their efforts will fail, the only sure way to avoid such a failure is not to try in the first place (Covington, 1986). Classroom failure can lead to reduced confidence and diminished self-esteem (Covington and Omelich, 1981).

## *When Guidance hinders Independence*

In an outstanding person, the complex qualities that are identified by words such as independence and self-directedness function both as outcomes and as causes, and take the form of bundles of attributes that are rather vaguely defined. Although a high degree of independence and self-directedness is probably vital if a person is to make a substantial individual achievement of any kind, the former qualities are not all-or-none ones. There is some room for people to vary, prior to the point being reached at which an individual must be judged as being sufficiently lacking in independence to make major achievements quite impossible.

The fact that one scientist does not have quite so strong a sense of direction as another does not entirely rule out the possibility of the former person's contributions being superior. Yet it is interesting to observe that those thinkers whose names immediately come to mind as being examples of individuals who, like Newton, Burton, Einstein, and Shaw, have been exceptionally independent-minded and self-directed (sometimes to the extent of appearing indifferent to events outside their own fields of special interest), have rarely come from families where the parents have maintained an intensive day-to-day supervision of the child's learning activities beyond early childhood. On the other hand those outstanding achievers whose parents did maintain very close control over their education into late childhood have quite often experienced some kind of crisis involving problems of identity or self-worth during adolescence or early adulthood (as John Ruskin, John Stuart Mill, and Norbert Wiener did, for instance) or, like William Sidis, failed to acquire the kind of self-motivated sense of purpose that would have enabled them to make productive use of their exceptional abilities.

It can never be taken for granted that someone who gains exceptional abilities as a result of close parental guidance and supervision throughout childhood will also acquire either the intellectual independence or the self-determined sense of direction that motivates a person to create major achievements. In sharp contrast with highly successful individuals like Einstein and Newton, in whom, as we have seen, inner-directed motives had the intense strength of ruling passions, are young people like the unquestionably brilliant 16-year-old doctoral student whose response to an interviewer's questions I quote below.

> Asked 'Do you have great ambitions? Would you like to contribute something that's really important?' Susan told us: 'Not really. I guess it would be nice, but I don't really want to spend the rest of my life chasing after the hope that I can make a great contribution ... my main goal in life is just to get married and have children.' (Walmsley and Margolis, 1987, p. 64).

It is safe to predict that no new Einstein is in the making here, for all this girl's exceptional intellectual skills.

## *Temperament and cognitive Style*

In his book *Advice to a Young Scientist* (1979), Sir Peter Medawar observes that scientists come in a variety of different temperaments. He categorizes some of them as collectors, classifiers and compulsive tidiers-up, detectives and explorers, artists and artisans, poet-scientists and philosopher-scientists. He even suggests that there are also some 'mystic-scientists'. Medawar is drawing attention to the fact that there exist different styles of intellectual working. He maintains that the preferred style of a particular individual helps determine the kind of contribution to which he or she is best suited.

A number of researchers have looked at the effects on task performance of what they call *cognitive style*. A person's characteristic cognitive style bears the imprint of a number of different factors, some of them purely intellectual, such as mental skills and knowledge, and others reflecting various aspects of the individual's temperament, attitude, and personality. We have already seen, in chapter 2, that even in infancy and early childhood, what an individual learns will often be affected by attributes of temperament (impulsivity, for instance, and cuddliness). Throughout life, differences between people in their cognitive styles, and in the manner in which they approach intellectual tasks, challenges, and opportunities, continue to act as major influences which help determine people's different patterns of achievements.

Of course, different spheres of intellectual achievement can demand very different kinds of thinking. Murdo Macdonald (1985) draws attention to the alternative approaches to meaning that are associated with different activities. One dimension involves the number of possible interpretations that result from mental work. Science, for instance, typically involves analytic activities, and there is usually only one correct solution of problems. In art, by contrast, ambiguity is typical, and multiple interpretations are usually possible. Another dimension along which thinking varies is that of reversibility. In certain intellectual accomplishments there is an irreversible order of events, as in novels, games such as chess, biographies, and studies of developments. In others, however, such as plastic art and design, and some forms of physics, there is multi-directionality and potential reversibility. A third dimension concerns relationships. With some activities, such as history and mythology, resemblance to some external event is an important element, whereas with others, such as music, games, and mathematics, relations are formal and internal, and resemblance to external things may be non-existent or irrelevant.

There has been very little systematic investigation of the outcomes of cognitive style differences as an influence on outstanding achievements. But their influence can be crucial. For instance, consider the effects of individual differences in 'reflection-impulsivity', a dimension which describes people's performance in situations where there is a trade-off between speed and accuracy (Baron, Badgio, and Gaskins, 1986). In many thinking and problem-solving tasks, a 'reflective' person, who is careful and takes time to make a decision, will make fewer errors than an 'impulsive' individual, who responds as quickly as possible.

Consequently, in those intellectual tasks in which it is important to avoid errors an individual who is habitually reflective will do better than someone who is more impulsive. On the other hand, in certain situations an impulsive individual would be more effective. For instance, in a society that depended on hunting skills someone who was overly reflective would be less effective than an individual who could act quickly and decisively.

# 7
# The Contribution of Intelligence towards Explaining High Abilities

Although particular intellectual abilities can operate with a degree of autonomy it is often found that people who are above average in one area of competence are superior in other spheres as well. There are a number of words that we commonly introduce to describe someone who does well at a each of a variety of tasks that demand intellectual expertise. Among them are, sharp, clever, smart, perceptive, adaptive, quick, astute, shrewd, wise, acute, canny, and intelligent. Of all these terms, 'intelligent' is the one that is most frequently used by psychologists and educators.

As a descriptive term, the word 'intelligent' is unquestionably valuable. It is often helpful to have an indication of someone's overall ability at a range of skills. And it is especially useful to have the use of practical tests that have been devised in order to assess the degree to which different people are capable of acting intelligently, compared with others. Such tests, which provide a kind of general measure of intellectual performance, serve a number of practical functions. Because they assess how well someone performs at a number of different tasks, the scores they yield can be used to predict how well a person is likely to do in the future, when dealing with new problems that make demands on a person's intellectual competence. For instance, a child's intelligence test score may give a helpful indication of the likelihood of that child succeeding at the kinds of challenges that are to be encountered in the school classroom, or an adult's score may be useful for helping potential employers to predict how the individual will cope with the demands of a new job.

So the concept of intelligence has definite practical value. Perhaps it can also contribute by aiding our efforts to account for human abilities, including exceptional ones. There is the possibility that it can provide some kind of unifying conceptual framework, so that instead of our being restricted to thinking in terms of single abilities it may be more realistic to assume that there is some kind of unifying general intellectual capacity that people possess to varying degrees. Indeed, intelligence is often regarded as being an underlying essence or quality which permeates different abilities, and constrains or controls a person's various capabilities.

In the commonsense psychology of everyday life the assertion that above-average intelligence is the cause of high achievements is rarely questioned: few teachers would raise any objection to the statement that 'she did well at school because she was intelligent'. Yet the statement 'she was intelligent because she did well at school' would be seen as much less acceptable. Why? The reason is that in the psychological thinking that ordinary people engage in as part of their everday lives it is widely accepted that the word 'intelligence' does refer to something that is not simply more general than specific abilities, but also more fundamental. Implicit in the way the word is often used, both in everyday life and in academic and scientific contexts, is the assumption that intelligence is some kind of underlying aptitude, which is largely unchangeable, and constrains people's achievements.

So, if intelligence is some kind of unifying intellectual capacity, and assuming that it is possible to measure how much intelligence each individual possesses, the concept of intelligence would seem to offer an economical scaffolding for structuring our knowledge of the origins of abilities. Rather than having to explain the causes of each of a person's different capabilities, it may be possible to account for abilities more satisfactorily by relating them to some broader and more fundamental quality that underlies them all. Making the concept of intelligence a crucial element in explanatory accounts of intellectual abilities appears to be a promising way of making this possible.

It is therefore hardly surprising that intelligence has been given a central role in many discussions of the causes of individual variability in intellectual competence. Intelligence is widely regarded as the source of mental skills and abilities. It is thought to have functional unity, enabling different abilities to work together. Knowledge of the nature of human intelligence is seen as an essential key to the understanding of particular abilities, which, according to this kind of account, are constrained by a person's level of general intelligence, and to some extent controlled by it. There seem, therefore, to be good grounds for believing that an effective strategy for discovering the origins of superior accomplishments is to explore the nature and origins of human intelligence.

As we shall see later, a closer examination of the conceptual status of intelligence reveals reasons for concluding that such a view may be unduly optimistic, and that at least some of the ways in which the concept is commonly used are not strictly valid and make no genuine contribution to the understanding of abilities. But there is no denying that uses of the construct of intelligence that are solely descriptive can be extremely useful, especially in conjunction with the practical measures of individuals' intelligence levels that are provided by intelligence test scores.

## Intelligence Tests: Descriptive Uses of the Concept

Broadly speaking, current tests of intelligence have evolved from tests that were constructed for straightforwardly pragmatic considerations. The purpose of the first intelligence test was to identify schoolchildren who lacked abilities needed for benefiting from the classroom teaching that was offered in (French) schools. Sensibly, the choice of items was made on the basis of their suitability for sampling skills and abilities necessary for succeeding at classroom learning situations. With that in mind, some of the items initially chosen were ones that had been suggested by teachers. Since the original tests were devised by Alfred Binet at the beginning of this century, there have been many changes, but these have often been minor ones, partly because one of the criteria adopted for choosing revised tests or new items had been their effectiveness at yielding patterns of scores similar to those produced by items already in use.

How effective are the tests? That partly depends upon what they are being used for. Intelligence-test scores enable reasonably accurate predictions to be made concerning how well a child will do at school. The tests are also useful for predicting how adults will perform at tasks that are broadly similar to ones encountered in schools. But intelligence tests are less effective for predicting someone's performance at practical and everyday tasks, even intellectual ones, that are encountered outside educational institutions. The only major exceptions to that generalization occur when the achievement of a certain degree of educational success is used by those who regulate jobs or professions as a necessary credential for entry. In these instances educational achievement (which *is* closely related to measured intelligence) forms a hurdle or barrier that has to be overcome in order that someone should qualify for opportunities for advancement, or have access to training.

The evidence firmly points to the conclusion that the majority of skills needed in order to do well at jobs in the real world are only weakly related to those abilities that are assessed in intelligence tests (Weinert and Waldmann, 1986). The fact that entry requirements are often based on educational achievements inflates the magnitude of relationships between intelligence-test performance and success in non-school areas of achievement. When this source of distortion is removed, correlations between a person's test scores and the same individual's success at skills required at work and in other contexts of everyday life tend to be very low, and sometimes zero. When positive correlations do still remain after corrections have been made to remove the above source of distortion, they are rarely sufficiently large to account for more than around ten per cent of the variability between individuals in their level of performance at job or everyday skills.

Even without making adjustments to compensate for the confounding influence of amount of schooling, correlations between tested intelligence and job effectiveness are rather modest, typically between $r = \cdot 2$ and $r = \cdot 4$ (Ghiselli, 1966; McClelland, 1973). Correlations of this magnitude are too low to form a basis for making accurate predictions about individuals' chances of vocational success. Klemp and McClelland (1986), who carefully watched senior managers actually performing their work, concluded that the intellectual abilities required for managerial success are very different from the skills that intelligence tests measure. Of course, intellectual abilities are also required by people doing non-managerial jobs. For instance, employees as diverse as warehouse workers, product assemblers and delivery drivers, all make use of a variety of intricate mental strategies. But these, too, are largely unrelated to intelligence test scores (Scribner, 1986). The same is true of the abilities needed for adjustment to military life (Zigler and Seitz, 1982).

At first glance, IQ scores seem to be good predictors of economic and social success. Correlations between a man's childhood IQ and his success as an adult are as high as $r = \cdot 8$ in some investigations, although other studies have found considerably lower correlations, in the region of $r = \cdot 5$, between IQ in adolescence and occupational status in late adulthood (Rutter, 1989). But these correlations turn out to be largely the result of other causes, such as schooling and family background. Amongst men with average IQs, those from the highest socioeconomic classes are more than seven times more likely to receive high incomes than men from the poorest families. Also, men having an average IQ whose years of schooling are exceeded by no more than 10 per cent of the population are over ten times as likely to be in the highest income group as men who are in the lowest 10 per cent of the population in the number of years of schooling they have received. If schooling and socioeconomic background are held constant, the proportion of the variation between people that is predicted by variations in IQ becomes negligible (S. Bowles and V. Nelson, reported in Lewontin, 1982).

Stephen Ceci and Charles Henderson (See Ceci, 1990) recently conducted a similar analysis in a study which was like the above one but examined individuals who varied widely in their intelligence-test scores. These authors regressed adults' earnings on their high school IQ scores, whilst controlling both the number of years of schooling and the childhood family background. Their findings, like the ones reported for men of average IQ levels, clearly indicate that variations in adult income are not related to difference in high school IQ. The variables that *are* important predictors of adult income are the number of years of schooling and the social background of the family.

In other words, the predictive value of IQ scores as such, when schooling and social class are controlled, is considerably less than the predictive value of the other two, when IQ is controlled. As it happens, there are other attributes which are only weakly related to IQ but which are considerably better predictors of adult success than IQ scores. One is competence at making sensible plans during late adolescence (J. A. Clausen, 1986, cited by Rutter, 1989). Also, as I mentioned in chapter 6, indications of childhood temperament are at least equally good predictors of adult success as are measures of childhood intelligence.

## *Intelligence Tests and superior Abilities*

How effective are intelligence tests for making predictions that involve discriminating between highly able people? Can such tests predict which individuals amongst a number of capable ones will produce the most exceptional achievements? On the whole intelligence tests have a rather poor record in this area. As I mentioned in the previous chapter, in one of Lewis Terman's investigations he compared the 150 most successful and the 150 least successful of his (intellectually) gifted subjects (Renzulli, 1986). Contrary to his expectations he found that the two groups did not differ in measured intelligence. Differences in their measured intelligence were not among the causes contributing to the two groups' differing degrees of success.

That finding seems to contradict beliefs which Terman spent much of his life persuading people to accept. Worse still, the apparent confirmation of the predictive value of IQ scores that was apparently provided by Terman's earlier finding (that the children identified as being intelligent in his California study did particularly well in adulthood) proved illusory. It was undermined by the discovery that the children he initially identified as being superior, partly on the basis of their intelligence-test scores, were actually no more successful in their later lives than individuals taken at random from children with similar family backgrounds (Sorokin, 1957; Ceci, 1990). And in addition to the finding that measured intelligence in childhood did not contribute to predicting which of the individuals in the California study would be most successful in later life, it also emerged that those of the individuals in his large-scale study who were eventually the least successful did not differ from the others in their childhood IQ scores (Howe, 1982; Elder, 1988; Elder, Hastings and Pavalko, 1989).

## *Conclusion*

Although intelligence tests can undoubtedly be useful, it is clear that they are very far from being perfect predictors of the kinds of skills and achievements that are important in real life. And such test are especially ineffective at making predictions that concern the achievements of individuals who are highly able. It is important to be aware of the limitations in the predictive value of intelligence tests, because otherwise we may err by attaching too much importance to test scores. This can easily happen. For instance, in evaluations of the effectiveness of a number of Headstart compensatory education progammes in the United States, gains in IQ scores were regared as a major criterion of the programmes' success (Lazar, Darlington, Murray, Royce and Snipper, 1982; Ramey, Bryant and Suarez, 1985). This had a number of negative consequences, and probably resulted in insufficient attention being paid to the effectiveness of the programmes at achieving genuinely useful outcomes. Using IQ scores to assess the extent to which an intervention increases the skills that children really do need is rather like having a plan to increase the output of a coal mine evaluated with a rating scale that was designed to measure the productivity of shipping companies. In both cases, the outcome is that the qualities that are actually assessed are not the ones that it is most important to measure.

## *Intelligence as an Explanatory Construct: some Problems*

There is nothing about the construction and use of intelligence tests that implies that the concept of intelligence must have a status that is other than a merely descriptive one. Strictly speaking, although someone may be described as being intelligent on the basis of their test score, all that has really been achieved is to specify how that person performed at a test.

Yet the majority of users of the word 'intelligence' in psychology would not agree that its only legitimate uses are descriptive ones. They would argue (or implicitly believe) that indications of a person's intelligence can help to explain abilities. Very frequently, when the word 'intelligence' appears in the context of psychological research it is quite clear that its use is intended to be explanatory. The concept is assumed to have functions that contribute to our understanding. In most cases, someone who describes a person as being intelligent is not just talking about what they can do but also identifying a quality which that person is thought to possess.

Few psychologists would admit to regarding intelligence as a concrete or tangible entity. But most applications of the term imply a belief by the user that the concept is more than just a descriptive construct. For example, psychologists and educators frequently describe intelligence as being central to, or giving rise to, or being necessary for, or the cause of, or at the root of or the heart of, or basic or fundamental to, or 'underlying' specific abilities. Or they may say that certain skills 'depend upon' or 'require' or 'demand' a degree of intelligence. The use of any of these words or phrases carries with it the implication that intelligence functions as a cause, and hence an explanation, of certain abilities that are present. If the concept of intelligence is to be given the central explanatory role in attempts to understand causes of individual variability that was suggested at the beginning of the chapter, whereby a person's level of general intelligence is seen as constraining and controlling specific abilities, it is first necessary to establish that the word intelligence, as introduced by psychologists, really does have the status of an explanatory construct. It cannot be taken for granted that this is the case.

Is the concept of intelligence a genuinely explanatory one, or are its legitimate uses restricted to descriptive ones? A possible response, if a naïve one, is to say that the very question is absurd. The folklore of our culture tells us that intelligence is a real entity, and a quality that plays a fundamental role in determining what we can do.

But, as we noted in chapter 2, in connection with qualities such as talents and gifts, words can mislead. We can easily make the error of reifying, and assume that the sheer existence of the word intelligence provides grounds for our inferring that an underlying quality also exists. In the case of intelligence, the difficulty we experience in deciding whether or not a particular use of the term involves an invalid reification is increased by the very familiarity of the term. Intelligence is a word people use often in their non-scientific, everyday psychological thinking. It is something very real for most people. It refers to qualities that have an important place in people's feelings about themselves. When we are thinking about the concept of intelligence, however scientific and logical we try to be, the fact that the term has connotations that are hard to separate from thoughts and feelings which surround the word makes this difficult.

We may also fail to make a distinction between descriptive and explanatory concepts, and wrongly believe that a word which describes something will also explain it. And we may fail to recognize that a strong conviction that something exists compensates for a lack of evidence that it actually does. In reality, the firm view that intelligence must exist as a real quality could eventually turn out to be comparable to the convictions of those millions of individuals throughout the ages who have been certain of the powers of stone idols or evil spirits, or the scientists in the past who were certain of the existence of phlogiston, or firmly believed that people's temperaments depended on the four humours.

Distinguishing between explanatory and descriptive constructs can be especially difficult when their nature is psychological. It is often easy to detect that non-psychological constructs are being misused. For instance, if descriptive words such as 'productive' or 'successful' appear in contexts that indicate that an explanation is being intended, as in

> My factory produces more goods than yours because it is more productive,

or

> She is doing well because she is successful,

it is clear that despite the presence of the word 'because' nothing is really being explained in either case. The circularity of what is being expressed is transparent: it is easy to see that there is a kind of verbal sleight of hand. But with a sentence such as

> He found the problem easy because he is intelligent,

the assumption that something is being explained would usually go unquestioned. It is implicitly assumed that the word 'intelligent', unlike 'productive' and 'successful', can serve the function of explaining things.

I am not denying the possibility that the concept of intelligence *may* be a genuinely explanatory one. My purpose is simply to draw attention to the tendency of users of the word to make the assumption that it must be, in the absence of any evidence that it actually is. If the construct is to play a role in attempts to explain human abilities it is essential to begin by establishing that it is more than just a descriptive term. Otherwise, saying 'she did well because she is intelligent' would only be equivalent to saying 'she did well because she is the kind of person who does well.' In other words, what appears to be an explanation would be simple a rephrasing, like Molière's remark that a sleeping potion makes people sleep because of its dormative properties (Olson, 1986; see also Stott, 1974; Keating, 1984; Bynner and Romney, 1986; Horn, 1986; Howe, 1988a; 1988b; 1989c).

It is important to be clear about the status of the concept of intelligence. If it is true that intelligence takes the form of some quality – perhaps of mental capacity, or mental power, or mental speed – that enters into and is necessary for particular intellectual abilities, it follows that an understanding of intelligence is essential if we are to be able to explain how exceptional abilities arise. And if that is true, it is equally important to know about the influences that affect intelligence, and about the ways in which it can contribute to a person's different abilities, and the ways in which it might be possible to increase someone's intelligence. In that event, knowledge about intelligence and the factors that affect it will also be crucial for the success of any practical efforts to promote or accelerate exceptional abilities.

Yet if these beliefs about the nature and function of intelligence are untrue, none of the above implications follow. In that case it would make sense for researchers to attend to the specific causes of particular abilities, without being greatly concerned with issues and questions about general intelligence. Specific abilities may be independent of any essence or quality of general ability and also largely independent of other abilities, except in certain specifiable circumstances (such as situations in which two abilities draw upon common component skills, or depend upon knowledge that is common to both abilities). Some reasons for suspecting that to be the case were given in chapter 2, where it was observed that in a number of investigations 'ordinary' people could, with sufficient training, gain skills that had been thought to be only accessible to individuals who are inherently exceptional. It was also reported then that these skills, when acquired, are remarkably specific, and do not readily generalize or transfer to different tasks. These findings clearly offer some support for the view that different human abilities are, to a considerable extent, independent and autonomous.

## Can the Concept of Intelligence help to Explain Abilities?

What has been established in the above section is that we cannot assume, on logical or conceptual grounds alone, that the construct of intelligence refers to a quality that contributes to human abilities or helps account for them. It cannot be taken for granted that it is legitimate to use the concept other than as a word merely to describe people and their capabilities. But science is replete with constructs which, like intelligence, are abstract and unobservable but nevertheless play a vital part in helping us understand the operations of the physical world. Neither the fact that intelligence is not an observable physical 'thing', nor the fact that there is no logical necessity for it to be a valid explanatory concept, rules out the possibility that it is such a concept. To establish whether or not intelligence does exist as a quality that contributes to explaining high abilities it is necessary to examine substantive evidence. We can then ask, 'what is the evidence for the existence of intelligence as a causal quality?'

## Defining Intelligence

Before we can do that we need to be precise about what is meant by term intelligence. In other words, the concept needs to be carefully defined. It is essential to have agreement about the meaning of any concept that is to be used in scientific investigations, and to have clear rules about the ways in which it can be observed and measured. In the physical sciences this preliminary step would not be expected to present major problems. However, defining intelligence satisfactorily is another matter, and raises difficulties which have never been resolved.

It is not that definitions of intelligence have not been forthcoming. The question 'What is intelligence?' has been debated many times, and numerous psychologists have been happy to provide definitions for the term. For example, the word has been defined variously as the ability to learn, to profit from experience, to perceive relationships, to find novel solutions, to think abstractly, to make judgements, to engage in complex reasoning, to inhibit an instinctive response and redefine it in the light of imaginally experienced trial and error, to adapt or adjust to a new environment, to gain and use knowledge, to produce correct responses, to think quickly, and so on. It is hard to resist the suspicion that when different psychologists have tried to provide definitions, the particular traits or abilities each has stressed are largely those which that individual particularly values.

The problem is not that people cannot define the concept but that their definitions are so different. Despite the fact that most of the definitions that have been offered are somewhat vague, it have proved impossible to agree on any one universally accepted meaning of intelligence. That failure ought to ring some alarm bells: if people cannot agree about what intelligence actually is, and if, in consequence, the term means different things to different people, the scientific validity of the concept has to be questionable. Another problem is that whilst it is evident that the ways in which the word 'intelligence' is typically used imply a belief on the part of those who introduce the term that it is not just a descriptive concept but also a 'scientific' one (Eysenck, 1988), few users are at all specific concerning their views about its actual conceptual status.

So far as its promise for furthering scientific progress towards increased understanding is concerned, a concept for which there is no agreement by its users concerning what it actually *is* must cause concern (even if there have been some instances in which ill-defined concepts have contributed towards scientific progress). Matters are made worse by the fact that when psychologists have tried to measure intelligence, no effort has been made to ensure that what is actually measured corresponds to any one definition of the term. Makers of intelligence tests have ignored the convention that if you want to measure something you start by specifying what it is. The obvious procedure of deciding what exactly it is that one wants to measure, and then, on the basis of what has been decided, proceeding to measure it, has not been followed.

Consequently, tests that measure intelligence bear no clear connection to any definition of intelligence. So there is no way of telling what kind of relationship, if there is any, exists between the 'meaning' of intelligence and the scores and ratings (such as IQ scores) that are assigned to people on the basis of their performance at intelligence tests. We cannot even assume that someone who gets a higher score than another person on such a test is, in any sense of the word that corresponds to our efforts to define it, more 'intelligent' than the other person. All that we can legitimately say is that the first individual has had more success at a test which its makers have decided to call an intelligence test, for largely arbitrary reasons that have little to do with either definitions or specifications or logic. And even the assumption that intelligence is a unitary capacity has been seriously challenged (Horn, 1986; see also Anastasi, 1967).

# The Evidence for Intelligence as an Explanatory Construct

What is the actual evidence that there exists some general quality of intelligence which is fundamental to a variety of accomplishments? In examining the evidence, it is obviously important to avoid taking for granted right at the outset of our discussion that any particular answer to the question at issue is the correct one. To prevent this, it may be useful to make the fictitious assumption that until just recently it has never occurred to anyone that underlying people's intellectual abilities there might exist some quality or entity of intelligence. Imagine that until now it has always been believed that separate abilities are largely independent and autonomous, but that someone is now proposing, for the first time, that there might exist a hitherto undiscovered quality, which they have chosen to call 'intelligence'. The new claim is that this entity is real and not illusory, and that it takes the form of a quality that somehow affects individuals' intellectual abilities, possibly by influencing the power, speed, or flexibility of mental processing operations. And it had just been suggested, again for the first time, that this underlying quality of intelligence which we are being asked to believe in also influences our capacity to succeed at a range of intellectual tasks and problems. It is argued by those who claim to have discovered it, that the concept of intelligence will help us to understand the nature and origins of intellectual abilities, including exceptional ones.

Essentially, the question I am asking is, 'if the concept of intelligence (as an explanatory construct) did not presently exist in our minds, would our efforts to explain the causes of abilities be aided by inventing (or 'discovering') it?' Can it make a positive contribution to our efforts to increase our understanding of the nature and origins of the differences between people in their abilities?

## 1 Correlations in Scores

Traditionally, an important reason for believing that intelligence is in some respect a 'real' entity, and more then just a descriptive construct, is that there appears to be something in common between whatever determines a person's level of performance at one intellectual task and whatever influences affect the same person's performance at other intellectual tasks. The justification for this assertion lies in the fact that if a number of people are each given a battery of intellectual tests the scores of a person at the different tests will usually be correlated. In other words, someone who does well at one test that measures intellectual abilities will tend to do well at other tests. Conversely, a person who performs poorly at any one test will tend to be below average at the other tests as well.

Because of these commonalities, it is not unreasonable to propose that there may be some quality that is common to someone's ability to do each of a number of different tasks. Clearly, if that were the case, it would help explain the observed correlations. And if it is true that there is some quality that affects each of a range of different tasks, it also seems reasonable to call that quality 'intelligence', to claim that intelligence has a fundamental role in intellectual abilities, and to argue that differences between people in the degree to which they succeed at mental tasks reflect individual differences in intelligence.

If substantial numbers of tests are administered, and correlations between the scores people obtain at them are calculated, it will usually be found that there are stronger relationships between some pairs of test scores than others. For reasons related to this, by making use of the algebraic technique of factor analysis it is possible to focus on various kinds of patterns that can be discerned in the scores. In particular, it is possible to derive an algebraic factor known as the first principal component, which is a kind of mathematical abstraction reflecting the fact that when all the scores are considered together, not only are there correlations between pairs of sub-test scores but there is a general tendency for the many scores to correlate with one another. The first principal component can be regarded as an index of the average inter-correlation among the various test scores.

In the case of the various sub-tests that contribute to a test of intelligence, because there are positive correlations between the scores, a moderately large (·3 or so) first principal component can usually be derived. When Charles Spearman first applied factor analysis to psychological test data at the beginning of the present century, he decided on the term '$g$' (to represent general intelligence) as a label to designate the factor which emerges as the first principal component when factor analysis is undertaken on matrices of correlations among mental tests. Each entry in the matrix is a correlation coefficient between scores of a large number of individuals on each of two tests. Subsequent researchers have followed this practice.

Spearman then went a step further. Instead of just assuming that $g$ is essentially no more then a way of drawing attention to whatever is in common to different test scores, Spearman claimed that $g$ formed some kind of unitary quality that underlies intellectual ability. That is, he regarded $g$ as being a causal entity. He saw it, not simply as a way of *describing* the tendency of scores to correlate, but as the underlying *source* of the correlations in performance at the tests, and the *reason* for them.

Over the past 80-odd years there has been much debate about the legitimacy of various interpretations of the information yielded by techniques based on factor analysis. It is now generally agreed that whilst such data can provide useful indications of patterns or regularities in test scores, and may provide hints that complement additional kinds of evidence concerning possible underlying structures and processes, the kinds of correlational data that emerge from factor analysis can never, on their own, be sufficient to identify the actual causes of whatever patterns or tendencies are detected. The fact that it is possible to derive $g$ is no basis for concluding that $g$ must be either a physical quality or an entity that can be regarded as being the source or cause of mental abilities.

In the 1930s there were intensive debates concerning which of a number of alternative ways of describing a set of scores in terms of factors was the correct one. In fact, it is partly a matter of preference. Factor analysis is not an entirely automatic process. At one point the investigator has to decide on what kind of patterning might be present in the data, and then initiate procedures that will ascertain whether or not it actually is. Even if it is, that does not rule out the possibility that other kinds of patterns might have been discerned had one looked for them instead. So the same data can be made to yield different factors. In that respect the procedure is rather like looking at the patterning in a piece of wallpaper. It may be possible to see the decorations as being formed from diagonal connections between shapes, or alternatively, horizontal ones, or vertical ones.

But even if the existence of correlations in scores obtained at tests of mental abilities does not permit us to infer that they provide evidence of some common cause ('$g$', or 'general intelligence') it is still true that there must be a reason for the correlations being present. If they do not reflect the influence of some common underlying cause, how otherwise can we account for them?

That may not be such a hard question to answer as it seems to be. Correlational techniques, including factor-analytic ones, depend upon comparisons that are made between two measures (or scores) at a time. If something that affects one of that pair of measures also affects the other measure, then, other things being equal, a positive correlation will be obtained when a number of such pairs are examined. But the fact that a correlation is found does not justify the inference that whatever underlies the similarity between one pair or measures is the same as whatever underlies the similarity between the other pair of measures: there is simply no way of telling. And the influences that have led to some of the pairs of scores being similar may be different from the influences that have produced similarities between other pairs of scores. For this reason, the fact that a statistically defined $g$ can be derived cannot be regarded as evidence for the existence of $g$ in any substantive, non-statistical sense. That is to say, it is not necessarily true that $g$ represents any unitary psychological (or physiological) process or quality.

So the existence of $g$ cannot be taken to imply that there must be any single quality or resource that runs through all of the contributing scores: all that is necessary for a statistical $g$ to emerge is that the different sub-tests in a test battery each sample one or more of the microlevel cognitive resources that contribute to at least one sub-test score. This situation can easily arise. As Stephen Ceci explains, one could imagine that a battery of three tests is administered (arithmetic, vocabulary, and spatial reasoning) to children and that their scores are factor analysed and $g$ is extracted. Suppose that the arithmetic performance depends on three microlevel cognitive components, $a$, $b$, and $c$. Now suppose, too, that the two other tests (vocabulary and spatial reasoning) also sample some, but not all, of these same microlevel cognitive components, in addition to some components that are highly specific to themselves. It is possible that scores at each of the three tests are correlated, but for different reasons. Consequently, Ceci points out, '$g$ could end up being substantial in magnitude without actually representing a single source of processing variance that is common to each of these three tasks' (Ceci, 1990). Moreover,

> If we replaced this example with a more realistic one, involving dozens of microlevel cognitive components, differentially sampled by various macro-level tasks, then the possibility for a series of partially shared components that give rise to $g$ in the absence of a single pervasively shared cognitive resource becomes not so far-fetched. Exploratory factor analysis by itself cannot elucidate such possibilities, as any resultant structure (simplex or otherwise) can be retrofit by positing a particular sampling galaxy. So we end up with a technique (factor analysis) that gives rise to a 'general' factor that may or may not represent a singular underlying entity, and then we are told that this general factor is correlated with IQ, and finally, that the latter (IQ) is its validation as a truly general factor! As Detterman (1982) points out, this type of reasoning is circular, at best. (Ceci, 1990, p. 110)

However complex or sophisticated the techniques of factor analysis that are followed, there are limits to the extent to which they can reveal information that did not initially enter into the analysis. Essentially, the techniques are 'blind' to the causes that account for the magnitude of the scores that are entered into the analysis, and there is little that subsequent manipulations can do to tease out such information. To expect otherwise is rather like expecting a machine that has been programmed to detect when a switch has been turned on or off to also say *who* was responsible for moving the switch. Knowledge about the patterns of correlations that are found in a large body of data can sometimes provide hints about the possible reasons for those correlations. Such hints can be helpful when used in conjunction with other kinds of evidence, but on their own, neither factor analysis nor other correlational techniques can ever generate conclusive information about underlying causes.

What might lead to scores being correlated? There are a large number of influences, any of which, either on their own or in combination with other influences, can jointly affect performance at more than one of the different sub-tests that are encountered in a test of intelligence, and therefore produce the correlations that are observed in the scores. First, it often happens that two ostensibly different tasks share elements in common. There are two main reasons for this. One is that different tasks draw upon the same knowledge; the other is that two tasks may draw upon the same mental skill. For instance, performance on a substantial number of sub-tests may be affected by reading ability or by related decoding processes. Both the specific skills and the knowledge of letters and words that a good reader possesses may contribute to someone's performance at more than one of the different problems that comprise a test battery. Whenever this is the case it will have the effect of producing correlations between the scores at the different sub-tests. It would be possible to rule out the possibility that observed correlations are caused by different tasks drawing upon the same knowledge or the same skills if one could be quite sure that the tasks did not do so. But in practice, with many of the questions that have been posed in tests of intelligence it is not at all possible to be sure of this.

There is another group of influences that jointly affect performance at more than one of the different items in a test battery, thereby producing the correlations between sub-test scores that enable a general factor to be derived. These take the form of a large number of personal traits and characteristics that are likely to have similar effects upon someone's performance at more than one test item. Many of these causes of similarities in scores are more closely related to mood, temperament or personality than to specifically cognitive attributes. For example, if a person's performance at a test is affected, as it can be, by that individual's degree of enthusiasm, or attentiveness, or ability to concentrate, or test-wiseness, or patience, or self-confidence, or doggedness, or competitiveness, or even by transitory influences such as fatigue, the effects of such influences will not be restricted to one particular item. On the contrary, these influences are much more likely to have similar effects on a number of different items. And when they do, the outcome, as in any situation where a particular source of influence affects performance at each of a number of tasks, will be to produce correlations between the performance scores at the different tasks. So these influences may well lead to states of affairs in which application of factor analysis to data obtained by giving intelligence tests to a number of individuals will result in a substantial first principal component being derived.

Is it possible to find a way round these difficulties? Can we still claim that there is some quality of intelligence which is a cause of differences between people in their ability to perform cognitive tasks? There is one approach that might seem promising. It is to admit that the correlations which emerge are caused by some combination of the various potential influences that I have mentioned, and to propose that we simply include all of them within a definition of intelligence. In other words, anything – whatever it is – that affects performance at the questions included in intelligence tests is defined as being an aspect of intelligence.

Such an approach has its attractions, but it has a fatal flaw. If we accept that anything that affects someone's score in a test is 'intelligence', thereby implicitly defining intelligence as everything that influences an intelligence test score, we are effectively retreating to a purely descriptive usage of the concept. The reason why this is so is made apparent by raising the question of what would be meant (if the above definition is accepted) by the phrase "because she is more intelligent" when used in an (apparently) explanatory statement. In these circumstances, "because she is more intelligent" would simply mean "because she possessed whatever qualities or attributes increase a person's level of performance at an intelligence test". Here it is clear that all that is being said is that the reason for a person's performance is that the person possesses the necessary qualities. Nothing is being done towards specifying what those qualities actually are.

## 2 Correlations with Performance at basic Tasks

The second kind of evidence which has been regarded as providing grounds for believing that intelligence can be said to be a source or cause of human abilities, in which event it would be permissible to regard the concept of intelligence as being an explanatory one, and not merely descriptive, also takes the form of correlations. But in this case the important correlations are not between different scores *within* an intelligence test, but *between* test scores and indicators of performance at very simple tasks that have been designed to provide measures of either (a) basic cognitive mechanisms that are thought to provide the elements or components of intellectual skills or (b) physiological processes that are regarded as underlying human cognition.

In either case, the essential argument is that if intelligence test scores are found to be highly correlated with measures of fundamental processes that underlie the effectiveness of a person's cognitive operations, then an intelligence test can be said to be providing a measure of something that is 'real', in the sense of being basic or fundamental to intellectual abilities. For example, imagine that it has been found that (1) people differ in the speed at which certain brain mechanisms are capable of transmitting information, and that (2) a task has been devised which successfully measures this rate in individuals, and also that (3) intelligence test scores are highly correlated with measures of the rate of information transmission in the brain. It would then be possible to argue that because intelligence test scores provided an accurate indication of a process that was basic to cognition, and also accounted for differences between people in the efficiency of their cognitive operations, the test scores could be said to provide an indication of some processes that are basic to cognition, ones that are at the root of individual differences in intellectual ability. In that event, it would be correct to say that indications of measured intelligence achieve the function of helping to explain, as well as describe, differences in ability. By describing someone as being highly intelligent, one would be identifying that person as being someone who was able to out-perform other individuals, quite possibly as a result of possessing a brain which transmitted information with above-average rapidity.

Some researchers have claimed that evidence meeting the above conditions (1), (2), and (3) has been obtained. In a number of published research studies it has been reported that there have been substantial correlations (of around +·8 or even higher) between overall measures of tested intelligence, on the one hand, and on the other hand, either measures of neuro-physiological activity ('evoked potentials') or measures which assess the time taken ('inspection time') to perform certain very simple cognitive tasks. Such measures purport to give an indication of the rate at which information is actually processed. (For detailed discussion of this research see, for example, Smith and Stanley, 1983; Irwin, 1984; Eysenck and Barrett, 1985; Ruchalla, Schalt, and Vogel, 1985; Anderson, 1986; Eysenck, 1986; Nettelbeck, 1987; Schafer, 1987; Howe, 1988c; Barrett and Eysenck, 1989; Howe, 1989e; Ceci, 1990).

Unfortunately for the researchers who have made these claims, there have been a number of serious problems with the evidence. For example, in some cases it has proved impossible to replicate in other laboratories the large correlations that were initially reported. In other cases close examination of the data has revealed that the conclusions have been based on samples of subjects which not only are far too small to permit reliable inferences to be drawn, but also contain a disproportionate number of mentally retarded individuals. The effect would be to invalidate the findings. That is because in this kind of research, if valid inferences are to be drawn about the population which is being sampled, it is necessary to obtain measures from subject samples that are reasonably large and in which the distribution of the variable at issue (measured intelligence in this case) broadly matches that of the population in general. Correlational measures are highly vulnerable to the distorting effects of using unrepresentative samples of subjects.

Practically the only situations in which very large correlations are reliably found between intelligence test scores and measures of the time taken to perform very simple cognitive tasks, are ones in which the cognitive task measures are not of speed at any one task, but composite ones of performance at a number of different tasks. For the present purpose, correlations obtained in these circumstances are relatively unhelpful: except when factor analysis of the component scores yields a very substantial principal component (which does not happen in these instances) the correlations provide no evidence of a close relationship between intelligence and performance at any particular component task.

In the case of possible correlations between intelligence test scores and indications of physiological functioning, it is also important to realize that the existence of such correlations would not necessarily indicate that whatever processes underlie the physiological measure are actually the causes of the differences in test scores. It is conceivable, for instance, that a person's mental activities actually produce differences in physiological functioning, or that some other influence affects both scores and physiological functioning. So there is no justification for assuming that the presence of such a correlation would be indicative of a cause-and-effect relationship which operates in the expected direction. Thus, the interesting finding that substantial correlations have been observed between measures of abilities and indications of evoked potential habituation does not, on its own, provide strong evidence for the view that measured physiological differences underlie performance differences.

On the whole, the correlations that have emerged from research examining the relationships between people's performance at intelligence tests and their performance on very simple tests that purport to be measures of either basic cognitive functioning or of physiological processes that underlie it have been small. In some cases $r$ has been zero, especially when care has been taken to choose, as indicators of the kinds of cognitive functioning that underlie skills needed in intelligence tests, tasks which are genuine components of the broader abilities, in the sense of being essential parts of those abilities and sources of variability between individuals at performing them (Keating, 1984; Keating, List, and Merriman, 1985). When correlations are found, they are typically around $r = \cdot 2$ or less, and rarely much above $r = \cdot 4$.

Correlations of these levels of magnitude indicate only weak relationships. That is because when two measures are correlated, the extent to which knowledge of the magnitude of one of them aids in the prediction of the other is estimated by squaring the correlation. Thus, if the correlation between people's smoking behaviour and alcohol consumption was ·4, we could say that 16 per cent (i.e., ·4 squared) of the variability in smoking behaviour was attributable to variability in alcohol consumption. If the correlation between two variables is ·2, only 4 per cent (i.e., ·2 squared) of the variability in the first is attributable to variability in the second.

As in the case of correlations between sub-test scores within a test of intelligence, the fact that there are any positive correlations at all, however small, between different measures is a possible indication that there is some underlying quality of general intelligence that affects a number of scores in common. But, as in the former case, there are simply too many alternative reasons for the existence of the observed correlations for it to be at all reasonable to infer that some common quality of intelligence (or $g$) must underlie them. For a start, all the traits of personality, temperament, and mood that were listed in the previous section as possible influences that could lead to correlations could also be operating here.

The other main source of influences which can produce correlated scores as a result of having similar effects on a number of tasks, namely, the involvement of identical skills, or knowledge that is common to more than one task, seems at first to be ruled out in the case of these very simple inspection tasks. But in fact even this assumption may be unwarranted. In some of the tests that have been manufactured in order to provide an indication of speed of mental processing, subjects have been rated on the speed at which they can identify letters or digits. Because both letters and digits are highly familiar to all literate people it has been assumed that differences in subjects' knowledge (which, if influential, would have effects that would rule out the interpretation that differences in performance at such tasks reflect differences in processing speed alone) would not be a source of variability in performance at letter- or digit-identification tasks. But that is not actually true at all. It has been shown that even with items that are as highly familiar to everyone as letters and digits are, there are differences between people in the form and extent of their knowledge. For instance, K. Corsale and D. H. Gitomer (cited by Chi and Ceci, 1987) discovered that individuals who are poor at solving arithmetic analogy problems (such as 'if 3:6 is equivalent to 4:$X$, what is $X$?', for example) represent digits on only two dimensions, shape and odd-evenness. Successful individuals, in contrast, can also represent digits in reference to a number of additional dimensions, such as whether or not a number is a prime and whether two numbers are multiplicatively or exponentially related. Having a larger number of dimensions along which digits can be represented means that a more elaborate network is available for encoding them. This makes easier and faster access possible (Miller and Gelman, 1983). For similar reasons, differences in the way in which knowledge is represented affect performance at letter-identification as well as at digit-identification tasks.

So even in the case of a correlation being found between intelligence test scores and scores at a very simple task measuring the time a person takes to identify letters or digits, it is clear that the correlation would not necessarily be indicative of the influence of either an underlying basic cognitive process or a quality of general intelligence that jointly affected both tasks. It would be just as likely that the correlation reflected the influence on both measures of variability in the degree and structure of subjects' knowledge in relation to the task elements.

CONCLUSION
In the 1970s the strategy of trying to investigate mental operations that form the basic components of tasks used in intelligence tests seemed to be a promising one. It appeared to offer a way of using the findings of cognitive psychology to find the building-blocks of intelligent behaviour. Now that we are more aware of the problems involved in that approach, some of the earlier enthusiasm seems naïve. Apart from the serious difficulties I have already mentioned, there is the question of whether it is actually even possible to specify unambiguously the precise mental components that must underlie a task. Even with very simple tasks, it is quite conceivable that the underlying routines or procedures followed by one individual are different from those which are introduced by a different person (Rabbitt, 1988). Only by pitching componential analysis at a level analogous to that of machine level operations would it be possible to avoid selecting components which are themselves learned routines, and therefore affected by the very kinds of individual differences in knowledge and practice which a componential approach is supposed to avoid.

## 3 Evidence that specific Abilities are present

The third reason for believing that knowing about someone's score on a test of intelligence can help to explain high abilities rests on the view that a person's measured intelligence level gives an indication of the extent to which that person possesses specific capacities that abilities depend upon. If it does, then by identifying a person as being highly intelligent one would pinpointing characteristics that make intellectual accomplishments possible. The presence of certain characteristics is explicitly or implicitly proposed in various definitions of intelligence.

Is it true that measures of intelligence serve the function of identifying qualities that contribute to the individual's competence? There are a number of ways in which this might happen (Howe, 1988a; 1989e). For example, it has been claimed that differences in measured intelligence reflect variability between people in their inherent capacity to learn, or in their ability to retain information in memory. Another suggestion is that measured intelligence provides an indication of a basic capacity to reason effectively. Alternatively, it has been suggested that someone's level of intelligence reflects the degree to which that person is capable of abstract thought. Yet another possibility is that differences in intelligence are caused by, and are indicative of, variability between people in the complexity of the cognitive functioning that they are capable of. Additional possibilities are that intelligence measures provide a guide to the effectiveness of a person's 'metacognitive' or executive skills, which are necessary for planning and coordinating one's mental resources, or to the degree of mental flexibility of which a person is capable, or their adaptability, or their ability to generalize and transfer existing knowledge and mental skills to meeting the demands of a variety of new and unfamiliar situations.

There is a germ of truth in most, if not all, of these suggestions. In general, it is correct to say that people who obtain high scores in intelligence tests do tend to be more successful than others at tasks involving the above-mentioned abilities. By and large, such individuals are better than others at remembering large quantities of information, solving problems that demand reasoning abilities, demonstrating flexibility and planning skills, and so on. But there is a vital difference between people's performances at tasks that involve learning, remembering, reasoning, and so on, and their underlying capacity to do these things as such. Take, as an illustration, success as a learner. The extent to which a person has succeeded at a task that involves learning something is not necessarily an indication of that individual's capacity to learn. An individual's degree of success may largely depend upon other factors, such as knowledge gained in the past, the degree to which one has worked hard, attentiveness at school, self-confidence, and sense of direction, and many of the personal attributes and traits that were listed earlier in this chapter. In other words, the extent to which a person succeeds at tasks that involve learning can depend on any of a number of possible influences, and is not a straightforward indication of 'ability to learn'.

If we wish to be in a good position to argue that someone's performance at a task is clearly indicative of their learning ability as such, rather than being the outcome of some combination of the numerous other influences on learning, what is needed is a test of learning in which someone's level of performance reflects their 'learning ability' and nothing else. We seek some measure of pure learning ability, a measure that cannot be contaminated by any of the various other factors that affect performance. In practice, it is hard, if not impossible, to find instances of learning that are 'pure' in the sense of not being affected by factors other than processes that are specifically and exclusively ones of learning. But we can examine very simple kinds of learning that appear not to be affected to any great extent by extraneous factors such as differences in knowledge, attitude, previously acquired skills, temperament, and so on.

Classical conditioning is a relatively simple form of learning which is relatively unaffected by most of those broader influences that affect a learner's performance. When classical conditioning procedures are administered to people of varying intelligence one clear finding emerges. Quite simply, learning and intelligence level are not related at all. So far as that kind of learning is concerned, it seems to make no difference whether someone's tested intelligence is low, high, or middling (Estes, 1970; 1982). Except in the very earliest months, there is no clear relationship between conditioning and intelligence, age, or any other measure of achievement (Howe, 1976). And performance at other simple laboratory learning tasks has a similar tendency to be uncorrelated with measured intelligence (Resnick and Neches, 1984).

The other cognitive abilities listed above show a similar lack of a relationship with measured intelligence, when tasks are carefully chosen in order to minimize the effects of extraneous factors that can affect people's level of performance. With memory, for example, like learning, whenever tasks have been carefully devised so that performance at them provides a relatively pure measure of ability to retain information, individuals' scores are found to be largely unrelated to measured intelligence. In fact, as was remarked in chapter 2, with the kinds of tasks in which there is little scope for acquired knowledge and learned strategies to increase a person's chances of success, young children do just as well as adults (Belmont, 1978). The importance of previously acquired knowledge is demonstrated by the fact that when memory is tested for information that is related to an area of knowledge on which children are better informed than adults, children out-perform adults at the memory tasks (Ceci and Howe, 1978; Chi, 1978). As became apparent in chapter 2, rather than thinking of individuals as differing in 'memory ability', it is more realistic to regard abilities to remember different kinds of information as forming relatively separate skills.

People who do well on one particular memory task usually do no better than average at other memory tasks, the correlation between a person's scores at the different tests being near zero (Martin, 1978; Wilding and Valentine, 1988).

For various reasons, the evidence that any of the other cognitive attributes that have been mentioned are clearly identified by knowledge of a person's intelligence is far from being compelling. For instance, in the case of cognitive complexity, one careful study which investigated people's reasoning in a difficult practical task revealed that the correlation between IQ scores and cognitive complexity was precisely zero (Ceci and Liker 1986).

## 4 Hereditary Influences on measured Intelligence

A final reason for some people believing that intelligence serves as the cause or origin of specific abilities is the simple fact that intelligence scores are affected by hereditary influences. The assumption is that if intelligence is partly inherited, it must be something real, and therefore an important element of any explanation of high abilities. And because it is often wrongly believed that anything that is inherited must also be fixed and unchangeable it is frequently concluded that intelligence must be immutable.

These views need not detain us long, because they are simply wrong, for reasons which were discussed in chapter 2. The fact that some quality is affected by hereditary influences provides no firm grounds for inferring that it must be some kind of tangible fundamental process. Happiness and contentment are affected by inherited causes: so are success and beauty. But it does not follow that the conceptual status of these constructs has to be other than descriptive.

# Conclusion: Can the Concept of Intelligence help us to Explain Ability Differences?

I began this chapter by raising the possibility that the concept of intelligence may aid our efforts to account for exceptional human abilities, by providing some kind of unifying conceptual framework. Such a viewpoint is clearly accepted within the commonsense psychology of everyday life, wherein intelligence is seen as being an underlying essence or quality which permeates different abilities, and constrains or controls a person's various accomplishments. Above-average intelligence is regarded as an important cause of high achievements.

But on examination, the arguments and items of evidence that have appeared to justify the assertion that intelligence is more than just a descriptive concept are less than convincing. Whatever is measured by tests of intelligence does not seem to be a unitary entity, and does not seem to control or constrain human abilities, or provide their origins or their source. Of course, the descriptive uses of the concept that are seen in intelligence tests are often very useful, but is important to realize that intelligence tests can only measure what a person does, and cannot simultaneously explain the individual's performance.

If intelligence level is not a source of differences in human abilities, what is? As we have seen in the previous chapters, there are many answers to this question. Faced with a new task, the chances of a person being successful depend on a myriad of contributing influences. These include the person's existing knowledge in relation to the particular task, existing cognitive skills, interest, motivation, attentiveness, self-confidence, and sense of purpose, to mention only a few. Some of these influences will have had cumulative effects that are not easy to measure. And both the extent and the form of each of the above influences depend on additional factors that have contributed to the individual's experiences, such as the opportunities and the encouragement he or she has received, various aspects of the person's own temperament, and, going several stages further back in time and causal chains, the values and the lifestyle of the individual's family.

In short, how well a person copes in any particular situation depends upon many different factors. Matters are not simplified by the sheer specificity of different abilities. In contrast to the notion that there exists the kind of underlying general ability that misunderstandings of the conceptual status of the construct of intelligence have appeared to indicate, different abilities are in fact remarkably independent of one another, autonomous, and specific to the particular kinds of knowledge that the individual happens to possess (Chi, 1978; Chi and Koeske, 1983; Glaser, 1984; Carey, 1985; Chi and Ceci, 1987; Howe, 1989a).

The idea that some kind of general intelligence constrains a person's abilities is further contradicted by evidence from various other sources. For instance, as I have mentioned earlier, it has been found that in many instances 'ordinary' people are perfectly capable of acquiring those 'exceptional' abilities that have been cited in the past as evidence that the possessor must have possessed inherently exceptional capabilities, and that people of low measured intelligence are capable of tasks demanding high levels of cognitive complexity. It has also been observed on numerous occasions that mentally retarded 'idiots savants' can master feats that necessitate complex and highly abstract reasoning abilities (Sacks, 1985; Smith and Howe, 1985; Howe and Smith, 1988; Howe, 1989b; 1989c), that, conversely, highly intelligent people who display considerable intellectual ability in one sphere may demonstrate mediocre intellectual competence in other spheres, and that destruction of mental abilities, such as that caused by damage to the brain, may be extremely selective, wiping out particular skills whilst leaving others, even ones that are highly similar, completely intact (Fodor, 1983; Gardner, 1984; Howe, 1989a).

In the face of these kinds of findings, the notion that intelligence is in any sense a unitary cause of high abilities is hard to maintain. Attempts have been made to get around this problem by postulating the existence of a number of different intelligences (for example, Gardner, 1984). But doing so introduces additional problems, such as that of defining the boundaries between the intelligences. Also, even within any one of the intelligences, different abilities and skills may remain largely autonomous, and unrelated to one another. So the lack of unitariness may remain a problem, even when the concept of one general intelligence is replaced by that of a number of different intelligences.

Where does this leave intelligence as a concept? Should we discard it altogether, except so far as its strictly practical functions are concerned, and conclude that it has no place at all in discussions about the nature of superior abilities? That is probably unnecessary, but we do need to be fully aware of the term's limitations. It might be wise to limit our use of 'intelligence' in the same way as we presently place limits on the uses to which we put certain other concepts that were once thought to have an explanatory function that we now realize they do not, in fact, possess. Think of 'the will' for example. A hundred years ago it was not uncommon to invoke different states of the will as reasons for all kinds of performances and behaviours, just as we now invoke differences in intelligence as being reasons for variability in intellectual performance. At that time, someone's will was regarded as being an entity that might be strong or weak, healthy, unhealthy or diseased, atrophied, corrupted, perverted, and so on. The state of a person's will could be invoked as a reason for any of a wide range of phenomena.

But today we no longer use the concept of will in those ways. We are fully aware of the invalid reification that would be involved in doing so. We are no longer inclined to believe that a will is any kind of thing or concrete entity. It is readily apparent that the real nature of the concept does not permit meaningful appeals to be made to the state of someone's will as a cause or explanation of their behaviour. All the same, the word has not dropped out of existence. It is still quite widely used. We regard it as being a meaningful and reasonably useful term, so long as we take care to avoid the misconceptions underlying previous generations' pseudo-explanatory invocations of it. Were we to place similar limits on our uses of the concept of intelligence, accepting that its legitimate applications do not extend to providing scientific explanations, the chances are that we would continue to find the term useful, in ways that are broadly similar to those in which we still find the concept of will to be useful.

# 8

# Final Words

Although our knowledge about the circumstances in which a few individuals gain outstanding abilities is far from being complete, we do know enough to be certain that it is within our power to add enormously to the numbers of young people who become capable of mastering the kinds of difficult human accomplishments that we find particularly impressive. There will never be any simple formula for manufacturing genius, but, as we have seen, there is plenty of evidence that various abilities which have been thought to be quite beyond the capacities of any but the most exceptional individuals can in fact be gained by the majority of ordinary people, provided that opportunities for learning are made available, as well as suficient support and encouragement, and enough time for training and practice.

In reality, unfortunately, the vast majority of today's young children do not have access to the opportunities and the other forms of support that kindle exceptional abilities. Consequently, these children never achieve the goals they might otherwise have reached. Of course, even if rich opportunities for learning were more widely available, not every child would take full advantage of them. But as was made clear in several of the earlier chapters, those young people whose parents can ensure that their early lives are lived in circumstances which are rich in interest and stimulation, with plenty of encouragement to gain the kinds of skills and knowledge that allow a person to make good sense of the world, are far more likely to grow up into unusually capable young adults than are children who do not have such opportunities.

So why are we not doing more to increase the proportion of young people who are capable of mastering exceptional skills? Why are there so few policy decisions aimed at achieving this? What is holding us back? Here are some of the reasons for the failure to take steps that would make it possible for these goals to be achieved.

1 First, the belief still lingers on that exceptional abilities are only achievable by individuals who are born possessing exceptional talents or inherited gifts. As was seen in chapter 1, that belief is certainly false, even though it is true that genetic variability is among the factors that can influence human accomplishments. Despite the possibility that genetic influences may convey advantages or disadvantages, there is solid evidence that most young children, if they are given enough opportunities and sufficient encouragement, are able to learn far more than children normally do. The vast majority of young people are quite capable of reaching extremely high levels of competence in any of a large variety of areas of achievement.

2 A second inhibiting factor is a widely shared view that radical educational improvements can only be achieved via schools and school-based educational systems. Consequently, the possibility that educational policy changes that are not firmly based in the schools might be enormously influential is often ignored, and rarely given serious attention. That is unfortunate because, as finding after finding has repeatedly shown, many of the most potent influences that affect the likelihood of a child developing into an exceptionally able young person are ones that are exerted within the child's own home, and stem from the actions of individuals in the child's own family.

As we have noticed, there are severe limitations – notably those imposed by the inevitably sizeable ratios of pupils to teachers – to what even the best schools can achieve. So if we raise the question of where it is that the greatest room lies for improvement, so far as most young children's learning is concerned, by far the most likely answer is, within the child's own home.

3 The third reason is that many parents simply fail to appreciate to how great an extent their children's progress depends upon their own actions and attitudes as parents. But as we saw in chapter 3, the acquisition of even the most fundamental and far-reaching human skills, including language, is greatly accelerated when ordinary parents take simple steps to intensify the help and encouragement they provide.

Obviously, parents who do not realize how much they can do to aid their children's progress will be unlikely to make special efforts to accelerate early development. A parent needs to have some confidence that a major investment of energy and patience will have some positive effects. Many adults are unaware of the real improvement that even a relatively small effort on a parent's part may bring about. For example, most parents do not know that the development of language skills is greatly influenced by parents' interactions with their children. If it was more widely known that (as reported in chapter 3) relatively modest parental interventions designed to accelerate the development of language skills can lead to substantial gains, or if more adults appreciated the fact that it is worth making efforts to stimulate a child's comprehension of language well before the child actually begins to speak, many parents might show increased interest in early childhood education.

4 The fourth reason is that many of those parents who are aware, however dimly, that their own parental practices can have far-reaching consequences, so far as their children's progress is concerned, are only too aware of their own limitations as teachers. They feel that they do not know what to do, or how, in order to give effective help and encouragement.

The problems identified here are very real ones. Addressing them ought to be a prime focus of educational policies aimed at helping young children to learn. Undoubtedly, some parents are better equipped to help, by virtue of temperament, attitude, and their own knowledge, and the degree of literacy they have arrived at. As I mentioned in chapter 5, some parents are more adequately prepared than others to act as guides for their children, especially to those aspects of the contemporary world in which numeracy and literacy are paramount. But it is not only those parents who are inarticulate or poorly educated who experience problems caused by lack of know-how and expertise in teaching young children. In one of the studies described in chapter 3, which investigated the effects of giving parents simple advice about techniques to employ when reading to young children, it was found that the children of those parents who had received simple instructions made considerably more progress at language skills than another group of children. This was despite the fact that the other children had conscientious parents who all read to their children, and spent just as much time doing so as did the parents in the specially-instructed group. Findings such as this demonstrate that even those children whose parents are relatively expert as guides for their children, and highly committed to helping children to learn, stand to gain a great deal from policies designed to help parents to teach their children more effectively.

Parents may overestimate the degree of expertise that is required in order to give a child assistance with learning. Generally speaking, the most important qualities required are sensitivity, patience, enthusiasm, common sense, and perseverance, rather than particular instructional skills or teaching techniques. Parents are especially effective as teachers of their children when they are willing to spend time patiently explaining things, drawing their child's attention to important objects and events, answering children's questions, posing questions that encourage children to concentrate and reflect, and doing all they can to make the child's world more understandable.

Even if it is true that many parents underestimate their own competence as teachers of their children, the sheer fact that they *feel* themselves to be incapable indicates that they need guidance, and at present that is in short supply, particularly where it is most needed. For many parents, particularly those who are not highly educated, vestiges of a 'leave it to the school' and 'teacher knows best' attitude remain too influential.

5 A fifth reason for failing to implement activities that would accelerate children's progress is that many parents and others are anxious that efforts to extend and intensify learning in young children can have adverse outcomes as well as positive ones. As was seen in chapters 4 and 5, some of the fears and anxieties are by no means unjustified. It is all too easy for parents who, for whatever reasons, are particularly strongly bent on maximizing a child's accomplishments, to act in ways that create difficulties for the child. In some cases the child suffers from the pressure of parental expectations, in others the child is deprived of opportunities for play, or other social experiences that contribute to normal development. In yet other instances the child fails to gain abilities that are needed in order to become able to function as a fully independent adult, make mature personal decisions, and gain an innerdirected sense of purpose. Those parents who are unusually committed to their childrens's success are sometimes prone to become dependent on the vicarious success that is provided by a child's achievements. Such parents may be rather insensitive to children's needs that are unrelated to the particular kinds of accomplishments that the parent values most, or unaware of personal difficulties that the child is experiencing.

The parent who sets out with the firm intention of making a child into an outstanding musician, scientist, sportsperson, mathematician, or whatever, may be sending the child into a dangerous minefield. But a parent who has the more realistic goal of giving a child the advantages of having an unusually good start in life, and is preparerd to let the child make decisions about how to make use of those advantages, is far more likely to see the child develop into a capable and independent adult (Howe, 1988e; 1988f; 1989d; 1990a; 1990b). So far as the early lives of most children are concerned, there is considerable leeway for parents to increase their efforts to assist and encourage children to learn basic skills, without invoking any danger of a child being harmed either by too much pressure or by the kind of extreme specialization that could lead to diminished opportunities for some of the experiences of a normal childhood. The fact that a highly intensive 'hot house' early childhood regime may have undesirable effects ought not to dissuade parents from making reasonable efforts to help their children to progress further and faster than is usual.

6 A final reason for some parents doing little or nothing to encourage high achievements is simply that not every adult places much value on such achievements. For obvious reasons there are substantial relationships between the kinds of accomplishments that parents value and the actual achievements of their children. This is as true of sporting attainments as it is of ones that are primarily intellectual or artistic. Not every parent attaches high importance to, say, the ability to perform instrumental music. Similarly, parents differ in the value they attach to the goal of helping their children to gain abilities that are intellectual in nature. Some parents would argue that modern civilization already places too much pressure on children to succeed and excel, and would resist the very idea of helping young children to extend their abilities.

## Helping Young Children to Learn

Precisely how do you help infants and young children to learn? Although a fair amount has been said on this matter, particularly in chapters 3, 4, and 5, detailed discussions of teaching methods are outside the scope of this book (but see Howe, 1990a; 1990b). But it is worth emphasizing that the majority of those parents who are unusually successful at helping their children to learn do not depend on any special or unusual instructional techniques. And, as we saw in chapter 5, the likelihood of a child gaining abilities considerably younger than usual does not seem to be greatly affected by whether the help given by the parents takes the form of structured instruction of a relatively formal kind or is largely informal and unstructured. That seems to have made little or no difference in the past, in the case of nineteenth-century child prodigies, nor does it seem to be an important source of variability in the achievements of children today.

Reports on their children's upbringing written by the parents of child prodigies, and autobiographical accounts by prodigies themselves, have been fertile sources of information, some of it quite detailed, about the varied ways in which people have tried to assist their children's progress during the years of early childhood. Despite the marked variability in the different parents' approaches – as seen, for example, in the large differences in the degree to which their didactic plans have taken a formal structure, many of the parents whose efforts have been particularly successful have shared a number of qualities. Almost always, these parents have been willing to give large amounts of time and attention to the early education of their children. Often, even with parents whose methods of instruction have been highly informal, there has been — eventually, if not at first — a degree of systematic planning in their approach.

In many cases the parents have been convinced that their child was inherently ordinary, and in a number of instances parents have held firm views concerning the potency of early intellectual training that sharply contrasted with prevailing opinions. A number of the parents have drawn attention to the extent to which opportunities to learn are wasted in most people's childhoods, and some of them have also been highly critical of the wastefulness of school-based educational systems. Some of the parents have held very strong views concerning individuals' duties towards other people: they have tended to believe that the gaining of high intellectual achievements, and the proper exploitation of them, are as much obligations as rewards.

Certain innovations that we might have expected to find as elements of what are, in many cases, unconventional and controversial approaches to early childhood education are, perhaps surprisingly, absent from these accounts. For instance, there are few reports of instructional procedures that are strikingly radical in their particulars. Often, of course, the methods that parents have followed *have* been different from the ones habitually followed in schools of the time. For example, many of the parents have taken pains to avoid rote learning and unnecessary repetition, and have done their best to ensure that their children's learning activities have been active, meaningful, and interesting for the learner. But one sees little use of those complicated mnemonic techniques that have always had adherents willing to claim that they 'make learning easier'; and there is nothing comparable to the teaching-machine or programmed learning techniques methods from which so much was expected in the middle years of the twentieth century.

These parents' educational methods and techniques of instruction were nothing like so untypical of their times as were their broader attitudes towards education in early childhood and their awareness of the potential strength of its effects. It seems that most of these parents, quirky, arrogant, and insensitive as some of them were, had the good sense to be distrustful of the notion that it is possible to make easy short-cuts in the education of a human child. Their awareness that learning needs to be interesting and enjoyable did not make them insensitive to the fact that the process of becoming extraordinarily able demands considerable effort and patience on the part of learner and teacher alike, and is inevitably time-consuming, and sometimes arduous as well.

The elder Karl Witte, writing about his son's upbringing at the beginning of the nineteenth century, was sure of his priorities. His first intention had been to ensure that the younger Karl would be healthy, strong, active, and happy. He reported with justified pride, 'and in this, as everybody knows, I have succeeded' (Witte, 1975, p. 53). He was also determined from the outset that his son should become outstandingly able. In the face of a climate of opinion in which it was almost universally agreed that a person's achievements largely depended upon inborn 'aptitudes', he was convinced that these were considerably less important than a child's education in the first five or six years.

Witte's description of some of the ways in which his infant son was encouraged to learn reads almost as if it came from an account of the methods adopted by modern researchers such as Fowler and his co-workers to promote language development a century and a half later. The father records that his son

> learned many things in the arms of his mother and in my own, such as one rarely thinks of imparting to children. He learned to know and name all the objects in ten different rooms, the rooms themselves, the staircase, the yard, the garden, the stable, the well, the barn, – everything from the greatest to the smallest, was frequently shown and clearly and plainly named to him, and he was encouraged to name the objects as plainly as possible. Whenever he spoke correctly he was fondled and praised. When, however, he failed, we said in a decidedly cooler manner, 'Mother (or Father), Karl cannot yet pronounce this or that word!' ... Consequently he took great pains to know and correctly name all objects. (Witte, 1975, p. 71)

Language was seen by the elder Witte as the key to intellectual competence. Acquiring the mother tongue, he said, 'makes the child intelligent at an early time, for it puts his attention and his several mental powers continuously in action. He is obliged always to search, distinguish, compare, prefer, report, choose, in short he must work, that is, think' (Witte, 1975, p. 75).

The child's parents took great pains to expose him to as varied a range of experiences as they could provide: these ranged from the familiar to the exotic. Consequently, while he was still a young child, Karl encountered not only watermills and windmills, and owls and bats, but also concerts, dramas, and operas, and lions and ostriches and elephants. And the parents took care to draw Karl's attention to important aspects of the objects they showed him. They also explained to

Karl all the things he came across, and discussed them in his presence, so that he understood the objects he perceived not 'by merely staring at them, as children generally know them, but thoroughly' (Witte, 1975, p. 81). In this and other ways the parents provided countless instances of the kind of 'mediated' learning which, as we saw in chapter 4, Reuven Feuerstein regards as crucial for today's infants and children. Karl Witte's parents were careful to talk to him about all the events they showed him, and they made sure that he noticed whatever was important. They regularly asked him whether he liked what he was seeing, so that the child 'became accustomed to what he had seen and heard, and he himself addressed us, enquired, reported, retorted, etc.' (Witte, 1975, p. 81)

Like Feuerstein, but many years earlier, Witte recognized that valuable abilities such as that of being able to discriminate between different objects are most likely to be acquired when an adult can provide learning experiences that are designed to direct the child's attention in ways that promote learning. Like all good teachers, the father knew the value of play and games. He was convinced that it was never too early for parents to engage their infants in playful activities. He stated that, with enough imagination, nearly all common objects could be turned into toys, a course of action that he regarded as much more effective than the practice of buying expensive toys but failing to give the child proper guidance in the use of them. But building blocks did meet his approval.

When Witte judged that his son was ready to learn to read, the father was sufficiently astute to appreciate the importance of motivation, so he went to some lengths to make sure that his child would *want* to read. When Karl was aged three, his father bought ten sets of German letters, the largest being three inches high, which were pasted on pictures of wood. He invented a family game in which the letters were all thrown into a box. Mother, father and child would sit together on the carpet, where they carefully mixed up the letters in the box, and then picked out one letter at a time. Each letter 'was carefully and solemnly surveyed and loudly and distinctly named. It went from hand to hand, and everybody did the same' (Witte, 1975, p. 224).

After a few quarter-hour sessions of the game each day for several days, Karl had learned all the letters, quickly and painlessly. The father then began to help his son learn to read syllables and words. At one stage Witte found that the child had been temporarily put off learning to read because his mother had been teaching him in a manner that was too formal and heavy-handed. After that, the father was even more careful to delay teaching new reading skills until Karl had shown a desire to learn them. Only after the child had made repeated requests did he start helping him learn to write, and even then he avoided formal teaching.

We can learn much from the elder Karl Witte's bold experiment. This fiercely independent man, who had the courage to trust his own judgement in the face of insults and ridicule, and persist with a course of action that many people told him could only fail, brought to the task of educating his son qualities of imagination, persistence, patience, and above all, an ability, uncommon now and much rarer in his time, of being able to understand a young child's point of view. In particular, Witte realized how enormously important it is for a child to want to learn, and he was therefore careful to make his son's learning experiences informal and playful, and to delay introducing new skills until the son's eagerness to acquire them was already apparent.

There is more than one way to educate a young child. The way in which James Mill approached the upbringing of his son John Stuart Mill, described in the son's famous *Autobiography* (Mill, 1971), first published five months after his death in 1873, was much more formal and more tightly structured than Witte's. John Stuart Mill's early education contained larger elements of severity and compulsion than the younger Witte's seems to have done. This might account, at least in part, for the fact that while the mature John Stuart was second to none intellectually, he nevertheless suffered periods of serious depression.

John Stuart Mill set out to provide as full an account of his unusual childhood as he could give, because, he said,

> in an age in which education, and its improvement, are the subject of more, if not of profounder study than at any former period of English history, it may be useful that there should be some record of an education that was unusual and remarkable, and which, whatever else it may have done, has proved how much more than is commonly supposed may be taught, and well taught, in those early years which, in the common modes of what is called instruction, are little better than wasted. (Mill, 1971, p. 5)

Mill begins by emphasizing just how hard his father had to labour in order to educate his children at home at the same time as working on his lengthy *History of India*. At least in the case of John Stuart, who was the oldest child, James Mill exerted 'an amount of labour, care, and perseverance rarely, if ever, employed for a similar purpose, in endeavouring to give, according to his own conception, the highest order of intellectual education' (Mill, 1971, p. 7).

We learn nothing of Mill's early language development, for the obvious reason that no-one remembers this stage of their own life, or of his first steps towards reading. The first records of his education that appear in the *Autobiography* are not taken from memory but are reproduced from what others told Mill later in his life. For instance, Mill informs us that he has no memory of the time when he began to learn Greek, but adds that he has been informed that it was when he was three years old. His earliest recollection about learning Greek is of memorizing lists of words, paired with the English equivalents, written out on cards by his father. Greek grammar was taught him some years later. He reports that he began Latin in his eighth year, and lists a number of Greek and Latin authors that he was required to translate at around that time. He adds that until he had learned Latin, and became able to make use of a Greek and Latin lexicon, he was forced to ask his father about the meaning of every word encountered in his lessons which he did not already know. For several years this resulted in the father having to submit to incessant interruptions, despite which, the son notes admiringly, James Mill continued to make steady progress on his *History*.

Formal instruction in John Stuart Mill's early childhood seems to have been restricted to Greek and arithmetic. He disliked the latter intensely. But equally importantly, the child was strongly encouraged to read, and he spent a large part of each day doing so, mainly from books of history, although his reading was wide and varied. Before breakfast, he would accompany his father on walks in the country, and during the walks the son would give an account of what he had read on the previous day, jogging his memory with notes that he had made on slips of paper while he had been reading. He reports that this exercise was a voluntary rather than a prescribed one, but it is safe to assume that the idea of doing it came from the father rather than from the son. Most of the books that John Stuart Mill read at this time (they would probably have been chosen for him from his father's library) were ones that contained narrative passages which an unusually knowledgeable and intelligent child would be able to understand, and even enjoy, without too much difficulty. For example, Mill writes with enthusiasm of a book entitled *Philip the Second and Third* by a Robert Watson, in which 'The heroic defence of the knights of Malta against the Turks, and of the revolted provinces of the Netherlands against Spain, excited in me an intense and lasting interest.' He adds that his father 'was fond of putting into my hands books which exhibited men of energy and resource in unusual circumstances, struggling against difficulties and overcoming them', as well as books of discovery, such as descriptions of the voyages of Drake, Cook, and Anson, which any boy would have found exciting. But he was given very few children's books, and notes that his father only permitted them 'very sparingly', although the boy was allowed to read *Robinson Crusoe*, which was a source of delight throughout his childhood.

As a child John Stuart Mill both admired and feared his father, and in the *Autobiography* he tries hard to give a balanced view of the father's qualities as a teacher. Sometimes James Mill seems to have acted with unreasonable severity. For instance, John Stuart was forced to practise writing verses, which he found a most disagreeable task. When, inspired by Pope's translation of Homer's *Iliad*, he spontaneously attempted, although (he says) without much success, to do something of the same kind himself, he found that the activity, which might have been expected to cease at that point, 'was continued by command' (Mill, 1971, p. 19).

James Mill did at least take care to explain to his son why he was compelling him to do this and other hated tasks. On occasions he could be a highly sensitive parent, and he often encouraged his son to express himself without fear of criticism. Writing of a childish attempt to produce a history of Rome, John Stuart Mill records that, to his relief, his father had the tact to avoid asking to see what had been written, so that the son did not experience the unpleasant situation of being under the father's critical eye.

Whatever its faults, it cannot be denied that the upbringing and education that James Mill provided for his son gave the latter a superb intellectual grounding. The fact that John Stuart Mill became one of the great thinkers of his age was due in no small part to his father's pedagogical efforts. James Mill's strengths as an educator were in many respects different from the elder Witte's, but in common to both fathers' approaches, apart from their admirable diligence and conscientiousness as teachers, was the enormous emphasis they placed on the necessity of the student having a clear understanding of what was to be learned, and becoming able to think for himself. Both stressed the importance of meaningfulness and comprehensibility, and each was severely critical of current educational practices that involved rote learning and drills, and the meaningless repetition of information. A passage in which John Stuart Mill draws attention to his father's insistence on the importance of understanding as well as his avoidance of drill methods can serve as a summary of what was best in the education which James Mill provided for his son.

> There was one cardinal point in this training ... which, more than anything else, was the cause of whatever good it effected. Most boys or youths have had much knowledge drilled into them, have their mental capacities not streng-

thened, but overlaid by it. They are crammed with mere facts, and with the opinions or phrases of other people, and these are accepted as a substitute for the power to form opinions of their own ... Mine, however, was not an education of cram. My father never permitted anything which I learnt, to degenerate into a mere exercise of memory. He strove to make the understanding not only go along with every step of the teaching, but if possible, precede it. Anything which could be found out by thinking, I was never told, until I had exhausted my efforts to find it out for myself ... A pupil from whom nothing is ever demanded which he cannot do, never does all he can. (Mill, 1971, p. 35)

Mill's education was also unusual for its time in not containing a large element of religion. The parents of other child prodigies who were broadly contemporary with John Stuart Mill saw religious knowledge as both a means of providing education and a reason for gaining it. With John Ruskin, for instance, born in 1819, the Bible provided the focus of most of the early instruction which his devoutly evangelical mother provided for him. The following extract from a letter she wrote to her husband when John was still only two years old gives an idea of the serious and the predominantly religious tone of the child's early upbringing.

We get on very well with our reading he knows all the commandments but the second perfectly and the Lords prayer – his memory astonishes me and his understanding too ... (Burd, 1973, p. 109)

In fact, the young Ruskin had to read aloud from the Bible – two or three chapters a day, seven days per week – throughout his entire childhood. And religion received even more emphasis in the childhood of Thomas Macaulay, born in 1800. His mother, the wife of one of the most active leading Evangelicals of the time, reacted to her first glimpse of her son by launching into a recital of Isaac Watts's hymn, which set the tone for a childhood of piety:

Mayst thou live to know and fear Him,
Trust and love Him all thy days
*Then* go dwell forever near Him,
See his face, and sing His praise.
(Quoted in Clive, 1973, p. 21)

So intense a preoccupation with religious matters is unusual in parents today, but in other respects the childhoods of those twentieth-century child prodigies whose early education has been recorded in reasonable detail seem not to have been very different, on the whole, from those of the earlier generations. As we have seen, behind the accelerated early progress of exceptionally precocious children there have often been parents who have been unusually active as educators, and unusually serious-minded and conscientious in their efforts to help their children acquire important intellectual skills while they were still very young.

As we would expect, the parents of twentieth-century prodigies have transmitted to their children their twentieth-century interests and values and preoccupations. For example, it is not uncommon to find modern parents encouraging a child to gain expertise in mathematics or the sciences. But that kind of emphasis is a surprisingly recent phenomenon: Darwin's father, although enthusiastic about science, never encouraged his son to think of biology as a vocation, probably because prior to Victoria's reign there was scant possibility of an Englishman making any kind of living as a research scientist. By the time Norbert Wiener was a boy, things had changed dramatically: opportunities for scientists and mathematicians to gain paid employment were becoming relatively numerous. Science books played a part in Wiener's education from a very early stage. On his fourth birthday his father gave him a volume on natural history, and soon afterwards Norbert read a children's book on elementary science which included discussions of such non-childish topics as the nature of light. By seven he had read a number of books on chemistry, physiology, botany, zoology, and various branches of physics, and was conducting chemical experiments under the supervision of an instructor whom his father had hired to teach him chemistry (Wiener, 1953).

The changes that have occurred over the generations in the broad approaches taken by the parents of child prodigies towards the early education of their offspring have been considerably fewer and smaller than the changes in the particular topics they have encouraged their children to learn. Nowadays it is probably more common than in the past for parents to employ games and play sessions in order to arouse a child's interest in a new skill, just as the elder Karl Witte did at the beginning of the nineteenth century, than to adopt the more coercive approach of parents such James Mill or Margaret Ruskin, both of whom were Witte's contemporaries. But there is no direct link of cause-and-effect between parental teaching style and a child's successes. Although it is tempting to assume that the relative severity of the early education received by John Stuart Mill and John Ruskin was the cause of their neuroticism, we would be wise to remember that the education received in early childhood by William Sidis, who was more neurotic than either of them, was not at all severe. That the playful tradition of the elder Witte is still alive in today's parents is demonstrated by numerous remarks collected in the course of the Chicago-based interview studies of exceptional young adults. There are many examples of a child's interest being caught through games. A young mathematician recalls, for instance,

> When we were very young, both my brother and I liked to play games. My father was especially good at playing games with us and keeping it fun. I remember him telling me some really exciting things, which would turn out to be some kind of math, and I would play with the ideas. My father was a sensitive teacher, and I'm sure he did all kinds of subtle things that didn't seem like teaching. (Gustin, 1985, p. 281)

## Conclusion: Chance and Fortune in Human Life

To end on a different note, we would be prudent to acknowledge that our best efforts to explain, understand, and predict the course of individual human lives are pre-empted at many points by chance influences that we can neither foresee nor control. In chapter 2 I mentioned that the very likelihood that someone will be regarded as a genius depends as much on other people's largely unpredictable reactions to the individual's contributions as it does on that person's actual achievements. Chance factors can produce sudden changes which confound any scientific prediction. An injury, a plane accident, or even a sudden infatuation may alter an individual's progress in ways that no-one could predict.

The significance of a particular lifetime event may not be apparent until long after it has taken place. I mentioned in chapter 5 that when the writer H. G. Wells was seven years old he broke his leg – hardly the kind of happening that one would wish on a boy of that age. But the effect of that accident in his particular case was to encourage an already bookish young child, confined by his injury to spending long hours in bed, to devote even more of his time to reading. His injury almost certainly contributed to the fact that Wells became an unusually knowledgeable young person, and in later years a major author and an intellectual force to be reckoned with. Another eminent writer, Charles Dickens, reported that in his childhood, too, being confined to bed (because of illness) had a strong influence on his development as a reader. Dickens commented that sickness brought the great advantage of encouraging him to read. And for some of today's children as well, having to spend weeks or months in bed can be the spark that kindles an intense interest. David Feldman (1986) mentions the case of a brilliant young chess player who first began to take the game seriously when at the age of five his normally energetic physical activities were suddenly curtailed by a broken collarbone.

But in all likelihood, for every child who has profited from injury or illness there have been many for whom the only consequences have been negative ones. The power of human individuality dictates that whatever we discover about the effects that a particular event have had on one individual may tell us little or nothing about the likely influence of a similar event upon someone else. As Howard Gruber once noted, each person incorporates or is otherwise affected by the happenings of his or her lifetime in a distinctive and unique way.

The smallest events that chance dictates can have momentous consequences. It is sometimes tempting to speculate 'What might have happened if only ...?' about the conceivable outcomes of seemingly minor happenings. Such a thought occurred to me this morning, when I found a space to park my car (not always an easy feat in Exeter, where I live) outside an attractive Georgian façade at Number 3, Northernhay Place. ('Hay' is an old English word meaning a field.) I recalled that on 26 September, 1831, a pretty and vivacious young woman named Fanny Owen had been staying next door, at Number 2. From that address she wrote an urgent letter to a close friend, the young Charles Darwin, who was about to set out on his five-year voyage round the world on board HMS *Beagle*. He adored her, and she reciprocated his affection, although her feelings towards him did not quite match the urgency of his longings for her. The correspondence of Darwin and his family and friends evokes lives that were often touched with kindness, good humour, and a sweet generosity of mind, but the letters between Charles and Fanny are the most poignant of all. These letters are sprinkled with jokey observations and gossipy witticisms, and are written in a mock-heroic, mock-romantic style that parodies the fiction of the time: they often finish with a sentence urging 'Burn this for pity's sake!' She called herself his 'dutiful Housemaid of the Forest' and he was her 'dear Postillion'.

Fanny's letter of 26 September has a seriousness that is absent from any of her earlier correspondence with Darwin. She is distraught because she fears (rightly, as it turned out) that she will not see him again before he disappears on his long voyage. She repeatedly expresses her sadness and frustration. 'I cannot tell you how disappointed and vexed I am,' she says, and a few lines later, 'I would give anything to see you once more before you go, for it does make me melancholy to think the time you are to be away.' And again, she continues, repeating herself, 'I cannot bear to think you are going clear away.' She tries to arrange a meeting, but their letters cross, and she writes to him once more from Exeter on 6 October, having just discovered that 'you were actually walking about Plymouth the very day I was, I never did know any thing so unlucky we should not have crossed each other's path!!' She tells him again, 'I cannot bear to think my dear Charles that we are not to meet again for so long', and urges him to reply: 'if you have a little spare half hour before you go do write to me again I should like so much to hear from you.'

The tone of Fanny's letters is more than urgent: there is a note of desperation. I think it is quite possible that her feelings about Charles, whom she had until then preferred to hold at arm's length, had become much stronger than before; and that in the knowledge of her dear companion's imminent departure she was beginning to see him as more than a friend. It does not seem altogether fanciful to suggest that had Charles Darwin travelled down to Exeter that autumn with a proposal of marriage she might have agreed to become his wife.

Of course, it didn't happen. They did not see each other for five years; and when they met again Fanny was already a disgruntled wife and mother. But in trying to imagine what might have taken place if only things had turned out a little differently, we are forced to recognize how much the achievements that individual people accomplish depend upon circumstances that are both outside the individual's control and also unique to the particular time and situation in which that person is placed. What might have happened to Darwin's career had he met Fanny that autumn and asked her to marry him? It is unlikely that he would have cancelled his plan to join the *Beagle* even if he and Fanny had agreed to marry; but would his dedication to science during that lengthy voyage have been quite so single-minded as it turned out to be? Would his mind have turned so regularly and intensely as in the event it did to the thoughts that were eventually to give rise to the theory of evolution by natural selection? Chance and fortune act in unpredictable ways to direct people's lives, to open up certain possibilities and close down others. Often the apparently random events that cross someone's path have enormous consequences, not only for the individual but also for all who stand to be affected by that person's achievements. And the timing of such events – the point in the course of a life at which they intersect – can be especially crucial.

Darwin's lucky opportunity to join the voyage of the *Beagle* provides an illustration of the fact that important – and sometimes unpredictable

– consequences can follow from the external events that take place at particular moments in time. Darwin was fortunate. On the one hand, he began the voyage as an already competent young biologist whose knowledge and skills made him well prepared to appreciate the significance of the many novel biological phenomena he was able to observe. On the other hand, the timing of the voyage ensured that he was at a sufficiently early stage in his career for his mind to be wide open to new possibilities and unfamiliar ideas. Had the voyage taken place a few years earlier he would have been less well prepared to understand the importance of what he saw: had it occurred later he might have been too set in his ways to make the all-important intellectual leap which established his place in history. Who can say? So much of what is crucial in human life hinges on the mechanisms of capricious chance.

Even so, although we cannot map our lives in advance, much can be done to make desirable outcomes more likely. Acquiring an exceptional ability is one such outcome. We can and we should act to make it happen more often.

# References

Ainsworth, M. D. S., Bell, S. M., and Stayton, D. J. (1974). Infant-mother attachment and social development: socialisation as a product of reciprocal responsiveness to signals. In M. P. M. Richards (ed.), *The Integration of a Child into a Social World*. London: Cambridge University Press.

Albert, R. S. (1971). Cognitive development and parental loss among the gifted, the exceptionally gifted and the creative. *Psychological Reports*, 29, 19–26.

Anastasi, A. (1967). Psychology, psychologists, and psychological testing. *American Psychologist*, 22, 297–306.

Anderson, M. (1986). Inspection time and IQ in young children. *Personality and Individual Differences*, 7, 677–86.

Bamberger, J. (1986). Cognitive issues in the development of musically gifted children. In R. J. Sternberg and J. E. Davidson (eds), *Conceptions of Giftedness*. Cambridge: Cambridge University Press.

Baltes, P. B., Reese, H. W., and Lipsitt, L. P. (1980). Life-span developmental psychology. *Annual Review of Psychology*, 31, 65–110.

Baron, J., Badgio, P., and Gaskins, I. (1986). Cognitive style and its improvement: a normative approach. In R. J. Sternberg (ed.), *Advances in the Psychology of Human Intelligence*, Vol. 3. Hillsdale, N. J.: Erlbaum.

Barrett, P. T., and Eysenck, H. J. (1989). Brain electrical potentials and intelligence. In A. Gale and M. Eysenck (eds), *Handbook of the Psychophysiology of Individual Differences*. Chichester: Wiley.

Belmont, J. (1978). Individual differences in memory: the cases of normal and retarded development. In M. M. Gruneberg and P. E. Morris (eds), *Aspects of Memory*. London: Methuen.

Berry, C. (1981). The Nobel scientists and the origins of scientific achievement. *British Journal of Sociology*, 32, 381–91.

Berry, C. (1990). On the origins of exceptional intellectual and cultural achievement. In M. J. A. Howe (ed.), *Encouraging the Development of Exceptional Abilities and Talents*. Leicester: The British Psychological Society.

Biederman, I., and Shiffrar, M. M. (1987). Sexing day-old chicks: a case study and expert systems analysis of a difficult perceptual-learning task. *Journal of Experimental Psychology: Learning, Memory and Cognition*, 13, 640–5.

Bloom, B. S. (1976). *Human Characteristics and School Learning*. New York: McGraw-Hill.

Bloom, B. S. (ed.) (1985). *Developing Talent in Young People*. New York: Ballantine.

Blum, D. (1989). A process larger than oneself. *The New Yorker*, May 1, 41–74.

Bornstein, M. H. (1985). How infant and mother jointly contribute to developing cognitive competence in the child. *Proceedings of the National Academy of Science of the United States of America*, 82, 7470–3.

Bouchard, C., and Malina, R. M. (1986). Concluding remarks. In R. M. Malina and C. Bouchard (eds), *Sport and Human Genetics*. Champaign, Illinois: Human Kinetics.

Brady, P. T. (1970). The genesis of absolute pitch. *Journal of the Acoustical Society of America*, 48, 883–7.

Bradley, L., and Bryant, P. E. (1983). Categorizing sounds and learning to read in preschoolers. *Journal of Educational Psychology*, 68, 680–8.

Brannigan, A. (1981). *The Social Basis of Scientific Discoveries*. New York: Cambridge University Press.

Brent, P. (1981). *Charles Darwin*. London: Heinemann.

Brodie, F. M. (1971). *The Devil Drives: a Life of Sir Richard Burton*. Harmondsworth: Penguin Books.

Bryant, P., and Bradley, L. (1985). *Children's Reading Problems: Psychology and Education*. Oxford: Blackwell.

Burchinal, M., Lee, M., and Ramey, C. (1989). Type of day-care and preschool intellectual development in disadvantaged children. *Child Development*, 60, 128–37.

Burd, V. A. (1973). *The Ruskin Family Letters: the Correspondence of John James Ruskin, His Wife, and Their Son, John, 1801–1843*, Vol. 1. London: Cornell University Press.

Bynner, J. M., and Romney, D. M. (1986). Intelligence, fact or artefact: alternative structures for cognitive abilities. *British Journal of Educational Psychology*, 56, 13–23.

Carey, S. (1985). Are children fundamentally different kinds of thinkers and learners than adults? In S. F. Chipman and J. W. Segal (eds), *Thinking and Learning Skills*, Vol. 2, 485–517. Hillsdale, N. J.: Erlbaum.

Ceci, S. J. (1990). *On Intelligence ... More or Less: a Bio-ecological Theory of Intellectual Development*. Englewood Cliffs, N. J.: Prentice-Hall.

Ceci, S. J., and Bronfenbrenner, U. (1985). Don't forget to take the cupcakes out of the oven: strategic time-monitoring, prospective memory, and context. *Child Development*, 56, 175–90.

Ceci, S. J., and Howe, M. J. A. (1978). Semantic knowledge as a determinant of developmental differences in recall. *Journal of Experimental Child Psychology*, 26, 230–45.

Ceci, S. J., and Liker, J. (1986). A day at the races: a study of IQ, expertise, and cognitive complexity. *Journal of Experimental Psychology: General*, 115, 255–66.

Ceci, S. J., Baker, J. G., and Bronfenbrenner, U. (1987). The acquisition of simple and complex algorithms as a function of context. Unpublished manuscript. Ithaca, New York: Cornell University.

Chase, W. G., and Ericsson, K. A. (1981). Skilled memory. In J. R. Anderson (ed.), *Cognitive Skills and their Acquisition*. Hillsdale, N. J.: Erlbaum.

Chase, W. G., and Simon, H. A. (1973). Perception in chess. *Cognitive Psychology*, 4, 55–81.

Chi, M. T. H. (1978). Knowledge structures and memory development. In R. Siegler (ed.), *Children's Thinking: What Develops?* Hillsdale, N. J.: Erlbaum.

Chi, M. T. H., and Ceci, S. J. (1987). Content knowledge: its role, representation, and restructuring in memory development. *Advances in Child Development*, 20, 91–142.

Chi, M. T. H., and Koeske, R. D. (1983). Network presentation of a child's dinosaur knowledge. *Developmental Psychology*, 19, 29–39.

Clark, E. F. (1983). *George Parker Bidder: The Calculating Boy*. Bedford: KSL Publications.

Clark, R. W. (1979). *Einstein: the Life and Times*. London: Hodder & Stoughton.

Clarke-Stewart, K. A. (1973). Interactions between mothers and their young children: characteristics and consequences. *Monographs of the Society for Research in Child Development*, 38, Serial No. 153.

Clive, J. (1973). *Thomas Babington Macaulay: the Shaping of the Historian*. London: Secker & Warburg.

Cloward, R. D. (1967). Studies in tutoring. *Journal of Experimental Education*, 36, 14–25.

Cole, J. R., and Cole, S. (1973). *Social Stratification in Science*. Chicago: University of Chicago Press.

Coles, G. (1987). *The Learning Mystique*. New York: Fawcett Ballantine.

Costall, A. (1985). The relativity of absolute pitch. In P. Howell, I. Cross, and R. West (eds), *Musical Structure and Cognition*. London: Academic Press.

Covington, M. V. (1986). Strategic thinkng and the fear of failure. In J. W. Segal, S. F. Chipman, and R. Glaser (eds), *Thinking and Learning Skills*, Vol. 1: *Relating Instruction to Research*. Hillsdale, N. J.: Erlbaum.

Covington, M. V., and Omelich, C. L. (1981). As failures mount: affective and cognitive consequences of ability demotion in the classroom. *Journal of Educational Psychology*, 92, 149–54.

Csikszentmihalyi, M. (1988). Society, culture, and person: a systems view of creativity. In R. J. Sternberg (ed.), *The Nature of Creativity: Contemporary Psychological Perspectives*. New York: Cambridge University Press.

Darwin, C. (1958). *The Autobiography of Charles Darwin, 1809–1882, with Original Omissions Restored*. (Edited with Appendix and notes by his granddaughter Norma Barlow.) London: Collins.

Davidson, H. P. (1931). An experimental study of bright, average, and dull children at the four-year mental level. *Genetic Psychology Monographs*, 9, 119–289.

# References

Davidson, L., and Scripp, L. (1988). Young children's musical representations: windows on music cognition. In J. A. Sloboda (ed.), *Generative Processes in Music: the Psychology of Performance, Improvisation, and Composition.* Oxford: Clarendon Press.

Dennis, W. (1941). Infant development under conditions of restricted practice and minimum social stimulation. *Genetic Psychology Monographs,* 23, 143–89.

Dennis, W., and Dennis, M. G. (1951). Development under controlled environmental conditions. In W. Dennis (ed.), *Readings in Child Psychology.* New York: Prentice-Hall.

Detterman, D. K. (1982). Does 'g' exist? *Intelligence,* 6, 99–108.

Dowling, W. J. (1988). Tonal structure and children's early learning of music. In J. A. Sloboda (ed.), *Generative Processes in Music: the Psychology of Performance, Improvisation, and Composition.* Oxford: Clarendon Press.

Dunn, J. F. (1979). The first year of life: continuity in individual differences. In D. Shaffer and J. F. Dunn (eds.), *The First Year of Life.* London: Wiley.

Durkin, D. (1966). *Children Who Read Early.* New York: Teachers College Press, Columbia University.

Elder, G. H. (1988). Wartime losses and social bonding: influence across 40 years in men's lives. *Psychiatry,* 51, 177–98.

Elder, G. H., Hastings, T., and Pavalko, E. (1989). Adult pathways to career distinction and disappointment. Paper presented at the Biennial Meeting of the Life History Research Society, Montreal, Canada.

Elkind, D. (1981). *The Hurried Child.* Reading, Massachusetts: Addison Wesley.

Ellis, A. W., and Young, A. W. (1988). *Human Cognitive Neuropsychology.* Hove: Erlbaum.

Ericsson, K. A. (1985). Memory skill. *Canadian Journal of Psychology,* 39, 188–231.

Ericsson, K. A. (1988). Theoretical issues in the study of exceptional performance. Invited address to the International Conference on Thinking, Aberdeen University, Scotland.

Ericsson, K. A. (1990). Peak performance and age: an examination of peak performance in sports. In P. B. Baltes and M. M. Baltes (eds), *Successful Aging: Perspectives from the Behavioral Sciences.* New York: Cambridge University Press.

Ericsson, K. A., and Crutcher, R. J. (1988). The nature of exceptional performance. In P. B. Baltes, D. L. Featherman, and R. M. Lerner (eds), *Life-span Development and Behavior,* Vol. 10.

Ericsson, K. A., and Faivre, I. A. (1988). What's exceptional about exceptional abilities? In L. K. Obler and D. Fein (eds), *The Exceptional Brain: Neuropsychology of Talent and Special Abilities.* New York: Guilford Press.

Ericsson, K. A., Tesch-Römer, C., and Krampe, R. T. (1990). The role of practice and motivation in the acquisition of expert-level performance in real life: an empirical evaluation of a theoretical framework. In M. J. A. Howe (ed.), *Encouraging the Development of Exceptional Abilities and Talents.* Leicester: The British Psychological Society.

Escalona, S. K. (1973). The differential impact of environmental conditions as a function of different reaction patterns in infancy. In J. C. Westman (ed.), *Individual Differences in Children*. New York: Wiley.

Estes, W. K. (1970). *Learning Theory and Mental Development*. New York: Academic Press.

Estes, W. K. (1982). Learning, memory, and intelligence. In R. J. Sternberg (ed.), *Handbook of Human Intelligence*. New York: Cambridge University Press.

Eysenck, H. J. (1986). The theory of intelligence and the psychophysiology of cognition. In R. J. Sternberg (ed.), *Advances in the Psychology of Human Cognition*. Vol. 3. Hillsdale, N. J.: Erlbaum.

Eysenck, H. J. (1988). Editorial: the concept of 'intelligence': useful or useless. *Intelligence*, 12, 1–16.

Eysenck, H. J., and Barrett, P. T. (1985). Psychophysiology and the measurement of intelligence. In C. R. Reynolds and V. L. Willson (eds), *Methodological and Statistical Advances in the Study of Individual Differences*. New York: Plenum.

Eysenck, H. J. versus Kamin, L. (1981). *Intelligence: the Battle for the Mind*. London: Pan Books.

Feldman, D. H. (1980). *Beyond Universals in Cognitive Development*. Norwood, N. J.: Ablex.

Feldman, D. H. (1986). *Nature's Gambit: Child Prodigies and the Development of Human Potential*. New York: Basic Books.

Feuerstein, R. (1980). *Instrumental Enrichment: an Intervention Program for Cognitive Modifiability*. Baltimore: University Park Press.

Feuerstein, R., Hoffman, M. B., Jensen, M. R., and Rand, Y. (1985). Instrumental enrichment, an intervention program for structural cognitive modifiability: theory and practice. In J. W. Segal, S. F. Chipman and R. Glaser (eds), *Thinking and Learning Skills*. Vol. 1: *Relating Instruction to Research*. Hillsdale, N. J.: Erlbaum.

Fodor, J. A. (1983). *The Modularity of Mind*. Cambridge, Mass.: MIT Press.

Fowler, W. (1981). Case studies of cognitive precocity; the role of exogenous and endogenous stimulation in early mental development. *Journal of Applied Developmental Psychology*, 2, 319–67.

Fowler, W. (1983). *Potentials of Childhood*. Vol. 1: *A Historical View of Early Experience*. Vol. 2: *Studies in Early Developmental Learning*. Lexington, Mass.: Heath.

Fowler, W. (1986). Early experiences of great men and women mathematicians. In W. Fowler (ed.), *Early Experience and the Development of Competence: No. 32, New Directions for Child Development*. San Francisco: Jossey-Bass.

Fowler, W. (1990). Early stimulation and the development of verbal talents. In M. J. A. Howe (ed.), *Encouraging the Development of Exceptional Abilities and Talents*. Leicester: The British Psychological Society.

Fowler, W., Ogston, K., Roberts, G., Steane, D., and Swenson, A. (1983). *Potentials of Childhood*, Vol. 2: *Studies in Early Developmental Learning*. Lexington, Mass.: Heath.

Fox, L. H. (1976). The values of gifted youth. In D. P. Keating (ed.), *Intellectual*

*Talent: Research and Development. Proceedings of the Sixth Annual Hyman Blumberg Symposium on Research in Early Childhood Education*. Baltimore: Johns Hopkins University Press.

Freeman, J. (1979). *Gifted Children: Their Identification and Development in a Social Context*. Lancaster: MTP Press.

Freeman, J. (1985). A pedagogy for the gifted. In J. Freeman (ed.), *The Psychology of Gifted Children*. Chichester: Wiley.

Freeman, J. (1990). The intellectually gifted adolescent. In M. J. A. Howe (ed.), *Encouraging the Development of Exceptional Abilities and Talents*. Leicester: The British Psychological Society.

Frith, U. (1989). *Autism: Explaining the Enigma*. Oxford: Blackwell.

Fullard, W. G. (1967). Operant training of aural music discriminations with preschool children. *Journal of Research in Music Education*, 15, 201–9.

Gardner, H. (1982). *Art, Mind, and Brain: a Cognitive Approach to Creativity*. New York: Basic Books.

Gardner, H. (1984). *Frames of Mind*. London: Heinemann.

Gardner, H. (1985). *The Mind's New Science: A History of the Cognitive Revolution*. New York; Basic Books.

Gardner, H. (1988). Creative lives and creative works: a synthetic scientific approach. In R. J. Sternberg (ed.), *The Nature of Creativity; Contemporary Psychological Perspectives*. Cambridge: Cambridge University Press.

Gesell, A., and Thompson, H. (1929). Learning and growth in identical infant twins: an experimental study by the method of co-twin control. *Genetic Psychology Monographs*, 6, 1–124.

Ghiselli, E. E. (1966). *The Validity of Occupational Aptitude Tests*. New York: Wiley.

Glaser, R. (1984). Education and thinking: the role of knowledge. *American Psychologist*, 39, 93–104.

Goldstein, D. M. (1976). Cognitive-linguistic functioning and learning to read in preschoolers, *Journal of Educational Psychology*, 68, 680–8.

Gottfried, A. W. (1984). *Home Environment and Early Cognitive Development*. New York; Academic Press.

Gould, S. J. (1984). *The Mismeasure of Man*. Harmondsworth: Penguin Books.

Gruber, H. E. (1981). *Darwin On Man: a Psychological Study of Scientific Creativity*, 2nd edn. Chicago: University of Chicago Press.

Gruber, H. E. (1982). On the hypothesized relation between giftedness and creativity. In D. H. Feldman (ed.), *New Directions in Child Development. Developmental Approaches to Giftedness and Creativity*, No. 17. San Francisco: Jossey Bass.

Guess, D. (1969). A functional analysis of receptive language and productive speech: acquisition of the plural phoneme. *Journal of Applied Behavior Analysis*, 1, 297–306.

Guess, D., and Baer, D. M. (1973). An analysis of individual differences in generalization between receptive and productive language in retarded children. *Journal of Applied Behaviour Analysis*, 6, 311–29.

Gustin, W. C. (1985). The development of exceptional research mathematicians. In B. S. Bloom (ed.), *Developing Talent in Young People*. New York: Ballantine Books.

Hagan, R. D., Smith, M. G., and Gettman, L. R. (1981). Marathon performance in relation to maximal aerobic power and training indices. *Medicine and Science in Sports Exercise*, 13, 185–9.

Hamilton, M. L. (1977). Social learning and the transition from babbling to words. *Journal of Genetic Psychology*, 130, 211–70.

Hart, B., and Risley, T. R. (1980). In vivo language intervention: unanticipated general effects. *Journal of Applied Behaviour Analysis*, 13, 407–32.

Hayes, J. R. (1981). *The Complete Problem Solver*. Philadelphia: The Franklin Institute Press.

Hershman, J. D., and Lieb, J. (1988). *The Key to Genius*. New York: Prometheus Books.

Hildesheimer, W. (1983). *Mozart* (trans. M. Faber). London: Dent.

Horn, J. (1986). Intellectual ability concepts. In R. J. Sternberg (ed.), *Advances in the Psychology of Human Intelligence*, Vol. 3. Hillsdale, N. J.: Erlbaum.

Howald, H. (1982). Training-induced morphological and functional changes in skeletal muscle. *International Journal of Sports Medicine*, 3, 1–12

Howe, M. J. A. (1975). *Learning in Infants and Young Children*. Basingstoke: Macmillan.

Howe, M. J. A. (1976). Good learners and poor learners. *Bulletin of the British Psychological Society*, 29, 16–19.

Howe, M. J. A. (1977). *Television and Children*. London: New University Education.

Howe, M. J. A. (1980). *The Psychology of Human Learning*. New York: Harper & Row.

Howe, M. J. A. (1982). Biographical evidence and the development of outstanding individuals. *American Psychologist*, 37, 1071–81.

Howe, M. J. A. (1983a). *Introduction to the Psychology of Memory*. New York: Harper & Row. Republished in 1987 by University Press of America.

Howe, M. J. A. (1983b). (ed.): *Learning from Television: Psychological and Educational Research*. London: Academic Press.

Howe, M. J. A. (1984). *A teachers' guide to the psychology of learning*. Oxford: Blackwell.

Howe, M. J. A. (1987a). Using cognitive psychology to help students learn. In J. T. E. Richardson, M. W. Eysenck and D. Warren Piper (eds), *Student Learning: Research in Education and Cognitive Psychology*, pp. 135–46. Milton Keynes: SRHE and The Open University Press.

Howe, M. J. A. (1987b). Motivation, cognition and individual achievements. In E. De Corte, H. Lodewijks, R. Parmentier and P. Span (eds), *Learning and Instruction*, pp. 133–46. Oxford: Pergamon.

Howe, M. J. A. (1988a). Memory in mentally retarded 'idiots savants'. In M. M. Gruneberg, P. Morris, and R. N. Sykes (eds), *Practical Aspects of Memory: Current Research and Issues*, Vol. 2, pp. 267–73. Chichester: Wiley.

Howe, M. J. A. (1988b). Intelligence as an explanation. *British Journal of Psychology*, 79, 349–60.

Howe, M. J. A. (1988c). The hazards of using correlational evidence as a means of identifying the causes of individual ability differences: a rejoinder to Sternberg and a reply to Miles. *British Journal of Psychology*, 79, 539–45.

Howe, M. J. A. (1988d). Context, memory and education. In G. M. Davies and

D. M. Thomson (eds), *Memory in Context: Context in Memory*, pp. 267–81. Chichester, Wiley.

Howe, M. J. A. (1988e). 'Hot house' children. *The Psychologist*, 1, 356–8.

Howe, M. J. A. (1988f). Perspiration beats inspiration. *New Scientist*, 120, No. 1644/1645, 58–60.

Howe, M. J. A. (1989a). *Fragments of Genius: the Strange Feats of Idiots Savants*. London: Routledge.

Howe, M. J. A. (1989b). Cognitive processes in 'idiots savants'. In A. M. Colman and G. Beaumont (eds), *Psychology Survey 7*. Leicester: The British Psychological Society.

Howe, M. J. A. (1989c). 'Idiots savants'. In M. W. Eysenck, A. Ellis, E. Hunt, and P. Johnson-Laird (eds), *Dictionary of Cognitive Psychology*. Oxford: Blackwell.

Howe, M. J. A. (1989d). The hot house effect. *Child Education*, 66, No.3, 20–1.

Howe, M. J. A. (1989e). Separate skills or general intelligence: the autonomy of human abilities. *British Journal of Educational Psychology*, 59, 351–60.

Howe, M. J. A. (1990a) (ed.): *Encouraging the Development of Exceptional Abilities and Talents*. Leicester: The British Psychological Society.

Howe, M. J. A. (1990b). *Sense and Nonsense about Hothouse Children: A Practical Guide for Parents and Teachers*. London: The British Psychological Society.

Howe, M. J. A. (1990c) Children's gifts, talents, and natural abilities: an explanatory mythology? *Journal of Educational and Child Psychology*, 7, No 1, 52–54.

Howe, M. J. A., and Smith, J. (1988). Calendar calculating in 'idiots savants': how do they do it? *British Journal of Psychology*, 79, 371–86.

Hunt, J. McV. (1986). The effect of variations in quality and type of early child care on development. In W. Fowler (ed.), *Early Experience and the Development of Competence: No. 32, New Directions for Child Development*. San Francisco: Jossey-Bass.

Hunter, I. M. L. (1984). Lengthy verbatim recall (LVR) and the mythical gift of tape-recorder memory. In K. M. J. Lagerspetz and P. Niemi (eds), *Psychology in the 1990's*. Amsterdam: Elsevier.

Irwin, R. J. (1984). Inspection time and its relation to intelligence. *Intelligence*, 8, 47–65.

Jersild, A. T., and Bienstock, S. F. (1931). The influence of training on the vocal ability of three-year-old children. *Child Development*, 2, 272–91.

Kagan, J. (1989). Temperamental contributions to social behavior. *American Psychologist*, 44, 668–74.

Kagan, J., Reznick, J. S., and Snidman, N. (1987). The physiology and psychology of behavioral inhibition. *Child Development*, 58, 1459–73.

Keating, D. P. (1976). Creative potential of mathematically precocious boys. In D. P. Keating (ed.), *Intellectual Talent: Research and Development. Proceedings of the Sixth Annual Hyman Blumberg Symposium on Research in Early Childhood Education*. Baltimore: Johns Hopkins University Press.

Keating, D. P. (1984). The emperor's new clothes: The 'new look' in intelligence research. In R. J. Sternberg (ed.), *Advances in the Psychology of Human Intelligence*, Vol. 2. Hillsdale, N. J.: Erlbaum.

Keating, D. P., List, J. A., and Merriman, W. E. (1985). Cognitive processing and cognitive ability: a multivariate validity investigation. *Intelligence*, 9, 149–70.

Klemp, G. O., and McClelland, D. C. (1986). What characterizes intelligent functioning among senior managers? In R. J. Sternberg and R. K. Wagner (eds), *Practical Intelligence: Nature and Origins of Competence in the Everyday World*. Cambridge: Cambridge University Press.

Koldener, W. (1970). *Antonio Vivaldi, His Life and Work*, trans. W. Hopkins. London: Faber & Faber.

Korner, A. F. (1971). Individual differences at birth: implications for early experience and later development. *American Journal of Orthopsychiatry*, 41, 608–19.

Kress, G. (1982). *Learning to Write*. London: Routledge.

Kunkel, J. H. (1985). Vivaldi in Venice: an historical test of psychological propositions. *Psychological Record*, 35, 445–57.

Laboratory of Comparative Human Cognition (1983). What's cultural about cross-cultural psychology? *Annual Review of Psychology*, 30, 145–72.

Lave, J. (1977). Tailor-made experiments and evaluating the intellectual consequences of apprenticeship training. *The Quarterly Newsletter of the Institute for Comparative Human Development*, 1, 1–3.

Lave, J. (1988). *Cognition in Practice: Mind, Mathematics and Culture in Everyday Life*. New York: Cambridge University Press.

Lave, J., Murtaugh, M., and De la Roche, D. (1984). The dialectic of arithmetic in grocery shopping. In B. Rogoff and J. Lave (eds), *Everyday Cognition: Its Development in Social Contexts*. Cambridge, Mass.: Harvard University Press.

Lazar, I., Darlington, R., Murray, H., Royce, J., and Snipper, A. (1982). Lasting effects of early education: a report from the Consortium for Longitudinal Studies. *Monographs of the Society for Research in Child Development*, 47, 2–3. (Serial No. 195).

Lehman, H. C. (1953). *Age and Achievement*. Princetown, N. J.: Princetown University Press.

Lennon, P. (1989). Sweeping the board by book or by rook. *The Guardian*, 11 November.

Lewis, D. (1976). Observations on route finding and spatial orientation among the aboriginal peoples of the western desert region of central Australia. *Oceania*, 46, 249–82.

Lewontin, R. (1982). *Human Diversity*. New York: Freeman.

Lowes, J. L. (1927). *The Road to Xanadu*. Boston: Houghton Mifflin.

Luria, A. R. (1968). *The Mind of a Mnemonist*. New York: Basic Books.

McCabe, A. (1987). *Language Games to Play with your Child*. New York: Fawcett Columbine.

McCartney, K. (1984). Effects of quality of day care environment on children's language development. *Developmental Psychology*, 20, 244–60.

McClelland, D. C. (1973). Testing for competence rather than for 'intelligence'. *American Psychologist*, 28, 1–14.

MacDonald, M. (1935). A model of the relationships between art and science. *Edinburgh Review*, 71, 81–90.

McGraw, M. (1935). *Growth: A Study of Johnny and Jimmy*. New York: Appleton-Century-Crofts.

McGraw, M. (1939). Later development of children specially trained during infancy: Johnny and Jimmy at school age. *Child Development*, 10, 1–19.

MacKenzie, N., and MacKenzie, J. (1973). *The Life of H. G. Wells: The Time Traveller*. London: Weidenfeld and Nicholson.

Marjoram, D. T. E., and Nelson, R. D. (1985). Mathematical gifts. In J. Freeman (ed.), *The Psychology of Gifted Children*. Chichester: Wiley.

Martin, M. (1978). Assessment of individual variation in memory ability. In M. M. Gruneberg, P. E. Morris and R. N. Sykes (eds), *Practical Aspects of Memory*. London: Academic Press.

Matheny, K., and Edwards, C. (1974). Academic improvement through an experimental classroom management system. *Journal of School Psychology*, 12, 222–32.

Mead, M. (1975). *Growing up in New Guinea*. New York: William Morrow.

Mehler, J., Morton, J., and Juscyk, P. W. (1984). On reducing language to biology. *Cognitive Neuropsychology*, 1, 83–116.

Metzl, M. N. (1980). Teaching parents a strategy for enhancing infant development. *Child Development*, 51, 583–6.

Mill, J. S. (1971). *Autobiography*. London: Oxford University Press.

Miller, K., and Gelman, R. (1983). The child's representation of number: A multidimensional scaling analysis. *Child Development*, 54, 1470–9.

Mitchell, F. D. (1907). Mathematical prodigies. *American Journal of Psychology*, 18, 61–143.

Moon, C., and Wells, G. (1979). The influence of home on learning to read. *Journal of Research in Reading*, 2, 53–62.

Morris, P. E. (1988). Expertise and everyday memory. In M. M. Gruneberg, P. E. Morris and R. N. Sykes (eds), *Practical Aspects of Memory: Current Research and Issues*, Vol. 1. Chichester: Wiley.

Morris, P. E., Gruneberg, M. M., Sykes, R. N., and Merrick, A. (1981). Football knowledge and the acquisition of new results. *British Journal of Psychology*, 72, 479–83.

Morris, P. E., Tweedy, M., and Gruneberg, M. M. (1985). Interest, knowledge and the memorizing of soccer scores. *British Journal of Psychology*, 76, 415–25.

Nelson, K. (1977). Facilitating children's syntax acquisition. *Developmental Psychology*, 13, 101–7.

Nelson, K., Carskaddon, G., and Bonvillian, J. D. (1973). Syntax acquisition: impact of experimental variation in adult verbal interaction with the child. *Child Development*, 44, 497–504.

Nettelbeck, T. (1987). Inspection time and intelligence. In P. A. Vernon (ed.), *Speed of Information Processing and Intelligence*. Norwood, N. J.: Ablex.

O'Connor, N., and Hermelin, B. (1984). Idiot savant calendrical calculators: maths or memory? *Psychological Medicine*, 14, 801–6.

Olson, D. R. (1986). Intelligence and literacy: the relationships between intelligence and the technologies of representation and communication. In R. J. Sternberg and R. K. Wagner (eds), *Practical Intelligence: Nature and Origins of Competence in the Everyday World* (pp. 338–60). Cambridge: Cambridge University Press.

Olson, D. R. (1977). From utterance to text: the basis of language in speech and writing. *Harvard Educational Review*, 47, 257–82.

Ong, W. J. (1982). *Orality and Literacy: the Technologizing of the Word*. London: Methuen.

Peak, L. (1986). Training learning skills and attitudes in Japanese early educational settings. In W. Fowler (ed.), *Early Experience and the Development of Competence. No. 32. New Directions for Child Development*. San Francisco: Jossey Bass.

Perkins, D. N. (1981). *The Mind's Best Work*. London: Harvard University Press.

Petersen, G. A., and Sherrod, K. B. (1982). Relationship of maternal language to language development and language delay of children. *American Journal of Mental Deficiency*, 86, 391–8.

Plomin, R. (1986). *Development, Genetics, and Psychology*. Hillsdale, N. J.: Erlbaum.

Rabbitt, P. M. A. (1988). Critical notice of R. J. Sternberg (ed.): *Handbook of Human Intelligence*; *Advances in the Psychology of Human Intelligence*, Vols 1 and 2; Human abilities; beyond IQ: a triarchic theory of human intelligence. *Quarterly Journal of Experimental Psychology*, 40A, 167–85.

Radford, J. (1990). *Child Prodigies and Exceptional Early Achievement*. London: Harvester.

Ramey, C. T., Bryant, D. M., and Suarez, T. (1985). Preschool compensatory education and the modifiability of intelligence: a critical review. In D. K. Detterman (ed.), *Current Topics in Human Intelligence*. Norwood, N. J.: Ablex.

Renninger, K. A., and Wozniak, R. N. (1985). Effect of interest on attentional shift, recognition and recall in young children. *Developmental Psychology*, 21, 624–32.

Renzulli, J. S. (1986). The three-ring conception of giftedness: a developmental model for creative productivity. In R. J. Sternberg and J. E. Davidson (eds), *Conceptions of Giftedness*. New York: Cambridge University Press.

Resnick, L. B., and Neches, R. (1984). Factors affecting individual differences in learning ability. In R. J. Sternberg (ed.), *Advances in the Psychology of Human Intelligence*, Vol. 2. Hillsdale, N. J.: Erlbaum.

Revesz, G. (1925). *The Psychology of a Musical Prodigy*. London: Kegan Paul, Trench and Trubner.

Rimland, B., and Fein, D. (1988). Special talents of autistic savants. In L. K. Obler and D. Fein (eds), *The Exceptional Brain: Neuropsychology of Talent and Special Abilities*, pp. 474–92. New York: Guilford Press.

Roe, A. (1952). *The Making of a Scientist*. New York: Dodd, Mead.
Rolfe, L. M. (1978). *The Menuhins: a Family Odyssey*. San Francisco: Panjandrum/Aris Books.
Rose, D. H., Slater, A. M., and Perry, H. (1986). Prediction of childhood intelligence from habituation in early infancy. *Intelligence*, 10, 251–63.
Rothenberg, A. (1979). *The Emerging Goddess: The Creative Process in Art, Science, and Other Fields*. Chicago: University of Chicago Press.
Rotter, J. (1975). Some problems and misconceptions related to the construct of internal versus external control of reinforcement. *Journal of Consulting and Clinical Psychology*, 43, 56–67.
Ruchalla, E., Schalt, E., and Vogel, F. (1985) Relations between mental performance and reaction time: new aspects of an old problem. *Intelligence*, 9, 189–205.
Rutter, M. (1989). Pathways from childhood to adult life. *Journal of Child Psychology and Psychiatry*, 30, 23–51.
Sacks, O. (1985). *The Man Who Mistook His Wife for a Hat*. London: Duckworth.
Saxe, G. B. (1988). The mathematics of child street vendors. *Child Development*, 59, 1415–25.
Schafer, E. W. P. (1987). Neural adaptability: a biological determinant of $g$ factor intelligence. *Behavioral and Brain Sciences*, 10, 240–1.
Schaffer, H. R., and Emerson, P. E. (1964). Patterns of response to physical contact in early human development. *Journal of Child Psychology and Psychiatry*, 5, 1–13.
Schenk, E. (1960). *Mozart and his Times*. Ed. and trans. from the German by R. and C. Winston. London: Secker and Warburg.
Scribner, S. (1986). Thinking in action: some characteristics of practical thought. In R. J. Sternberg and R. K. Wagner (eds), *Practical Intelligence: Nature and Origins of Competence in the Everyday World*. Cambridge: Cambridge University Press.
Seligman, M. A. P. (1975). *Helplessness: on Depression, Development and Death*. San Francisco: Freeman.
Shuter-Dyson, R., and Gabriel, C. (1981). *The Psychology of Musical Ability*. 2nd edn. London: Methuen.
Shuter-Dyson, R. (1985). Musical giftedness. In J. Freeman (ed.), *The Psychology of Gifted Children*. Chichester: Wiley.
Simon, H. A. and Chase, W. G. (1973). Skill in chess. *American Scientist*, 61, 394–403.
Simonton, D. K. (1984). *Genius, Creativity and Leadership: Historiometric Enquiries*. Cambridge, Mass.: Harvard University Press.
Skidelsky, R. (1983). *John Maynard Keynes*. Vol. 1. *Hopes Betrayed*. London: Macmillan.
Slater, A. M., Cooper, R., Rose, D., and Morison, V. (1989). Prediction of cognitive performance from infancy to early childhood. *Human Development*, 32, 137–47.
Sloane, K. D. (1985). Home influences on talent development. In B. S. Bloom (ed.), *Developing Talent in Young People*. New York: Ballantine.

Sloboda, J. A. (1985). *The Musical Mind: the Cognitive Psychology of Music*. London: Oxford University Press.
Smith, S. B. (1983). *The Great Mental Calculators*. New York: Columbia University Press.
Smith, G. A., and Stanley, G. (1983). Clocking g: relating intellience and measures of timed performance. *Intelligence*, 7, 353–68.
Smith, J., and Howe, M. J. A. (1985). An investigation of calendar-calculating in an 'idiot savant'. *International Journal of Rehabilitation Research*, 8, 77–9.
Sorokin, P. (1956). *Fads and Foibles in Modern Sociology*, Chicago: H. Regnery Co.
Sosniak, L. A. (1985). Learning to be a concert pianist. In B. S. Bloom (ed.), *Developing Talent in Young People*. New York: Ballantine.
Sosniak, L. A. (1987). The nature of change in successful learning. *Teachers College Record*, 88, 519–35.
Sosniak, L. A. (1990). The tortoise, the hare, and the development of talent. In M. J. A. Howe (ed.), *Encouraging the Development of Exceptional Abilities and Talents*. Leicester: The British Psychological Society.
Staats, A. W. (1971). *Child Learning, Intelligence, and Personality*. New York: Harper and Row.
Stanley, J. C., George, W. C., and Solano, C. H. (1977). *The Gifted and the Creative*. Baltimore: Johns Hopkins University Press.
Sternberg, R. J., and Salter, W. (1982). Conceptions of intelligence. In R. J. Sternberg (ed.), *Handbook of Human Intelligence*. Cambridge: Cambridge University Press.
Storr, A. (1988). *The School of Genius*. London: André Deutsch.
Stott, D. H. (1974). *The Parent as Teacher: A Guide for Parents of Children with Learning Difficulties*. London: University of London Press.
Super, C. (1976). Environmental effects on motor development: the case of 'African infant precocity'. *Developmental Medicine and Child Neurology*, 18, 561–7.
Tamis-LéMonda, C. S., and Bornstein, M. H. (1989). Habituation and maternal encouragement of attention in infancy as predictors of toddler language, play, and representational competence. *Child Development*, 60, 738–51.
Taniuchi, L. (1986). Cultural continuity in an educational institution: a case study of the Suzuki method of music instruction. In M. I. White and S. Pollak (eds), *The Cultural Transition: Human Experience and Social Transformation in the Third World and Japan*. Boston: Routledge and Kegan Paul.
Thomas, A., and Chess, S. (1977). *Temperament and Development*. New York: Brunner/Mazel.
Treffert, D. A. (1989). *Extraordinary People*. London: Bantam Press.
Valdez-Menchaca, M. C., and Whitehurst, G. J. (1988). The effects of incidental teaching on vocabulary acquisition by young children. *Child Development*, 59, 1451–9.
Vygotsky, L. (1962). *Thought and Language*. Cambridge, Mass.: MIT Press.
Wachs, T. D., and Gruen, G. E. (1982). *Early Experience and Human Development*. New York: Plenum Press.

Wallace, A. (1986). *The Prodigy: A Biography of William James Sidis, the World's Greatest Child Prodigy.* London: Macmillan.
Wallace, D. B. (1986). Giftedness and the construction of a creative life. In F. D. Horowitz and M. O'Brien (eds), *The Gifted and the Talented: Developmental Perspectives.* Washington: The American Psychological Association.
Walmsley, J., and Margolis, J. (1987). *Hot House People: Can we Create Super Human Beings?* London: Pan Books.
Weinert, F. E., and Waldmann, M. R. (1986). How do the gifted think?: intellectual abilities and cognitive processes. In A. J. Cropley, K. K. Urban, H. Wagner and W. Wieczerkowski (eds), *Giftedness: a Continuing Worldwide Challenge.* New York: Trillium Press.
Weisberg, R. (1986). *Creativity: Genius and Other Myths.* New York: Freeman.
Wells, H. G. (1966) *Experiment in Autobiography.* London: Gollancz/The Cresset Press. [First published in 1934.]
West, A. (1985). *H. G. Wells: Aspects of a Life.* Harmondsworth: Penguin Books.
Westfall, R. S. (1980). Newton's marvellous years of discovery and their aftermath: myth versus manuscript. *Isis*, 1980, 71, (No. 256) 109–21.
White, B. L. (1971). *Human Infants: Experience and Psychological Development.* Englewood Cliffs, New Jersey: Prentice-Hall.
White, B. L. (1985). Competence and giftedness. In J. Freeman (ed.), *The Psychology of Gifted Children.* Chichester: Wiley.
White, P. A. (1988). The structured representation of information in long-term memory: a possible explanation for the accomplishments of 'idiots savants'. *New Ideas in Psychology*, 6, 3–14.
Whitehurst, G. J., and Valdez-Menchaca, M. C. (1988). What is the role of reinforcement in early language acquisition? *Child Development*, 59, 430–40.
Whitehurst, G. J., Falco, F. L., Lonigan, C. J., Fischel, J. E., DeBaryshe, B. D., Valdez-Menchaca, M. C., and Caulfield, M. (1988). Accelerating language development through picture book reading. *Developmental Psychology*, 24, 552–9.
Wiener, N. (1953). *Ex-Prodigy: My Childhood and Youth.* New York: Simon & Schuster.
Wilding, J., and Valentine, E. (1988). Individual differences in everyday memory. In M. M. Gruneberg, P. Morris, and R. N. Sykes, (eds), *Practical Aspects of Memory: Current Research and Issues*, Vol. 2. Chichester: Wiley.
Witte, K. H. G. (1975). *The Education of Karl Witte*, trans. Leo Wiener. New York: Arno Press. (Originally published in 1914 by Thomas Cromwell.)
Zigler, E., and Seitz, V. (1982). Social policy and intelligence. In R. J. Sternberg (ed.), *Handbook of Human Intelligence.* New York: Cambridge University Press.

# Author Index

Ainsworth, M. D. S., 112, 115
Albert, R. S., 188
Anastasi, A., 207
Anderson, M., 214

Badgio, P., 195
Baer, D. M., 76
Baker, J. G., 33
Baltes, P. B., 176
Bamberger, J., 84
Baron, J., 195
Barrett, P., 214
Bell, S. M., 112
Belmont, J., 45, 219
Berry, C., 98
Biederman, I., 90
Bienstock, S. F., 84
Bloom, B. S., 8, 12, 103
Blum, D., 101
Bonvillian, J. D., 71
Bouchard, C., 43
Bradley, L., 78
Brady, P. T., 46, 90
Brannigan, A., 41
Brent, P., 106, 107
Brodie, F. M., 179, 180
Bronfenbrenner, U., 33
Bryant, D. M., 70, 202
Bryant, P., 78
Burchinal, M., 71
Burd, V. A., 102, 235
Bynner, J. M., 205

Carey, S., 221
Carskaddon, G., 71

Caulfield, M., 74
Ceci, S. J., 6, 33, 45, 201, 211, 214, 216, 219, 220, 221
Chase, W. G., 24, 25, 86
Chess, S., 48
Chi, M. T. H., 216, 219, 221
Clark, E. F., 128, 130
Clark, R. W., 40, 140, 141, 182, 183
Clarke-Stewart, K. A., 71
Clive, J., 235
Cloward, R. D., 192
Cole, J. R., 186
Cole, S., 186
Coles, G., 78
Cooper, R., 7, 46
Costall, A., 90
Covington, M. V., 193
Crutcher, R. J., 88
Csikszentmihalyi, M., 40, 41

Darlington, R., 70, 202
Darwin, C., 182
Davidson, H. P., 80, 81, 82, 84
Davidson, L., 84
De la Roche, D., 90
Dennis, M. G., 67
Dennis, W., 67
Detterman, D. K., 211
Dowling, W. J., 84
Dunn, J. F., 48
Durkin, D., 82

Edwards, C., 192
Elder, G. H., 102, 202

Elkind, D., 162
Emerson, P. E., 49
Ericsson, K. A., 27, 33, 34, 43, 44, 46, 86, 87, 88, 89, 90, 91, 184
Escalona, S. K., 7, 49
Estes, W. K., 45, 219
Eysenck, H. W., 51, 214

Faivre, I. A., 27, 34, 46, 87, 88, 89, 90, 184
Falco, F. L., 74
Fein, D., 28
Feldman, D. H., 22, 34, 40, 109, 110, 146, 155, 156, 166, 171, 172, 238
Feuerstein, R., 117, 120
Fischel, J. E., 74
Fodor, J. A., 222
Fowler, W., 6, 63, 65, 66, 69, 71, 72, 74, 76, 77, 83, 84, 85, 145, 146, 147, 148, 153
Fox, L. H., 156
Freeman, J., 12, 88, 121, 122, 156, 183
Frith, U., 42

Gabriel, C., 84
Gardner, H., 16, 98, 173, 185, 222
Gaskins, I., 195
Gelman, R., 216
George, J. C., 152
Gesell, A., 64, 65
Gettman, L. R., 91
Ghiselli, E. E., 200
Glaser, R., 221
Goldstein, D. M., 79
Gottfried, A. W., 110
Gould, S. J., 8, 174
Gruber, H. E., 8, 181
Gruen, G. E., 110
Gruneberg, M. M., 89
Guess, D., 76
Gustin, W. C., 237

Hagan, R. D., 91
Hamilton, M. L., 76
Hart, B., 76
Hastings, T., 102, 202
Hayes, J. R., 24, 100, 110
Hershman, J. D., 185
Hildesheimer, W., 23
Hoffman, M. B., 117

Horn, J., 205, 207
Howald, H., 44
Howe, M. J. A., 26, 34, 45, 87, 88, 116, 117, 159, 173, 180, 184, 193, 205, 218, 219, 221, 222, 227, 228
Hunt, J. McV., 76
Hunter, I. M. L., 88
Irwin, R. J., 214

Jensen, M. R., 117
Jersild, A. T., 84

Kagan, J., 48
Kamin, L., 51
Keating, D. P., 156, 205, 215
Klemp, G. O., 199
Koeske, R. D., 221
Koldener, W., 11
Korner, A. F., 7, 47
Krampe, R. T., 91
Kress, G., 94
Kunkel, J. H., 11

Laboratory of Comparative Human Cognition, 90
Lave, J., 90
Lazar, I., 70, 202
Lee, M., 71
Lehman, H. C., 144
Lennon, P., 99
Lewis, D., 33
Lewontin, R., 51, 52, 201
Lieb, J., 185
Liker, J., 220
List, J. A., 215
Lonigan, C. J., 74
Lowes, J. L., 26
Luria, A. R., 86

McCabe, A., 20
McCartney, K., 71
McClelland, D. C., 200
MacDonald, M., 195
McGraw, M., 68
MacKenzie, N., 150
Malina, R. M., 43
Margolis, J., 4, 156, 159, 194
Marjoram, D. T. E., 152
Martin, M., 88, 220
Matheny, K., 192

Mead, M., 33
Merrick, A., 89
Merriman, W. E., 215
Metzl, M. N., 76
Mill, J. S., 8, 136, 169, 232, 234
Miller, K., 217
Mitchell, F. D., 185
Moon, C., 81
Morison, V., 7, 46
Morris, P. E., 89
Murray, H., 70, 202
Murtaugh, M., 90

Neches, R., 219
Nelson, J., 71, 76
Nelson, R. R., 152
Nettelbeck, T., 214

Ogston, K., 69
Olson, D. R., 94, 205
Omelich, C. L., 193
Ong, W. J., 94, 95

Pavalko, E., 102, 202
Peak, L., 11, 86, 185
Perkins, D. N., 26, 27
Peterson, G. A., 76
Plomin, R., 51, 52

Rabbitt, P. M. A., 217
Radford, J., 176
Ramey, C. T., 70, 71, 202
Rand, Y., 117
Renninger, K. A., 49
Renzulli, J. S., 189, 201
Resnick, L. B., 219
Revesz, G., 162
Reznick, J. S., 48
Rimland, B., 28
Risley, T. R., 76
Roberts, G., 69
Roe, A., 144
Rolfe, L. M., 101
Romney, D. M., 205
Rose, D. H., 7, 45, 46
Rothenberg, A., 27
Rotter, J., 192
Royce, J., 249, 202
Ruchalla, E., 214
Rutter, M., 19, 124, 200, 201

Sacks, O., 222
Saxe, G. B., 90

Schafer, E. W. P., 214
Schaffer, H. R., 49
Schalt, E., 214
Schenk, E., 182
Scribner, S., 200
Scripp, L., 84
Seitz, V., 200
Seligman, M. A. P., 191, 192
Sharrod, K. B., 76
Shiffrar, M. M., 90
Shuter-Dyson, R., 84
Simon, H. A., 25
Skidelsky, R., 101
Slater, A. M., 7, 45
Sloane, K. D., 104
Sloboda, J. A., 22, 84, 90
Smith, G. A., 214
Smith, J., 34, 184, 222
Smith, M. G., 91
Smith, S. B., 152, 164
Snidman, N., 48
Snipper, A., 70, 202
Solano, C. H., 152
Sorokin, P., 6, 202
Sosniak, L. A., 170, 171, 186, 187
Staats, A. W., 76, 82
Stanley, G., 214
Stanley, J. C., 152
Stayton, D. J., 112
Steane, D., 69
Storr, A., 185
Stott, D. H., 175, 205
Suarez, T., 70, 202
Super, C., 29, 30
Swenson, 69
Sykes, R. N., 89

Taniuchi, L., 11, 86, 185
Tesch-Romer, C., 91
Thomas, A., 48
Thompson, H., 65
Treffert, D. A., 28
Tweedy, M., 89

Valdez-Menchaca, M. C., 74, 76
Valentine, E., 220
Vogel, F., 214
Vygotsky, L., 9

Wachs, T. D., 110
Waldmann, M. R., 200

Wallace, A., 153, 161, 165
Wallace, D. B., 116
Walmsley, J., 4, 156, 159, 194
Weinert, F. E., 200
Weisberg, R., 26
Wells, G., 81
Wells, H. G., 150, 151
West, A., 152
Westfall, R. S., 182, 183

White, B. L., 19
Whitehurst, G. J., 74, 75, 76
Wiener, N., 101, 132, 133, 134, 135, 137, 160, 161, 166, 236
Witte, K. H. G., 9, 115, 131, 132, 167, 168, 169, 230, 231
Wozniak, R. N., 49

Zigler, E., 200

# Subject Index

aboriginal Australians, 33
absolute pitch perception, 46
abstract thinking, 88, 94, 95, 181, 204, 218, 221
accelerating early progress, 4, 5, 32–76, 83, 93, 115, 158, 174, 180, 181, 199, 202
aerobic capacity, 44
ambition, 59, 96, 180, 194
approaches to meaning, 194
aptitude, 5, 14, 35
Ashford, Daisy, 142
astronomer, 127
astronomical calculations, 164
athletes, 43, 44, 90
athletic capacity, 43
attentiveness, 55, 212, 218, 221
attentiveness at school, 218
aural training, 83
Austen, Jane, 109
autobiography, 35, 40, 59, 68
awareness, 4, 18, 21, 26, 51, 62, 65, 77, 95, 190, 228

babies, 13, 16, 18, 19, 23, 28, 29, 30, 42, 45, 47, 48, 49, 67, 71, 72, 84
Bach, J. S., 100, 101
Bach family, 107
*Beagle*, HMS, 238, 239
behaviour modification, 82
behaviours, 13, 16, 18, 19, 191, 222
being different, 156
Berle, Adam, 165, 169

Bidder, George Parker, 127–130, 137, 141, 142, 152–4, 164, 165, 169, 184
biographical evidence, 7, 20, 42, 52, 53, 56, 60, 109, 113, 114, 175, 195
body build, 43
body shape, 52
*Book of the Sword, The*, 178
Boswell, James, 8
brain mechanisms, 213
Burt, Cryil, 5–7
Burton, Richard, 177–80, 188, 193
Butler, Samuel, 133

calculating, 127–9, 151, 152, 163, 164
Cannon, Walter, 134
canoe, 32, 33
categorization, 37, 59
cello, 100
chain of processes, 55
chance, 12, 19, 39, 41, 62, 126, 143, 150, 159, 166, 191, 236, 239, 240
Chaplin, Charlie, 113
character, 17, 190
chess, 2, 3, 44, 61, 120, 121, 134, 195, 236
Chicago studies, 102–4, 122, 164, 169
chicken sexing, 46
child prodigies, 9, 19, 21–3, 96–175, 227, 234, 235
child-rearing practices, 15, 18

Chinese characters, 179
Chomsky, Noam, 71
classical conditioning, 219
classroom failure, 193
climbing, 46, 64–6, 68
cognitive complexity, 219–21
cognitive processes, 45
cognitive style, 78, 194, 195
Colburn, Zerah, 163, 164, 184
Coleridge, Samuel Taylor, 26
colour hues, 89
commitment, 18, 47, 66, 84, 90, 185
commonsense, 2, 21, 88, 196, 220
compensatory programmes, 70
component skills, 204
composer, 11, 22, 24, 40, 76, 85, 182
concentration, 20, 55, 58, 79, 90, 92, 182, 183, 184
concept of intelligence, 18, 34, 196–207, 213, 220, 222
Copland, Aaron, 172
correlational measures, 214
correlations in scores, 208, 209
crawling, 29
creating, 26, 39
creativity, 2, 23, 25, 26, 30, 36–40, 103, 109, 188
cricket, 150
critical period, 16
critical periods, 112–16
crying, 48
cultural traditions, 100–2, 183
Curie, Marie, 109
curiosity, 176, 181, 185, 187
customs, 113, 117, 118

Dante, 131
Darwin, Charles, 105, 106, 182, 183, 189, 235–240
decision-making, 17, 19, 37, 39, 40, 69, 223, 226
dedication, 13, 30, 41, 75, 76, 114, 178, 179, 239
defining intelligence, 205, 212
demanding individuals, 3, 11, 26, 36, 39, 58, 59, 85, 221
depressed patients, 191
deprivation, 18, 22, 40, 56, 66, 67, 93
Descartes, René, 183
descriptive concepts, 205, 220

determination, 18, 58, 178, 180, 182, 183, 185, 186
developmental noise, 53
Dickens, Charles, 237
digit lists, 32
disadvantaged children, 70
discriminations, perceptual, 46, 78, 90
distractible children, 78
diving, 32, 68
doggedness, 176, 180, 183, 187, 212
drive, 18, 185, 189
dyslexic children, 78, 79

early development, 1, 2, 4, 52, 53, 67, 75, 76, 101, 104, 114, 124, 126, 134, 139, 160, 168, 169, 172, 224
early language development, 74, 232
early reading, 77–9, 82
Einstein, Albert, 40, 109, 140, 182, 183, 194
emotional stress, 26
engineering, 33
environment, 7, 15, 30, 51–60, 82, 83, 113, 115, 119–23, 142, 151–3, 166, 171, 172, 185, 190, 205
environmental factors, 7, 29, 44, 52, 57, 65, 108, 110, 172
eugenics, 189
evoked potential, 214, 215
Exeter, 237–9
expectations, 3–6, 12, 48, 61, 66, 113, 154, 187, 200, 226
experience, as distinct from environment, 13–16, 20–8, 58–60
experimental approaches, 5, 13, 15, 16, 71, 83, 92
explanatory concepts, 35, 41, 202, 204

family background, 1, 9–12, 28, 34, 54, 56, 97–175, 199
Faraday, Michael, 98
fear of failure, 193
feedback, 74, 190
feelings of inferiority, 189
flexibility, 206, 218
folklore, 177, 202
foreign languages, 178, 179

formal instruction, 4, 77, 79, 81, 148–54, 231, 232
'g' 197–223
Galileo, 40
Galton, Francis, 189
games, 7, 22, 55, 60, 70, 78, 182, 195, 230, 235, 236
Gauss, Karl Friedrich, 152, 153
general intelligence, 5, 18, 19, 196–223
genes, 10, 51, 52, 53, 55, 57, 72
genetic influences, 2, 10–12, 30, 43, 48–63, 96, 224
genius, 2, 4, 7, 14, 21–5, 32, 34, 39–41, 101, 102, 107, 131, 137–42, 154, 163, 180, 181, 223, 236
genotypes, 52
Gesell, Arnold, 5, 6, 7, 64–7, 147
Gosse, Edmond, 133
grammatical forms, 71
guidance, 4, 22, 23, 24, 71, 80, 193, 226, 230
Guizot, François, 106
gymnastic skills, 68

Harvard, 130, 133, 134, 156, 160, 164
Headstart, 70, 71, 201
hereditary factors, *see* genetic influences
heritability, 51, 52
high school students, 192
hothousing, 4, 7, 19, 194
Houghton, Cedric, 165

identical twins, 52, 64
idiographic approach, 189
Inaudi, Jacques, 154
independence, 135, 137, 149, 176, 190, 191, 193
infants' preferences, 49
information transmission, 213
inheritance, *see* genetic influences
injury and illness, 237
innate ability, 7, 27, 42, 46, 50
intellectual expertise, 197
intelligence, 4–6, 18, 19, 33–5, 45, 51, 70, 81, 82, 90, 144, 148, 151, 172–5, 176, 189, 195, 196, 197–223
intelligence tests, 206–16

interventions, 19, 51, 56, 67–70, 73, 74, 201
IQ, 12, 45, 48, 69, 70, 73, 80–2, 199–201, 206–11, 220
isolation, 61, 63, 184

James, William, 144
Johnson, Samuel, 8
jumping skills, 68

Kelvin, Lord, 162
Kekule, Friedrich, 26
Keynes, John Maynard, 101
Kipsigi infants, 29, 30

labelling, 37, 72, 76
language development, 70–8, 229, 232
la Pietà, 11, 62
leaps of thought, 26
learned helplessness, 191
learning and intelligence level, 219
learning disabilities, 78
learning to read, 20, 54, 77–83, 93–5, 230
Leibnitz, Gottfried, 152
Leonardo da Vinci, 4
literacy, 93–5, 225
locus of control, 191, 192

mathematicians, 131–9, 144, 152–4, 236
memory feats, 23, 32, 33, 86–9
memory skills, 15, 33, 83, 87, 88
memory span, 32, 86, 87
Mendel, Gregor, 40, 41
mental calculations, 127–31, 152, 164–5
Menuhin, Yehudi, 101
metabolism, 52
metropolitan centres, 98
Mill, James, 102, 122, 129, 131, 132, 135, 147, 154
Mill, John Stuart, 8, 102, 122, 126, 129, 131–5, 161, 166–9
Millais, John Everett, 122
mood, 58, 212, 216
motivation, 17, 18, 55, 84, 90, 176–96, 221, 230
motor skills, 29, 30, 65, 68
Mozart, Leopold, 23
Mozart, Wolfgang Amadeus, 21–4, 31, 140, 154, 169, 182

music, 11, 21–5, 28, 36, 42, 83–5, 91, 92, 110, 140, 161, 170, 172, 181, 182, 185–7, 195, 227
neural structures, 64
Newton, Isaac, 18, 40, 182, 183, 193, 194
Nobel prize, 97, 98, 113, 160, 176
nutrition, 53
Nyiregyhazi, Erwin, 162, 163

oral culture, 94, 95
ordinary people with exceptional abilities, 11, 14, 15, 22–4, 31–4, 62, 86, 87, 196, 223
Owen, Fanny, 238, 239

Pascal, Blaise, 162
perceptual abilities, 46, 89, 90
perceptual sensitivity, 10, 46–8
perfect pitch, 46
personality, 17, 54, 58, 66, 176, 179–89, 194, 212, 216
Pestalozzi, Johann Heinrich, 106
phlogiston, 21
phoneme discrimination in reading, 77, 78
physical maturation, 64, 71
physical skills, 29, 49, 64, 67, 68
picture books, 169–72
planning skills, 218
Polgar, Laszlo, 99
practising, 91–3
prenatal environments, 53
prerequisite skills, 79
prodigies, see child prodigies
pronunciation, 65, 71

race, 28–30
Ramanujan, Srinivasa, 143
readiness, 64
reading, 77–83
reification, 14, 41, 202, 222
Rubinstein, Artur, 11, 173
running, 43, 44
Ruskin, John, 102, 121, 122, 168, 193, 234, 235

Satie, Eric, 24
sense of direction, 17, 180, 181, 190, 193, 218
sensory stimulation, 46
Sessions, Roger, 165

Shaw, George Bernard, 193
Shostakovich, Dmitry, 24
Sidis, Boris, 160, 161, 166, 167
Sidis, William, 102, 156, 160–9
slow learning, 78
Spearman, Charles, 209
sports, 1, 43, 44, 69, 70
Stephenson, George, 130
Stephenson, Robert, 130
story-telling, 22
Stravinsky, Igor, 173
swimming, 32, 68

talent, as a concept, 5, 14, 35, 36, 38, 41, 42, 50
Talmud, 99, 100
temperament, 10, 17, 48, 49, 55, 58, 101, 115, 162, 164, 174, 176–96, 200, 212, 216, 219, 221, 225
tennis, 103
test batteries, 208, 210, 211, 212
Terman, Lewis, 5, 6, 101–3, 189, 190
Thomson, James, 162
Tolstoy, Leo, 144
training programmes, 62–96
Turbina, Nika, 142

unfolding, 5, 64
unitary intelligence, 206, 209, 210, 220, 222

van Gogh, Vincent, 140
violin students, 91, 92
visual stimulation, 47
Vivaldi, Antonio, 11
Vygotsky, L. S., 9

Watts, Isaac, 235
Wells, H. G., 150–2, 237
Wiener, Leo, 101, 130, 136, 147, 159, 165–9
Wiener, Norbert, 131–8, 155, 160–2
Witte, Karl, 8, 9, 115, 140, 147, 167–9
Wittgenstein, Ludwig, 16
Woolf, Virginia, 109
Wordsworth, William, 140
Wright, Frank Lloyd, 102, 145

years of schooling, 200